WHO ARE YA?

This book is dedicated to Ali, whom I fell in love with halfway through the Blackburn chapter and still adore; to Ed, our brilliant son, and, more importantly, a Palace fan; and to Molly, whom I love like a daughter. And, of course, to my dad, known by many people reading this as 'dear old Kenny'.

BLOOMSBURY SPORT
Bloomsbury Publishing Plc, 50 Bedford Square, London, WC1B 3DP, UK
29 Earlsfort Terrace, Dublin 2, Ireland

BLOOMSBURY, BLOOMSBURY SPORT and the Diana logo are trademarks of Bloomsbury Publishing Plc

First published in Great Britain 2020

A catalogue record for this book is available from the British Library

Library of Congress Cataloguing-in-Publication data has been applied for

ISBN: HB: 978-1-4729-8064-9;
      eBook: 978-1-4729-8063-2

10 9 8 7 6 5 4

Typeset in Life BT by Austin Taylor
Printed and bound in Great Britain by CPI Group (UK) Ltd, Croydon CR0 4YY

To find out more about our authors and books visit www.bloomsbury.com and sign up for our newsletters

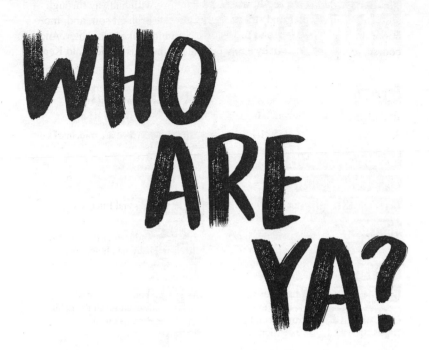

WHO ARE YA?

92 football clubs – and why you shouldn't support them

KEVIN DAY
Foreword by Gary Lineker

BLOOMSBURY SPORT
LONDON · OXFORD · NEW YORK · NEW DELHI · SYDNEY

CONTENTS

FOREWORD

I have known the author of this fine book for over 20 years. During that time, he has written countless jokes for me. Some of them were actually quite funny, only to be ruined by my delivery. Others were good enough to not be spoiled by my rotten delivery. Others have occasionally landed me in a bit of bother, whatever my delivery. This was all during 15 seasons of *They Think It's All Over* – for those of you who are unaware, this was a comedy sports quiz show that was pretty popular in its day, lots of fun to be part of, and got very respectable audiences who quite enjoyed watching sportspeople being made fun of. Kevin Day was one of the scriptwriters for the show and despite his allegiance to Crystal Palace, we became friends. I did, though, pretty much always score at Selhurst Park, and because of this I always had a soft spot for Palace (please don't tell him). Despite the show reaching its inevitable conclusion, Kevin would still write the odd joke for me if I had a speech to make, or a big show like BBC Sports Personality Of The Year, in the days when we had time to ask more questions than we do now.

'Who would have thought that after all this time, Kevin would ask me to write for him?'

Well, who would have thought that after all this time, Kevin would ask me to write for him? I, of course, was more than happy to do so, especially when I saw the idea for the book: a tome that would prove invaluable for research to those of us who work in the sport and for those who are just enthusiasts of the beautiful game. It would also inevitably be an amusing read, and so it proved to be. The cultural history of every one of the 92 Football League clubs. Well researched, wittily transcribed and accurate.

Or so I thought. Naturally, the first pages I looked at were those of the club that I have supported since I waddled around in just my pants (funny how your childhood catches up with you). As I was reading about Leicester City's miraculous triumph in 2016, when against all the odds they won the Premier League, I noticed that Kevin had written: 'How did a decent team with only … one genuinely top-class player win the Premier League? Jamie Vardy, who came from nowhere to score goal after goal.'

I beg your pardon, Kev, mate.

At this point I was about to call him to say 'forget your foreword', but as I went for the phone I spotted a small [*] and a footnote at the bottom of the page. Here he begrudgingly accepts that N'golo Kanté (World Cup winner) and Riyad Mahrez (Premier League winner again, with Manchester City) were also top-class players. That, readers, is the author's equivalent of a last-minute equaliser having been outplayed throughout.

Genuinely, though, I've always enjoyed Kevin's wit, his writing and his regular appearances on *Match of the Day 2*. He loves his football, he's a passionate supporter of his club and the game and his immense knowledge shines on every page. I just wish I could think of something funny to finish with... Oh, I know, I'll ask Kevin.

Gary Lineker

INTRODUCTION

I've always felt sorry for people who don't get football. People who say 'I'm sorry, I just don't understand it'. Poor sods. What *do* they talk about to strangers at weddings, I wonder?

Football has filled my life with joy (and misery and anxiety) for more than 50 years, and in that time the game has changed beyond recognition. But one thing will never change: the insatiable desire to watch Crystal Palace and all the lovely intangibles that go with it; or, as my wife so eloquently puts it: talking the same bollocks to the same people in the same corner of the same pub year after year.

I reckon I've seen over a thousand football games in my time and been to around 72 grounds, and the lads I still drink with have been to most of them with me. You'll have your own versions of Steve, Roy, Gaz, Chirpy, Dickie and Nick (and all the many others whose names I will mention in the acknowledgements because I promised) and my guess is that your match day experience is similar. Yes, we occasionally talk politics or films, and, even less occasionally, family, but mainly it's Palace. Past games, past players, past kits, and always the comparison with the modern game, which normally ends up losing.

My football club gives me a sense of identity. A belonging, a place in a community united by the glorious idiocy of being a fan.

Because there is a kind of idiocy to our support. Not only in its constancy, but in its rituals and its superstitions. Arriving at the pub through one 'lucky' door and leaving by another. Always turning left out of the railway tunnel. Trying to get searched by the same steward. Nonsense but necessary.

For a time I had the best job on TV. I spent 10 years as 'that bloke from *Match of the Day 2*', getting up at stupid o'clock to travel the country with fans of all shapes and sizes. I loved it, and I was proud that I became known as someone who understood football and gave its fans a fair hearing.

Being a Palace fan actually helped me on *Match of the Day 2*. There was an innate sense from most football fans I met that we were in the same boat, and had probably picked the wrong team to support. Except we also knew that the bad times are often more fun than the good, and actually bring you closer as fans.

Being a comedian also helps when I meet fans of other clubs. A lot of them seem to think I deliberately chose Palace just for the material. I didn't, but when your goalkeeper nutmegs himself to score an own-goal, it does help to know that it's given you a new five minutes.

I am still involved in various podcasts and radio shows, which brings me into contact with all sorts of people in the game. I love meeting people who love football, and you'll meet a lot of them here.

Patrick Stewart talks about Huddersfield, Freddie Flintoff about a one-man pitch invasion, Stephen Fry about his days as a football hooligan at Norwich,* Sylvester Stallone about Everton and Danny Dyer about cockneys who support Man United. It does his nut in.

There are a lot of people in this book who you will know, and many you won't: like the two disgracefully funny old ladies at Hull, or the blokes in a Portsmouth pub who refused to even speak the name of an ex-manager and the Palace fans who communicated by wheelie bin.

And there are people in this book I would love to have met, if only to find out whether the stories I discovered are true. Why did you start a team in Rotherham that only played by moonlight? What was it like to carry a stuffed fox on to the pitch at Carlisle every week? How many times did you have to launch that coracle at Shrewsbury? I probably wouldn't get the same answer twice. Cherished tales change and grow in the telling.

So here are tales about your club, about every club in the Football League† and a few that aren't any more. The 92nd chapter is a tribute to clubs currently lost to the League, and one in particular. The anger of every football fan at what happened to Bury FC proved something I have always suspected. We football fans have far more to unite us than to divide us.

Having said that, and to avoid accusations from Palace fans that I have a secret admiration for any other club, I have also included the reasons why you shouldn't support them!

Kevin Day

---

* Well, the Norwich bit is true, but what a chapter that would have been if the hooligan bit was as well!

† For people really new to football, or Americans, the English Football League is usually made up of 92 clubs, divided between the Premier League, the Championship, League One and League Two. The clubs in this book were in the League for the 2019/20 season.

ACCRINGTON STANLEY

'Accrington Stanley, who are they?'
'Exactly.'

Milk Marketing Board commercial, 1989

'This is Stanley – the club that wouldn't die.'

Fans' banner

Chances are that if you are from the south you won't have heard of either Accrington or Stanley, and that includes people for whom the south starts at Manchester. If you *have* heard of Accrington Stanley you are either a proper football fan or you are old enough to remember one of the most patronising TV adverts in the history of a very patronising industry.

It was an advert for milk. Just milk, because in those days no one had learnt how to milk an acorn. The only milk options were milk … or no milk. In the commercial, a young lad with the most Scouse accent ever – he makes John Bishop sound like Jacob Rees-Mogg – explains to his even more Scouse-sounding mate that Liverpool legend Ian Rush told him that if he doesn't drink his milk he'll only ever play football for Accrington Stanley.

Now, the standard Scouse mate response to that would be 'when did you meet Ian Rush, knobhead?'. Instead, the kid looks horrified and says 'Accrington Stanley, who are they?' (or more precisely 'Accccrington Stanley, oo-arr-dey?'), to which comes the reply 'exactly'.

To this day, it is simply impossible for anyone to mention the name 'Accrington Stanley' without someone hilarious shouting 'who are they' in a comedy Liverpool accent. Now, if that were my club being patronised like that, I would never have drunk milk again. Or put it in my tea. Or eaten milk chocolate. Or looked at space. I wouldn't even milk a laugh on stage. Because, as you will find out, when it comes to football I can bear a grudge for England. In fact, I always try to live by the motto of comedian Mark Lamarr: 'I can forgive, but I can't forget. Or forgive.'

But as it happens, Stanley fans and the people of Accrington are actually quite proud that an advert for a cow's by-product has put them on the map. The club even refer to it themselves in their pre-match announcements. I think that's very decent of them; but also slightly dull. They could have been getting bitter mileage out of that for years.

So, Accrington Stanley, who are they? Here are your pub quiz facts: they are arguably the smallest club in the League. Their cumulative attendance in 2016/17 was 36,978. That's their *cumulative* attendance, over 23 games.* I say 'arguably' but let's face it, they *are* the smallest club in the League. No shame in that. Someone has to be. The reason I said 'arguably' is that a Stanley fan may have got this book for Christmas and I wouldn't want them to be sad if they are reading it on the toilet halfway through Boxing Day.

They play at the 'Wham Stadium'. What a great name for a stadium! Wham!! I'm all for naming stadiums after bands. Imagine a cup run where I see Palace play Man City away at the Buzzcocks followed by Coventry at the Kajagoogoo and Spurs at the Blancmange† … and then next week we're off to see West Ham play at the Stolen from the Taxpayer Stadium. Sadly, there isn't a band called Stolen from the Taxpayer but there bloody well should be just so we can see West Ham play there.

As is often the case in football, the truth behind the Wham stadium is slightly more prosaic. It's the result of a £200,000 sponsorship deal between Stanley and What More UK Ltd. 'What More UK Ltd? Who are they?' 'Exactly.' Well, my little Scouse friend, What More are one of the UK's leaders in the world of online retail plastic boxes, that's who. And the fact that they have spent £200,000 and no one outside Lancashire knows that may be a source of some concern to their marketing department.

'What a great name for a stadium! Wham!! I'm all for naming stadiums after bands.'

Incidentally, Accrington has a proud industrial heritage and as well as plastic boxes it makes the hardest bricks in the world (the 'Accrington Nori' – it's an anagram of 'iron'), which were used to construct the Empire State Building and the Blackpool Tower.

One pub quiz fact about Accrington and/or Stanley is invariably wrong. If you are asked to name the only two teams with a person's

---

* Most Premier League sides get that per game.
† Kajagoogoo and Blancmange are actual band names, kids.

name in them, immediately stand up and berate the quizmaster because the question is wrong … there is only one League team with a name in it.

You'll have to read the book to find out who it is, I'm not an idiot. Or rather, I am. I was happy to tell you now but Bloomsbury said you may not read the Crewe Alexandra chapter if I do. Bollocks.

Yes, these things are important, thank you. I am still reminded of the time I was asked to leave a charity pub quiz because I was so red-in-the-face furious that the answer to a geography question was 'the moon'. The 'geo' in 'geo' refers to the earth so how can a question about the bastard moon be geography?! My team (Crystal Phallus) came second by one point, that bloody point. And if my wife is reading this, I still claim that glass of wine slipped out of my hand towards that wall. I didn't actually throw it.

Anyway. The original Accrington FC were among the 12 founding members of the Football League in 1888 but left after three years (no one seems to know why – I like to hope it was milk-related). At the time there was another team in town called Stanley Villa, based in a working mens' club on Stanley Street, and they took over the town name to become Accrington Stanley. Don't let any idiot quizmaster tell you otherwise. The moon is in space, it can't be geography. Of course, there is the possibility that the Stanley Street in question was named *after* someone called Stanley, but I have another 91 clubs to get through, I haven't got time for deep research like that.

'In 2018, the club announced that a pair of false teeth had been found on one of the terraces.'

After that name change kerfuffle in 1891, not a lot happened really. They knocked around the lower leagues for a bit then were in the Football League proper from 1921 until 1966, when they became one of the very few teams to actually just give up and resign from the League. The current club were reformed in 1968 (hence 'the club that would not die') and returned to the Football League proper in 2006. Since then, well, not much really, but at the time of writing, they are, almost miraculously for a club their size, holding their own in League One.

However, there is still a glorious touch of the past about them that befits a team called Stanley. In 2018, after a 2-1 home victory against AFC Wimbledon, the club announced that a pair of false teeth had been found on one of the terraces. Eager to reunite them with their owner, the club dutifully released a photo of said teeth to the press, although my guess is that the owner had already realised that he/she had lost them.

Can you imagine the PR department of any big club allowing them to publicly admit that one of their fans had left their teeth behind? If it was Man United they would have made a few discreet enquiries, hired a private detective, gone door-to-door. Accrington just treated it like a living episode of *Last of the Summer Wine*. I like that.

So, if anybody asks 'who are they?' in future, Accrington can proudly respond, 'we are the club who wouldn't die'. And they are the club who may still have your false teeth in the office.

Why You Shouldn't Support Them

- They didn't ban milk from their stadium forever. That shows a lack of childish resentment with which no fan can identify.
- The whole false-teeth thing.
- Really, the Wham Stadium?

AFC
BOURNEMOUTH

'Without any big titles, AFC Bournemouth has played in the English professional league since 1923.'

FootballHistory.org – summing it up nicely

'The whole of mankind is to be found in the alphabet.'

VICTOR HUGO

No disrespect, Bournemouth fans, but in the old days you'd be about the ninth chapter in and your absence of passion wouldn't matter as much, but now, by adding the AFC, you've elbowed your way up to second and I'm having to pretend to care about a club much earlier in the book than I planned – still, at least it's given me a proper reason to dislike you other than Eddie Howe's hair.

They never used to annoy me. Back when they were plain old Bournemouth and Boscombe Athletic, I quite liked them, if I thought about them at all. They knocked about the lower divisions not doing any harm, with the general demeanour of a Labrador that was good with kids.

I even thought it was quite charming, in a patronising way, when such a small club began their recent ascent through the divisions under the guidance of golden-hair, too-good-to-be-true boy Eddie, and found themselves in the Premier League. Like most fans of other Premier League clubs, I thought it would be a nice day out and six easy points. Instead, their ground is so bloody small I couldn't get near a ticket and they turned out to be quite good and are (currently at least) still in the Premier League.

That's when I started to really get the hump, because the media are all over them with tales of plucky little Bournemouth defying the odds. They're not plucky – they're owned by a Russian billionaire. Still, in the interests of balance, it *is* remarkable that such a small club* can be in the top division of the strongest league in world football even though their story contains a terrible case of identity theft.

Boscombe is a rather chic little seaside suburb of Bournemouth. In 1899, out of the remains of a previous club called Boscombe St John's Institute was formed Boscombe FC, a name that was obviously much easier to fit on a stick of rock. I like to think that the decision was taken by a group of Victorian gentlemen gravely discussing the need for a new club while simultaneously plucking candy-floss out of their impressive beards, and as the meeting did apparently take place out of doors, I may be right.

In 1910 they moved to a ground donated by one J. Cooper-Dean and very politely named it after him – and Dean Court is still their ground, although it goes under the rather less romantic name of the Vitality Stadium. It was around the same time that they acquired the nickname the Cherries, either because they wore cherry-red shirts or because J. Cooper-Dean's land also had a cherry orchard on it. 'Ooh, please, Miss, me, Miss, it's the shirts Miss, isn't it?' Probably, Kevin, yes.

Truth is, we don't know. Like so many football facts, it's a guess. Maybe their first manager was a big Chekhov fan. Or a greengrocer.

In 1923, presumably in an attempt to widen their appeal with a hint of big city glamour, they changed their name to Bournemouth and Boscombe Athletic FC, and were elected to the new Third Division of the Football League. Then they proceeded to the process of playing there 'without any titles'. Seriously, nothing very much happened until it all started to get a bit groovy with the dawn of the 1970s.

First, in 1971, they introduced a red and black striped kit in an attempt to emulate AC Milan. It didn't work, but they did get some attention when they started to climb the Third Division with a lad called Ted McDougall scoring goals all over the place, including 9 (nine!) in an 11-0 cup tie against Margate. As someone who scored one goal in my entire Sunday league playing days, I think scoring 9 (nine!) in one game is taking the piss.

But 1972 was the biggie. In February they played away in front of 48,000 fans at Villa Park in one of the most high-profile Third Division games ever. It was even on *Match of the Day*. Bournemouth were second, Villa top. Obviously McDougall scored, but Villa won and subsequently went up while Bournemouth had to wait a few more years.

---

* Their ground only holds 11,000.

In the same year came another name change. Boscombe were discarded like a greasy chip and they became simply AFC Bournemouth. That's no way to treat the memory of the Victorian candy-floss men. Apparently the logic was that they would now be the first team mentioned in any Football League listing, but (a) why would that matter? And (b) why not AFC Boscombe? And (c) ... comes after (b).

Also, if everyone had gone down that path, I'd be off to Selhurst Park this Saturday to watch Absolutely Crystal Palace play Aaarsenal. A long-established football club shouldn't behave like AAAA Plumbers trying to get to the top of a directory.

At the same time, they introduced a new badge. It didn't look right in the seventies and it looks even worse now. It's a sort of Mussolini-looking stylised head, in profile, heading a ball. Apparently the profile is meant to represent Dickie Dowsett, the 1950s version of Ted McDougall, but I don't know if Dickie will be pleased that he is commemorated in what looks like an economy shampoo commercial.

After the Villa disappointment, AFC Bournemouth, the identity thieves, went back to nothing much until Harry Redknapp finally took them into the Second Division for the first time. It was Harry's first job, and this is my first mention of him. It won't be the last. It's amazing how many times he will crop up in this book. He has managed a *lot* of clubs.

A 31-year-old Eddie Howe took over as caretaker manager at Bournemouth on New Year's Eve 2008, with the club in an extraordinary mess. An on-pitch decline following Redknapp's departure had seen them relegated to League Two and off-pitch financial mismanagement nearly saw them expelled from the League altogether. Enough of a deal had been cobbled together to save them, but they started the season with a deduction of 17 points. They were still 10 points adrift at the bottom when Howe took over and began that slow, fairy-tale rise to the Premier League with only some massive financial backing to help them.

So there you are. Probably the most straightforward history in the whole book. And it comes right at the start of the bloody book. Maybe I should warn people in the introduction?

Why You Shouldn't Support Them

- The whole plucky billionaire thing.
- The whole alphabet thing.
- Get a bigger away end!

AFC WIMBLEDON

'Where were you when you were us?'

AFC Wimbledon fans singing at MK Dons fans

'One two, one two three, bollocks to the referee.'

ME aged 4

This could have been a very different book and mine a very different life were it not for my infant potty-mouth.

Family legend has it that when I was an angelic little boy, my Uncle Bill decided I needed a football team. My Uncle Bill was a pugnacious little chap who knew everything and was apparently loosely related to a bloke whose cousin was the back-up getaway driver for the Krays. He was also a spiritualist medium, prone to nipping unexpectedly into betting shops because Charles Dickens had just come through with a tip.

Enough context. Uncle Bill took me to my first ever football match. Plough Lane, SW17, Wimbledon versus someone in the old Southern League, the fifth level of the pyramid. It was probably about 1966. I would ask Uncle Bill but he's dead now and, ironically, we've not heard a peep from him since.

I remember nothing of the afternoon, either because I was four years old or because my brain has mercifully erased the trauma of potentially spending my life not supporting Crystal Palace. According to that family tradition, I came home in a rather boisterous mood, singing 'one two, one two three, bollocks to the referee'. Apparently this outraged my mother and she decided I would not be going to football with Uncle Bill again. Like many family (and football) traditions, it doesn't stand up to the most rudimentary research. My mum was petite and beautiful, glamorous even. But she swore like a docker's parrot.*

Seriously, Mum was the Rembrandt and Mozart of swearing. And when she ran out of combinations in English she would slip effortlessly into Irish for an extra touch of the exotic.

---

* Reference courtesy of Barry Cryer, comedy legend and connoisseur of parrot jokes. You want to know what a randy French parrot sounds like? Ask Barry.

Dad always claims that he didn't want me going with Bill again because of his alarming habit of talking to dead people who weren't there, but I suspect it was also because Bill asked him for the ticket money. Whatever the reason, I escaped the clutches of Wimbledon and ran headlong towards dear old Palace.

As it happens, supporting Wimbledon would have been quite fun. In 1975, still a Southern League team, they beat First Division Burnley, away, in the FA Cup. Then they drew with reigning League champions dirty Leeds, away, in the FA Cup before losing the replay in front of about 40,000 people at Selhurst Park.

In 1977 they were elected* into the Football League. Eleven years later, they were in the First Division and defeating Liverpool at Wembley to win the FA Cup. As BBC commentator John Motson said, 'the Crazy Gang have beaten the Culture Club'. The 'Crazy Gang' being a motley group of battle-hardened nasty bastards with no respect for reputation taking on all-comers in a tiny dilapidated stadium, who used to initiate new team members with boisterous 'pranks' like setting fire to their car.

They were the Heathcliffs of football, both brutal and romantic. Sometimes more brutal than romantic. I met Vinnie Jones on a TV show at the time. Ever polite, I said, 'pleased to meet you' and held my hand out. He ignored it and said 'oh, you're that Palace wanker aren't you?' I said 'that's Mr Palace wanker to you' – a level of witty repartee that seemed to enrage him, because his agent needed a chair and a whip to get him to back away.

Whatever you think of them, the 'Crazy Gang' and their fans had it all taken away by of one of the most disgraceful acts of craven cowardice ever committed by the FA. This book is a celebration of the English game, its history, its culture and its fans in all its baffling, irrational glory; the story of how Wimbledon come to be one of the first chapters in this book and not one of the last may be baffling and irrational, but it's certainly not glorious.

After a lot of hard thought, I think it's a story that should be told in the MK Dons chapter; but MK Dons fans, once I've told it, I promise I will treat your short history with the utmost respect. And I will treat the short history of AFC Wimbledon with the same respect, even though it includes me being insulted by the short chairman of AFC Wimbledon.

In 2002, those Wimbledon fans who were so outraged by the FA's decision to allow the club to relocate to Milton Keynes (i.e. all of them)

---

* In those days the team at the bottom of the Fourth Division and the team at the top of the Southern League went head to head in an actual election-type thing.

decided to form a new team, even though the FA commission who made that decision had said that any attempt to do so would be 'not in the wider interests of football'.

I agreed to host a fundraising benefit for them and fellow comedian and Palace fan Mark Steel agreed to headline. Firstly because we were able to transcend petty rivalries for the greater good of football, and secondly because they didn't have any comedian fans of their own. The wonderful comedy actress June Whitfield seemed to be their only celebrity fan, but was clearly not the right choice for a theatre full of angry south Londoners, even though she told me one of my favourite football stories ever. June was invited into the dressing room at Wembley after that FA Cup win and sat on a bench sharing the champagne and the glory. One of the players, being hilarious, came out of the shower naked and called her name, causing her to turn around and accidentally brush his penis with her face. Then she paused, winked, and said 'well, he thought it was accidentally'.

The fundraiser was a wonderful night of football solidarity, except that, during the interval, the chap who became their first chairman decided to make a speech. He was 5ft 2in tall, and wide. And most of his speech was about how much he hated Palace and Palace fans.

Which was fine. Mark and I understood. He was nervous. Emotions were running high. And we were professional comedians who had plenty of stage-time left for our right-to-reply. Much of what we said wasn't big or clever (like him), but a lot of money was raised and I'm proud to have been a small part of repairing a big hurt.

A few weeks later, after recruiting players through trials in a local park, AFC Wimbledon played their first ever game, in the Combined Counties League, against Sandhurst Town (me neither). Eighteen years (and about as many promotions) later, AFC are in the EFL, and hopefully about to move into a new stadium back in SW19.

Not only are they in the EFL, they are in the same division as MK Dons, so for the moment at least, they get to sing that brilliant existentialist chant at least twice a season.

Why You Shouldn't Support Them

- Insulting the Palace fans who were gracious enough to save them.
- Vinnie Jones called me a wanker.
- Setting fire to a new teammate's car isn't 'crazy', it's psychotic.

ARSENAL

'Arsenal are the most beautiful club in England. At Man City and Chelsea they will never have that class and style.'

MARCO VAN BASTEN Dutch football legend

'They are, and forever will be, a south London team.'

ANDY LINDEN comedian, actor and Spurs fan

In 1886, a group of workers at a munitions factory in Woolwich, south-east London, started a football team by the name of … Dial Square. Because there was a sundial on top of the factory gate.

Then someone with an early sense of PR flair decided they needed a fancier name … Royal Arsenal. However, that was a bit *too* fancy for south-east London, so they changed it again … to Woolwich Arsenal. Then they borrowed a set of red shirts from Nottingham Forest, and thus began the story of one of the most famous football names in the world.

In 1913 they found a new home at Highbury, in north London, kicking off one of the most famous rivalries in world football. And much of the animosity between Spurs and Arsenal still rests on that move across the river.

It's difficult to explain the whole south London/north London thing to an outsider. When Ali first moved to London as a student, she found a bedsit in Crouch End. It's a smart part of town with a lively cultural scene, many independent shops doing edgy things with cheese, and eye-wateringly expensive houses, so obviously it is home to 90% of the country's left-wing stand-up comedians and TV producers. Ali loved it, and couldn't understand why I hated visiting her there, especially as, it being a new relationship, we spent most of the time in the bedsit anyway.

And I did hate visiting there. It's still London, which is good, but it's a sort of ersatz London that tries too hard to be different and quirky. Ali only understood that when I took her south of the river (not a euphemism). Basically, they got all the Tube stations and hills, and we got all the open spaces and proper pubs.

They feel the same way about us. When we play Arsenal at Selhurst I nearly always entertain a couple of Arsenal-supporting comedians in the Pawsons Arms, and they are visibly on edge the whole time, although that could also be because they are in a pub full of Palace fans who all know they support Arsenal.

Look, there's no logic to why it feels different up there, it just does and we're better. Which is why, even now, when me and the boys cross the river back from an away game we will spontaneously burst into a round of 'Oh south London ... is wonderful ... oh south London is wonderful'.*

It is 107 years since Arsenal dropped the 'Woolwich', but to Tottenham fans they are still interlopers, a feeling that is made worse by the implacable conviction of smug Arsenal fans that they are north London's true and only club. And believe me, there are a lot of smug Arsenal fans. Annoyingly, though, those Arsenal fans are right, there *is* something about Arsenal. It is a classy club.

Alan Davies is a comedy legend, a dedicated Arsenal fan and an old mate. He is also a very modest man except when it comes to the club he loves: 'Kev, I am absolutely secure in the knowledge that we are the best and classiest club.' In London? 'In London and beyond. Everywhere.' But you haven't won anything lately. 'Three FA cups and a European final in the past few years. We'd have killed for that in the sixties, you'd kill for it now!'

Ah, always with the history. But, for lovers of football history like me, the old Highbury was a place of beauty – an art deco masterpiece of a stadium, complete with marble walls and floors and an actual doorman who would tip his actual hat as you entered. Or he would if you were wearing a suit and accompanied by a camera crew, like I was on several occasions. I don't remember much hat-tipping when I went in wearing jeans and a Palace scarf. Even when I was thrown out of there one time, for sharing witty pleasantries with the home fans after Palace conceded yet another goal, I was ejected by the stewards and police† with a degree of style and charm you simply wouldn't encounter at other clubs.

It was also quite classy that their legendary manager Herbert Chapman managed to persuade London Transport to change the name of the nearest underground station from Gillespie Road to Arsenal, still

---

* Not the full version of the song but definitely the full *printable* version of the song. It's not woke, let me put it that way.

† Well, it started off as witty pleasantries, but the stewards had no sense of humour so they had to call for uniformed comedy back-up.

the only Tube station in the country named after a football club. If you win a pub quiz with that fact, make a small donation to charity. Chapman it was too who invented that iconic red shirt/white sleeve kit they've been wearing since 1933. Legend has it that one of the players turned up for summer training wearing a red sleeveless pullover on top of a white cricket shirt and Chapman thought it looked so cool he declared it immediately as their new kit. Good job the player wasn't wearing sunglasses as well, then.

Interestingly, though, for two years the socks had white tops above what looks like a suspiciously Tottenham blue. Was that a subliminal message that red and white would always be above blue and white? Am I reading too much into it? Almost certainly. Fun, though, isn't it?

But the average Spurs fan's resentment to Arsenal is not just geography- or sock-based. Oh no, it's much deeper than that and it's been festering since 1919. As a fan of the festering grudge, I really admire that. I still remind my dad of the Christmas he bought me a set of darts instead of the train set I asked for. I wouldn't have minded except (a) we didn't have a dartboard and (b) I was seven. My dad essentially gave a child three tiny weapons.

In 1915, when the Great War put an end to football, Arsenal were fifth in the Second Division and would have expected to remain in that league when it all kicked off again in 1919. However, it was Spurs who kicked off. The First Division was extended from 20 to 22 teams and tradition suggested that the two clubs who were bottom of that division – Chelsea and Spurs – when the war started would retain their place in the top flight, along with the two teams at the top of the Second Division. Chelsea and the Second Division teams duly took their place in the top league. But it was suggested that a ballot should take place for the remaining spot. And it was suggested by Henry Norris, the chairman of Arsenal.

Worse still, in an infamous speech before the ballot, Norris suggested (or 'demanded' if you're a Spurs fan) that as Arsenal were the longest-established team in the ballot, *and* the first League club from the south, they should get the coveted spot, despite having only finished fifth back at the start of this story. And the board of the League agreed, despite the technicality pointed out by Wolves that they were several years older than Arsenal, and the equally convincing technicality pointed out by Tottenham that this was all a bit fishy. As it was: even Arsenal's official club history admits that Norris may have 'influenced' the voters, either with words or money.

Whatever he did say, or pay, Arsenal are the only club to have stayed in the top division continuously ever since, and they are the only club not to be there on merit. But (and Spurs fans will hate me for saying this) that level of skulduggery does take a certain sort of class, doesn't it?

However, there is a late and slightly worrying development to this chapter. Alex Brooker is the twinkly-eyed little charmer from *The Last Leg* on Channel 4. He is also a massive Arsenal fan, even though he is from Croydon and his family all support Palace. He says me and his nan are the only people who ever give him stick for that, which is also his way of calling me old. He says there are Spurs fans like Andy Linden who 'give it the whole south London thing', but all he has to do is ask what they've won recently because 'trophies trump geography'. Then he added that, lately, Chelsea were becoming more of a rival than Spurs, a sentiment that was echoed when I asked some other young Arsenal fans in the office of a football show I was writing on.

This was slightly disconcerting to hear so early in a book like this. Are there other fans out there making up their own rivalries? Is there a factory somewhere in Manchester where City and United fans work in cheery harmony because now they both hate Bristol Rovers instead?

Luckily, a quick question on the WhatsApp group confirmed that Palace fans all still hate Brighton, even Chirpy's two-year-old grandson. Or, as Chirpy said, *especially* his two-year-old grandson.

But if Arsenal fans are not hating Spurs, I could have a problem. I turned to Alan Davies for clarification. He looked puzzled for a second, like Jonathan Creek finding a new clue, then said simply: 'No, it's not a thing. Ask those weirdoes which of these scores they would prefer: Chelsea 9 Spurs 0, or Spurs 9 Chelsea 0. Chelsea are intolerable in every respect but they're still just irritating. Spurs are the enemy.'

Thank Jesus for that!

Why You Shouldn't Support Them

- The wrong side of the river.
- Possibly the smuggest fans in the country. (Not you, Alex and Alan. The others.)
- One of the coppers who threw me out had seen me do a gig and said I wasn't funny then, either.

ASTON VILLA

'There are football grounds and there are football grounds.
Then there is Villa Park.'

SIMON INGLIS football ground historian extraordinaire

'Shaw, Williams, prepared to venture down the left.
There's a good ball in for Tony Morley. Oh, it must be,
and it is! It's Peter Withe.'

BRIAN MOORE commentating on the goal that won the European Cup*

Beating Bayern Munich to win that European Cup in 1982 was almost the worst thing that could have happened to Aston Villa. It was a remarkable victory considering that Villa had been in the Third Division only 10 years earlier and had won the First Division title in 1981 using just 14 players. Brian Moore's words are emblazoned round the four stands at Villa Park as a reminder of their greatest night, but also serve as an equally stark reminder that nothing like it has happened to Villa since, and doesn't seem likely to happen in the future. And that's an odd prediction to make about what has been, and should be, one of the biggest clubs in England.

Villa Park will always be a very happy place for me (see chapter on Crystal Palace), but when you see it for the first time as an opposition fan it is a very imposing site with one end dominated by a huge Victorian mansion-like building, which is all the more impressive for rising out of what looks like a surprisingly deprived area.

And Palace fans will always owe Villa a debt of gratitude. In 1905, when the club was formed, the secretary/manager, Edmund Goodman, was appointed from Villa and obligingly brought a full set of their kit with him, hopefully with their permission. So, for many years of our history, claret and blue were our colours too and will be again if I ever buy the club, which, sadly, I never will, unless this book turns into the Harry Potter of football.

---

* You'll hear a lot more about Brian Moore in this book.

In fact, we all owe Villa a debt of gratitude. One of their directors, William McGregor, a local shop-owner, noticed that they got far bigger crowds for competitive cup matches than they did for the irregular friendlies they usually played. He approached a number of other clubs with that notion and in 1888 Villa took their place as founder-members of the Football League with 11 other teams, all of whom are still in it. And the chairman? Why, William McGregor of course. Look him up: brilliant beard.

Villa's history before that is very unusual because they are one of the few clubs who can't pin

'... what a ground it became. Even as a kid watching black-and-white telly, you could tell it was something different.'

down the exact date of their beginning. (If you are actually reading this cover to cover, you are yet to learn that clubs are surprisingly definite about facts and dates from longer ago than they have any right to be.) And that means, of course, that I can't be definite either, which is why you probably shouldn't use this as a textbook.

It was probably early in 1874 that members of the Villa Cross Methodist Chapel in a suburb of Birmingham called Aston decided to form a football team, although whether or not it was after they'd witnessed an impromptu game on their way to prayers is impossible to know (doesn't stop people claiming that though).

Now, my father-in-law was a Methodist minister,† so it doesn't surprise me at all that they didn't waste time looking for a frivolous Fancy Dan name. No Rovers, Swifts or Albion for them. They were in Aston and they were in the Villa Cross Chapel. Ten seconds that name decision would have taken, knowing Methodists. Followed by a massive row about who was making the sandwiches.

Regardless, the club nickname soon became 'The Villans'. Straightforward, no nonsense. Don't make me say Methodist again.

Villa were the most successful club of the Victorian era. They won five League titles and three FA Cups in that time, and considering there were only 13 years of the Victorian era remaining when the League was formed, that is good going!

In 1897 (the year of Queen Victoria's Diamond Jubilee) they moved to a ground on the site of an old amusement park. There is no official record of it ever having been named Villa Park. The fans just decided that's what it was going to be called. Come on, you know what they

---

† My family are very Catholic. Ali and I were married in a Methodist church, or as one of my aunts called it as she entered, 'a fucking scout hut'.

were like. It was a park and Villa played there, why waste time?

But what a ground it became. Even as a kid watching black-and-white telly, you could tell it was something different. One of the stands had what appeared to be gables on it, and stained-glass windows, with a giant lion in the middle; and the Holte End, where the home fans gathered, seemed to go on forever.

By the time I started to go there regularly, the glory days of Europe were receding but the gaps in the terrace only seemed to emphasise the sheer size of the place. And it could have been bigger. In 1911, an ambitious director wanted to build a mega-stadium holding 104,000 people and incorporating a giant aquarium and saunas for the players. It sounds more like the lair of a James Bond villain, so I'm almost sad it didn't happen.

Sadly, as the grandeur of the famous old ground diminished, so did the fortunes of the club. With occasional exceptions (and, to be fair, winning the European Cup is a pretty massive occasional exception), Villa have underachieved greatly. The phrase 'sleeping giant' is often used to describe them. They are a giant, but the sleep is deep. Still doesn't stop Villa Park being full for most games or claiming an impressive list of celebrity fans. Prince William supports them, which really annoys me. They are not his local team and if anyone should support Palace, it's him. Ex-Prime Minister David Cameron supports them.* Tom Hanks supports them. Ozzy Osbourne supports them, as does the brilliant poet Benjamin Zephaniah, half of Duran Duran, one of Ron Weasley's twin brothers and Private Pike from Dad's Army.

That'll be an interesting executive box if they all turn up at once.

Why You Shouldn't Support Them

- They have enough fans already, most of them celebrities.
- Yes, they won the European Cup, but that was in 1982 – there were only about 12 countries in Europe then, and one of them was Luxembourg.
- Our goalkeeper once scored an own-goal there when he managed to nutmeg himself.

---

* Although he did once forget that and claim he supported West Ham. He blamed 'brain fade'.

BARNSLEY

'I remember I used to get on the bus to a home game and quite often Barnsley's centre-half would be on it.'

SIR MICHAEL PARKINSON legendary chat show host and Barnsley fan

'I grew up in Yorkshire, which is like the Texas of Britain. It's a proud free state.'

JOANNA COLES author and TV presenter

I've never been a fan of nominative determinism, the idea that your name may somehow influence your character or your occupation. Gordon Banks would have ended up at the NatWest, not the World Cup; David Seaman would still be on a trawler; and somebody called Kevin Friend surely wouldn't even consider becoming a referee.†

Having said that, if you name your baby town Barnsley, it could only ever grow up to be in Yorkshire. Barnsley could only sound more Yorkshire if it was called Barnsley-by-Eck and moaning about London beer prices. A town called Barnsley is never going to be in Surrey, is it? It's in YORKSHIRE! And away fans at Oakwell can have no doubt they are in YORKSHIRE!

If you were writing a sit-com in which an elderly football fan reminisced about the good old days when the players all got on the bus with you to the game, you would definitely set it in Barnsley. I don't know if there ever was a time when players did get the bus with you, and I can think of all sorts of reasons why they probably wouldn't, but it is definitely a memory all fans over the age of 70 seem to share. And it's a very useful way to compare the proper football of their day to the namby-pamby modern game when players all go to the game in their fancy warm cars that only hold five people.

Indeed, later in the interview quoted above, Parky claims that in his day you had a bond with the players because they had probably been working down the coal mine all week with your dad, which is (surely)

---

† Yes, I do know about the Belgian midfielder Mark de Man. Shut up.

nonsense, especially *after* becoming a professional footballer.* But Parky said it, and he was as much part of my childhood Saturdays as *Match of the Day* was, so I choose to believe him.

None of this, by the way, is meant as criticism. I'm all for regional pride. I am the proudest South Londoner going, it's just that the people of Yorkshire seem able to express their pride in a more effusive way, without any sort of ironic apology, and I'm a little bit jealous.

And given the recent assault on the industry and economy of most parts of Yorkshire, thank goodness they at least have football teams to be proud of. Mind you, I genuinely don't know if this is a fact to be proud of or not: Barnsley are the team who have spent more seasons than any other in the second tier of English football.

They were founded as Barnsley St. Peters in 1887 by the Reverend Tiverton Preedy, who, ironically, given the above, sounds like a village in Wiltshire. Since then, they won the FA Cup in 1912, had one unlikely season in the Premier League and have spent more than 70 seasons in whatever the second tier of English football has been called. The Second Division, the First Division, the Championship: Barnsley have been in them all, for a very long time. Is that something to celebrate or something to ignore? The club's website very much goes for the latter option, but *not* being in the bottom two divisions for more than 70 seasons isn't bad, is it? Or is it? Yes, you could argue they've not been in the top division for more than 70 years, but I'm a glass-half-full chap so the Second Division thing seems fine by me, and they don't have all that pressure of trying to survive in the Premier League (he says patronisingly).

'So in one scenario, Barnsley, the top-flight's longest serving team, are beating Barcelona in the final of the Champions League.'

One of the things I love most about football are those illogical reasons that fans of one club can find to dislike every other club; for example, my West-Ham-supporting mate who gets cross at the mere mention of Oldham Athletic (see the chapter on Oldham for details).

Well, if there are any 110-year-old Barnsley fans out there, they will have an entirely logical reason to hate Arsenal. In 1919, having finished pre-war football in third place in the second tier (where else?) they were the team with most expectations to be placed in the newly extended First Division, until the silver tongue and golden coins of Arsenal bought their

---

* Having said that, Barnsley is one of the many teams in Yorkshire about who it's claimed that if they wanted a new player they just shouted down the pit.

way in instead. Who knows, without those underhand dealings, we may be celebrating Barnsley as the team with the most years in the top flight. But, as one of my cousins always says, if your auntie had bollocks, she'd be your uncle. I don't know why he says it, but it seems to fit.

'I'm a glass-half-full chap so the Second Division thing seems fine by me.'

Football is full of sliding-door moments. Those what-ifs that allow football fans to still be talking about an alternative history decades after missing out on that player, or moving to that ground or sacking that manager. So in one scenario, Barnsley, the top flight's longest-serving team, are beating Barcelona in the final of the Champions League. And in another, Barnsley, the second tier's longest-serving team, are the source of pride for a region that desperately needs it. That will do for me.

Why You Shouldn't Support Them

- Yeah, Yorkshire, we get it. Your badge has got a bloke on it wearing a flat cap, FFS.
- They are friendly folk, but try asking for a half-pint in a Barnsley pub and see where it gets you.
- The whole settling for the Championship thing. Like a couple who married too early but can't be arsed to get divorced because they'll argue about who gets the dog.

BIRMINGHAM CITY

'Keep right on to the end of the road, keep right on to the end.'

Birmingham City anthem – first sung by winger Alex Govan, team bus, January 1956

'When they started being successful, I had to go out and write half an hour of stuff on another subject.'

JASPER CARROTT comedian and Bluenose

Not just successful, Jasper, Birmingham City are currently ranked as the 28th *most* successful club ever in English football.

I shall just pause here while fans of every other club say 'bollocks, they are' and fans of Birmingham City say 'bollocks, we are!' But you are. It's there in black and white on your official club website. I don't know whether to be slightly embarrassed on their behalf about that proud boast, or impressed by a fact I would never have guessed unless it was a Birmingham fan who asked me. Still, 28 out of 92 is not bad, is it? And without knowing exactly how they've worked it out, I suspect that Palace won't be in the 27 above them; so, you know, fair play.

Unfortunately for Bluenoses, one of the teams that will be in the 27 are Aston Villa, and that's the reason why, without actually admitting to liking them, I can identify with them. Since they were founded, a year after their bigger and bitter rivals, they have nearly always been just behind them. Or on some occasions, a massive way behind them. And, on fewer occasions, slightly ahead of them.

Jasper Carrott has always been able to take out his frustration on stage but other Bluenoses have often taken their frustration out in other, more surreal ways. Palace played them at Selhurst on the last day of the season in 1989. We had a very slim chance of promotion if other results went our way (they didn't, obviously) but Birmingham had already been relegated. Despite that, they had advertised the game as an end of season party. So, 3,000 of them turned up, many in fancy dress. Except, initially, some of them didn't turn up. The coaches took them instead to Crystal Palace Sports Centre, a couple of miles away, which meant swathes of them arrived just as we scored the first goal. That was clearly the final indignity of a frustrating season and to this day the sight of Laurel and Hardy being frogmarched off the pitch by two policemen lingers long in the memory.

And why 'Bluenoses'? A surprising amount has been written about that question, actually. Over the years, Birmingham City, Everton, Glasgow Rangers and many other clubs have all been called the same. There may be complex socio-economic and religious factors at play here, or they may all wear blue shirts. It's a conundrum, ain't it?

Predominantly blue shirts in Birmingham's case. We are only just into the book so you may not yet fully realise the extent of my football kit fetish,* but one of the reasons I identify with them (which is not the same as liking, by the way) is the sheer variety of kits they have conjured using only two colours. Their home kit between 1971 and 1975 was blue with a broad white stripe down the front and I loved it. But even better, and so much even better, was their away kit between 1972 and 1974. Never mind the 28th most successful club in England, the brilliant nostalgia site Football Attic voted it as the 41st best kit ever; and by my reckoning they were only about 38 places out. It was basically the flag of (West) Germany turned into a shirt, but whether by accident or design I haven't been able to discover. It's properly gorgeous in a weird sort of way, or weird in a gorgeous sort of way, and I don't think it would have seen the light of day in any other decade.

> '... the sight of Laurel and Hardy being frogmarched off the pitch by two policemen lingers long in the memory.'

And the same could be said of Trevor Hockey's beard. The Trevor most fans associate with Birmingham is Trevor Francis, who, in 1979, became English football's first ever one-million-pound transfer. But give me Trevor Hockey any day.† He was a no-nonsense, tough-tackling midfielder who played for many clubs, and was a cult hero at all of them. In the television set of my mind, he is always in a Birmingham shirt, heaving his huge beard round the pitch and smiling to himself as he walks away from a prone striker who is lying in agony on the pitch after Trevor has let him know he was there. 'Letting him know he was there' was a favourite expression of Hugh Johns, the Midlands TV equivalent of Brian Moore. It was basically a euphemism for 'he tried to break his leg'.

---

* Partly my fault. I really wish I'd written this in alphabetical order. I know I've written about kits in some detail but I assume a lot of those will be about kits that come after 'B'. Also, I guess the editor will take this footnote out, so I'm not sure why I've bothered.

† Especially as Trevor Francis went on to become one of the dullest managers Palace ever had.

Hugh, by the way, was the unluckiest commentator in football. In 1966, while Kenneth Wolstenholme was on the BBC ending the World Cup Final with 'Some people are on the pitch, they think it's all over ... it is now', Hugh was describing the same Geoff Hurst goal to a tiny audience on ITV.*

It's almost a metaphor for the rivalry known as the second-city derby. Villa have traditionally been the BBC, with City as the equivalent of ITV. Much more of a working-class feel but when push comes to shove, outsiders just seem to assume Villa have a touch more class.

They were formed in 1875, a year after Villa (how annoying is that?) as Small Heath Alliance, or, as they soon became known, The Heathens. I wonder what the Methodists at Villa made of that? They became Birmingham in 1905, but didn't add the City until 1943, although I doubt anyone noticed that, what with the whole war thing and all.

The most annoying thing for Birmingham fans must be that they have actually always been quite a successful club, if 28th out of 92 counts as *quite* successful. Sure, very recent years have been lean, but they've won things. They've won the League Cup twice. Palace fans would kill for a trophy cabinet like theirs (although it would be odd if we managed to win the Birmingham Senior Cup). Trouble is – and smug Villa fans know what's coming here – Villa have won much more. They have won League titles, FA Cups and that bloody European Cup.

For Birmingham fans, however, there are two consolations. Their silver polish bill is much more manageable. And Villa have never, ever won anything wearing a shirt remotely as sexy as that 1972 away kit.

So all the Bluenoses have to do is keep on keeping right on till the end of the road, and who knows what may await them? Villa fans holding up another trophy, probably.

Why You Shouldn't Support Them

▪ Who wants to support the team that are 28th best at anything?
▪ Starting a riot in fancy dress is neither big nor clever. Funny, though.
▪ Even pre-satnav it takes some doing to go to the wrong stadium.

---

* 'Here's Hurst, he might make it three, he has, he has! So that's it, that is it!' Right time, wrong place, Hugh.

BLACKBURN ROVERS

'Ali, I think I love you.'

ME 1 June 1989, 6 a.m., Euston Station, after a night game in Blackburn

'The supporters are issuing a vote of no confidence to the board of directors and the owners of this club.'

MARK FISH BRFC Action Group chairman, 5 October 2016, after years of mismanagement

When my son was about seven, I came home from a gig one evening to find him and Ali waiting up for me. There was a slightly tense atmosphere, as though they had bad news. I could see that the cat was in her usual place in the kitchen, staring at the fridge, so that was alright, but I felt a slight chill. 'Dad,' he said, 'I've got something to ask you.' He looked anxiously at his mum, took a deep breath and said: 'Can I support Blackburn instead of Palace?'

I smiled, gave him a big hug and reassured him: 'Of course you can, little mate. When you're old enough to get a job and buy a house in Blackburn. Because who do we support?'

'We support our local team, Dad.'

'Because?'

'Because otherwise we're a glory-hunting ...'

Ali glared at us both so he didn't finish the sentence.

I was intrigued, though. Why Blackburn?

'You never come home happy from Palace, and I want to have some fun when I go to football.'

Where he got the idea there was fun involved watching football, I don't know.

'Uh-huh. And why Blackburn?'

'Well, I looked at a list of the 91 other teams and Mum reckons you hate them all, except Blackburn, because of the whole telling-her-you-loved-her-when-you-were-drunk-at-the-station thing.'

Clever Mummy. Clever, crafty Mummy.

'I wasn't drunk. It was six o'clock in the morning. I was hung-over. Now put on your Palace pyjamas and snuggle up under your Palace duvet. And say goodnight to Selhurst the cat.'*

As it happens, I did Ed a favour. Blackburn are struggling at the moment, but they were a very good team at the time. They'd even won the Premier League a few years earlier. Or, if you supported any other team, had bought their way to the Premier League a few years earlier. More of that to come, but first a quick look at their history, before I tell you the whole 'love's young dream' thing.

They were formed in 1875 by four ex-public schoolboys, two from Malvern School and two from Shrewsbury School. Presumably the sons of wealthy mill owners. Recent labour reform laws meant that mill and factory workers now had Saturday afternoons off and the people who owned those mills saw an opportunity to make even more money by charging them to watch their new local football team. It's why we still have 3 p.m. kick-offs.

In 1882, Blackburn lost to Old Etonians in the FA Cup final. And thank all that's holy that *they* are not still a team. Imagine how much I'd have hated Old Etonians! That would have been fine but the following year the FA Cup was won by rival team Blackburn Olympians. This was a serious blow to those plans for making serious money, so the owners poached their best players by promising to pay them. The seriously amateur FA were not happy, but it worked, and Rovers won the next three FA Cup finals.

In 1888, they became founder members of the Football League, and players could finally be paid professionals. Rather than the paid amateurs that everyone knew they had been. They flourished initially, but the 20th century brought mainly Second Division mediocrity with the odd FA Cup highlight in between.

That was until millionaire businessman, and Blackburn fan, Jack Walker bought the club. He was clearly a history buff and decided that if throwing money at a problem was good enough for 1883, it was good enough for 1991. Spending a fortune on the facilities, and bringing in Kenny Dalglish as manager and Alan Shearer as striker, solved the problem big style. The Premier League win in 1995 was their first trophy in 81 years.

Trouble is, of course, that there is always someone richer out there waiting to outbid you. Rovers fell away, came back and fell away again. Jack Walker died and in 2011 the club was bought by the Venkys, purveyors of fried chicken to most of India. Their ownership led

---

* She was actually called Sheba. I'd wanted to call her Alice, short for Crystal P'Alice, but I was overruled after a conversation with Ali in which my views were 'carefully considered'.

to a period of on- and off-field turbulence, including an embargo on signing new players just as my cousin Tom was about to sign for them. It continues still because, sadly, the owners don't have to listen to a vote of no-confidence from the fans.

Maintenant, l'amour. The play-offs had been invented by the Football League in 1986 to keep more teams involved in the League until the end of the season. The top two teams were promoted automatically and the four below them played off for the final place. So it was that on Wednesday 31 May 1989 we were on a chartered train taking us to Blackburn for the away game of a two-legged final. The train left around 2.30 p.m., so naturally we'd been in the pub since 11 a.m.

The game was terrible, and even though we'd scored a very late consolation goal, we'd lost 3-1 and had played so badly that any hope of overturning the result at Selhurst seemed forlorn. (We did it. Typical Palace!) About 10 minutes into the return journey, a couple of Blackburn fans decided to celebrate their victory by chucking a concrete slab on to the train from a bridge. It damaged the engine so badly we had to wait for a new one, hence that 6 a.m. arrival into Euston.

Many tired and emotional Palace fans queued for the phone boxes to reassure loved ones they had gotten home safely. Pointless really, because, amazingly, a broken-down train in Blackburn hadn't made it on to the national news and most of the loved ones only realised there was a problem when they were woken up at 6 a.m. to hear about it. But I don't like to be left out of things, so I thought I'd call someone. And even though I'd only recently met Ali, I phoned her. Although when I'm in a bad mood, I tell her it was because she was first in my phone book. 'I love you, Ali.' I can't remember her response, and neither can she, which is amazing because she remembers every bloody thing else.

I wonder how many other marriages have happened because of football? If I hadn't got drunk on the way to watching a midweek football match in Blackburn, I may not have married the woman I love and had the child who is now a Palace season-ticket holder too.

Why You Shouldn't Support Them

- Tried to steal my own son away from me.
- Bought the Premier League.
- Literally, Cousin Tom had the pen in his hand. He'll tell you in more detail why you shouldn't support them!

BLACKPOOL

'The shirts are never, ever described as "orange".'

Historicalkits.co.uk describing Blackpool's shirt

'It's too bloody noisy.'

BBC sound recordist describing Blackpool's ambience

Now you've had a brief insight into my home life, I am going to use one of the most famous clubs in football history to give you a brief insight into the best job I ever had – travelling the country for 10 seasons filming with football fans as 'that bloke from *Match of the Day 2*'.

I don't think Blackpool fans will mind. Famous old club they may be, but their recent history has been dominated/blighted by the ownership of the Oyston family, and I don't want to write about that, if only to save myself a fortune in legal fees. I suggest you Google them and come to your own conclusions. Or, if you have a spare afternoon, you could ask a Blackpool fan.

Geordies, Cockneys and Brummies may quibble, but there is no denying that the north-west of England has been the epicentre of top-flight football in recent years. Leicester's freak win apart, the headlines have been about United, City and Liverpool.

And it was always thus, except in previous years the headlines were about the likes of Blackburn, Preston and Blackpool. Well, at least in my imagination. I devoured all sorts of history as a child, especially football, and everything I read about Blackpool gave the impression they were once one of the biggest clubs in the country.

So it came as a bit of a surprise when I learnt that the highest they had ever finished was second in 1956 and they only won the FA Cup once, albeit in the most famous final ever, in 1953, when Blackpool came from 3-1 down to win 4-3; and even though Stan Mortensen scored a hat-trick it has always been known as the 'Matthews Final' because of the wizardry of winger Stanley Matthews.*

---

* Wingers were always wizards. Midfielders were always maestros. Full-backs were always the ones not good enough to be wingers or midfielders.

Matthews was a genius. Even on scratchy black-and-white film you can see his artistry and grace. Any football fan over the age of 70 will still argue the merits of Matthews or Tom Finney as the greatest English player ever. I'm going to plump for Finney, but only because I met him, and he had a lovely twinkle in his eye.

Of course, the other distinguishing feature of Blackpool is the kit. I *loved* those tangerine shirts. 'Tangerine', remember; never, ever 'orange'.

Blackpool had the same history as many clubs, emerging in 1887 out of the remnants of various local amateur sides. They first wore a blue and white striped kit, which the fans cheerily referred to as 'merry stripes'; and in 1915, as a tribute to the many Belgian refugees that had taken refuge in the town, they adopted a kit of black, yellow and red hoops. Ah, the good old days of European unity. Sadly, it didn't last long, by 1916 they were wearing white shirts, possibly because colours were put on ration.†

Then in 1923, one of their directors, who was also a referee, came back from officiating an international match between Belgium and the Netherlands and enthused about the Dutch shirts, to the extent that Blackpool became the first and only club to adopt the colour as their kit albeit, for some reason, insisting it *wasn't* orange.

I was sent there to cover a crucial relegation battle and travelled with an eager middle-class producer, an ebullient cameraman and a taciturn sound engineer. If you work for the BBC, don't try to work out who they were. All producers are eager and middle-class, always looking for a sexy new angle: 'Can you hang upside down from the crossbar while we film your reflection in a puddle?' All cameramen think they are the F1 drivers of TV, the sexy ones carrying the sexy equipment; and sound engineers rarely speak except to tell you it's too noisy.

This producer's new angle was to film on the beach with a donkey. I'm not suggesting filming a donkey on Blackpool beach was unoriginal, but let's just say the price-list for riding one included 'adults', 'kids' and 'TV presenters'.

Three people weren't keen on this idea. The sound engineer, because 'the bloody sea is bloody noisy'. Me, because I'm wary of any animal not on a plate. And the donkey's owner, because I have this rare condition that makes me look much heavier than I am. The donkey didn't look too

'The donkey didn't look too keen either but donkeys rarely look keen about anything so I was willing to forgive him.'

---

† Blackpool were one of several clubs who kept a team going throughout the war, playing regular morale-boosting friendlies.

keen either, but donkeys rarely look keen about anything so I was willing to forgive him, especially as the poor sod was called 'Lightning'.

He was a perfectly charming donkey, though, and graciously allowed me to sit on him. Sadly, what he absolutely refused to do was move with me sitting on him. If I got off he happily consented to amble a yard or two, but once I got back on, no amount of carroty persuasion could shift him.

His owner said that Lightning liked crisps, which you could sort of tell by his shape. Crisps didn't work. But they did attract the attention of other wildlife.

On TV, it looked like I was delivering a witty link while enjoying a gentle ride on the beach. In reality I pretended to sway a little, like Lawrence of Arabia on a camel, while the cameraman ran round and round an immobile donkey and the producer tried to keep every seagull in Lancashire away from the sound engineer's packet of cheese and onion.

There's still a glamour about Blackpool, even if it is slightly faded these days. And despite everything they've been through, there is still a glamour about the football club as well, and finally, things are improving for them, only at Lightning's pace, but definitely improving.

Why You Shouldn't Support Them

- Stanley Mortensen scored a hat-trick and you call it the Matthews Final. Poor Stanley (Mortensen).
- No one can tell the difference between orange and tangerine. No one.
- The Oystons. I hope you've picked up on the idea that they are wrong'uns.

BOLTON
WANDERERS

'The new-fangled jersey of the Wanderers is something you would expect in a circus ring.'

The Football Field newspaper commenting on Bolton's new kit of white shirts with red spots in 1884; they have been wearing plain white shirts since 1885

'I would have left my leg at the halfway line rather than miss that chance.'

NAT LOFTHOUSE Bolton legend

Most football fans grudgingly accept that their club will have a mascot. A lovable yet slightly sinister creature that scampers around the pitch patting kids on the head and then wildly over-celebrates goals* in the hope they will get on *Match of the Day*, even though no one can see their actual face. My advice, though, is don't get too close. Not because they are dangerous but because those costumes take a lot of washing and not every club has a machine big enough. Also, up close, the fur can be a bit manky and some of the stains look worryingly unexplainable. But in public, at least, most fans will defend their mascot and at the very least will happily explain what the mascot actually represents, because you can't always tell.

Obviously, Crystal Palace, the Eagles, will have Pete the Eagle as a mascot. Although it took me a lot of research to discover the reason he's called Pete. It's not a very majestic, eagley sounding name, is it? Turns out the first bloke in the costume was called Pete. Sometimes research only ends in disappointment. It makes sense too that West Ham have a hammer (a six-foot weapon as a mascot – welcome to the East End!) and that Norwich have a canary. And I can almost live with Birmingham

---

* No one blames our mascots for wildly over-celebrating goals. We don't score many.

City having a rather smart bear called 'Beau Brummie'.* But to younger Bolton fans, 'Lofty the Lion' must take some explaining. After you've explained to them why they can't support one of the Manchester teams like all their mates.

Nat Lofthouse was a centre-forward. Not a 'striker'. Not a 'number 9'. A centre-forward. A genuine rock-hard bulldozing ball-header of the type that will make your grandparents misty eyed with emotion for the days of 'proper footballers'.

He was born in Bolton. He only ever played for one team: Bolton Wanderers. He only ever managed one team: Bolton Wanderers. Can you see why he may be popular in Bolton? And Lofthouse became known as the Lion of Vienna in 1952 when he scored against Austria while being elbowed in the face by one centre-back, punched in the back by the other *and* taken out at the knees by the goalie. All in a day's work. So, the furry Lofty the Lion represents a link to a past as illustrious as any club in this book.

'He was born in Bolton. He only ever played for one team: Bolton Wanderers. He only ever managed one team: Bolton Wanderers. Can you see why he may be popular in Bolton?'

Founder members of the Football League in 1888, FA Cup winners, and probably the most famous FA Cup losers of all time when they were beaten by Stanley Matthews in 1953 (see chapter on Blackpool for more details), they went on to be a fixture in the Premier League and a thorn in the side to many more 'glamorous' teams.

It's a shame, then, that most of the headlines they have made lately have been about money and not football. Because their very recent past nearly saw them disappear completely due to mismanagement and greed. They were moments away from extinction. As Kieran Maguire, lecturer on football finance at Liverpool University, told me, with a rather unexpected reference to Disney's *Beauty and the Beast*, 'the last petal was about to fall from the rose'.

Kieran gave me a brief explanation of their downfall. Well, as brief as a lecturer on football finance can be. It involved long words and spreadsheets, so I had to concentrate and drink a lot of coffee. At one stage it got so technical I had to go out for fresh air, but here's a summary.

---

* But that's because I know about history, which means I know who Beau Brummel was. He was the best-dressed man in Regency London. Which, because I also know a bit about geography, is a long way from Birmingham.

Basically, after their eventual relegation from the Premier League, the club's long-term owner, Eddie Davies, who had made millions making kettles, decided to step down because of ill health and because high player wages meant the club had been losing £400,000 a week (that may have caused the ill health, come to think of it). The club was then bought by a consortium led by Ken Anderson, who had previously been banned from being a director of *any* company in the UK (a fact that didn't seem to perturb the English Football League). Anderson was left in sole charge when the rest of the consortium bailed out; and he came up with an ingenious wheeze to help save money. He simply stopped paying bills. To anyone. Although he did find enough down the sofa to pay himself £525,000 as a consultant, and his son (Lee) £125,000 as an agent. Even though Lee Anderson was not a registered agent (again, the EFL were resolutely unperturbed). After Kieran told me that, it took about five minutes before I could lower my eyelids and double-check it, but, sadly, all true.

The club faced, and survived, six winding-up orders in the High Court until, eventually, HMRC noticed that they were owed over £1 million and the club were placed into administration and deducted the mandatory 12 points for doing so.

It's a tale similar to the one that saw Bury FC disappear in 2019, and it's a tale being told at many clubs, and will continue being told while the FA and EFL continue to stand aside and allow greedy corrupt chancers to try and make a killing from vulnerable football clubs.

I know I'm too romantic when it comes to the history and culture of football. But I still don't understand how any club, let alone one with the history and heritage of Bolton Wanderers, can be allowed to flirt with destruction when there is so much money in the game.

Happily, the tide of football tends to wash the pebbles from the beach after a while. This time next century, Bolton fans won't know about Ken Anderson, but they'll still be talking about Nat Lofthouse.

Why You Shouldn't Support Them

- They got rid of a polka-dot shirt? Madness.
- Their fans spend way too much time telling you Bolton's not in Manchester. It sort of is.
- They don't have a giant bolt as a mascot. Imagine the fun when they played West Ham and Harry the Hammer met Bolty the Bolt.

BRADFORD CITY

'Unbelievable.'

CHRIS KAMARA on getting to the play-offs as manager of Bradford City

'Claret and amber kinship is the order of the day as the Dalai Lama blesses Bradford City in the run-up to the League Cup final.'

Footballburp.com

I like Bradford. It's an interesting, vibrant and lively city. I've got cousins there who live in a suburb called Thornton, which is where the Brontë sisters were born. I don't know who the sisters supported,* but unfortunately all my cousins support either Leeds or Manchester City, and there's the problem for Bradford City. Despite having a distinct identity of its own, it seems to get overlooked in favour of the much bigger city down the road or any of the more successful clubs that lie around it on either side of the Pennines.

But if I was from there, I know for certain I would have supported them, for one reason and one reason only. They have a brilliant kit. Obviously it doesn't quite match the full glory of claret and light blue stripes, but claret and amber runs it close. Flamboyance is not a word you would associate with Bradford, but mate, that kit is fan...cee.

Sadly, it's not actually claret and amber any more. Or, rather it is, it's just not called 'claret and amber' any more. It's 'burgundy and gold' these days, for branding purposes. This time next year it will probably be 'dragon fire and sunflower', but it will still be lovely. Football shirt manufacturers giving fancy names to colours is one of those small things that really irritate me.† A greeny-brown away kit is still horrible whether you call it 'taupe' or not.

No one seems to know why claret and amber were chosen. Rather

---

* I would say they supported their brother Branwell, but that would be quite a highbrow joke, even in a Bloomsbury football book.

† Most of the others are travel-related. Why would you stand on the left side of an escalator, you idiot?

strangely, the team was formed in 1903 when Manningham Rugby League club, in danger of going bankrupt, tried one last desperate throw of the dice and became a football club instead, and the Football League, keen to get a football interloper into rugby country, bunged them straight into the Second Division before they had ever played a game.

It may be, as one theory goes, that Manningham wore claret and amber and the newly named Bradford City adopted them as a guilty tribute after they changed their name. Another theory has it that the colours represent the colours of wine and beer, to reflect the chosen beverage of its middle-class owners and its working-class fans. Or there's my favourite theory: the local sport shop only had one kit in stock when the new club came knocking.

I'm not the only one who likes those colours either, the Dalai Lama wears them a lot, although I'm fairly certain there's a spiritual reason for that, unless he saw Bradford on the telly in Tibet one day and thought 'that's the team for me'. He visited Leeds in 2012 and was apparently given a Bradford shirt, which is why he was gracious enough to send a message of support for that League Cup final a year later, when they became the first fourth-tier team ever to reach a Wembley final. Sadly, the blessing didn't help: they lost 5-0. Never mind, there's always the next life. And they do at least have one major trophy.

In 1911, when the colour combination was claret with a sort of massive yellow collar, they won the FA Cup, collecting a trophy that had only just been made in the city of ... Bradford. Since then, nothing much.

Well, I say nothing much. Unfortunately, every football fan knows the name Bradford City for one terrible, terrible reason; and it happened on what should have been a rare day of celebration, as just before the kick-off of their game against Lincoln City on 11 May 1985, they had been presented with the trophy for winning the Fourth Division title.

'Flamboyance is not a word you would associate with Bradford, but mate, that kit is fan...cee.'

Around 42 minutes later, the referee abandoned the game with smoke visible in the Main Stand. Moments later the stand was engulfed in flames. Fifty-four Bradford City fans and two Lincoln City fans were killed. The official cause was given as a carelessly discarded cigarette. In truth, it was caused by fans having to sit in a dilapidated wooden stand beneath which was the accumulated litter of many seasons, including a newspaper from 1968. It was the worst football stadium disaster since 65 fans were killed on the cramped stairs of Ibrox during an Old Firm derby.

It's difficult to explain to younger fans how different English football was in those days. There was no glamour, no wall-to-wall worldwide coverage. Just physical football, played on grass-free pitches in shabby stadiums. Of course, we didn't know that then. It was our game and we loved it.

At the time, football and its fans were under siege from the government, the police and the tabloid press. Every single one of us was a working-class hooligan or lout, going to games intent only on confrontation with each other. And we didn't pay much to get in, so why bother giving us fancy facilities like a roof, or a toilet with a door?

'We hated hooligans, not only for what they did but for what they did to the reputation of the rest of us.'

Of course, there were hooligans. We hated them, not only for what they did but for what they did to the reputation of the rest of us. Those hooligans were a tiny minority but attitudes to them rubbed off on us. You often heard the phrase 'if people behave like animals you treat them like animals'. But as I say, I was there, and my theory is that if you treat people like animals, even the nicest of them will sometimes behave like one.

'Football specials', like the one that took us to Blackburn, were trains chartered by fans to get to away games. Normally, it was a whole train, and if you were lucky, you got one that didn't look like it had been taken out of the shed for the first time since the Blitz. When around a hundred of us made the long and arduous trip to Wrexham, our 'special' was one carriage attached to a normal, scheduled train. The door to our carriage was padlocked in case we disturbed the normal, scheduled passengers. We changed trains at Wolverhampton, which simply involved shunting us on to another one, padlock and all, while we were prevented from leaving the train by a line of policemen. If some of us were seen pissing out of a train window, it wasn't because we were hooligans, it was because we'd been padlocked into a train with no toilet for five hours.

The dilapidated stand at Bradford was the result of years of neglect. We'd always put up with poor conditions because we put up with poor conditions. But some good did come out of it. Well, not *good* exactly, but at least the beginnings of a glimmer of good, of a change of attitude, of a dawning realisation that people shouldn't be fucking dying at football matches.

Condolences and financial donations came from around the world. Even the Pope made a statement, and I mention that because (a) it's good, and (b) I like the idea that a chapter in this book contains the Pope *and* the Dalai Lama.

Lord Chief Justice Popplewell (who chaired the official enquiry) was not a football fan. He did recommend some safety changes be made, but he concluded that the best way to save football fans from harm was to make it more difficult to actually go to games by making them all carry membership cards. And he could have ordered, as safety experts who testified recommended, that all the fences that ringed football pitches be removed. Instead, he ordered they should have wider access gates as a means of escape in case of emergency. It was a decision that had fatal consequences four year later in the overcrowded pens at Hillsborough.

Some of you may think that it is flippant to start this chapter with a light-hearted look at a football shirt and end it with the death of 56 people. But here's why. Like you, I love football nostalgia. I will discuss old games, old players, old kits, old TV shows and old dogs on the pitch with great delight. But one thing we should always remember is that for all the exuberant joy of football, it could also be tragically shit.

Why You Shouldn't Support Them

- In the circumstances, I'll sit this one out.

BRENTFORD

'Brentford fans, by definition, are glass-half-full types.'

DOMINIC HOLLAND comedian and Spiderman's dad

'I used to play for Brentford.'

BRADLEY WALSH comedian and Brentford reserve player

Take my advice. Don't mention the four pubs. They don't like it. Seriously. You can mention the seasons on a pizza, the horsemen of the apocalypse or the candles in a Two Ronnies sketch. But do not mention that there is a pub on every corner of Brentford's ground. I can feel the hands of Brentford fans gripping the page a little more tightly as we speak, because not only am I mentioning it, I'm opening with it. I imagine they thought I was better than that.

I have a sneaking suspicion that's the only reason they are just about to move to a brand-spanking-new ground. I reckon the chairman would have just looked at the architect's plans and said 'never mind all that, just make sure there are no bloody pubs'. You can almost feel Brentford fans flinching as they tell you who they support because they are 100% certain that you will say, 'Oh, they have a pub on every corner of the ground', as though Brentford fans may not have noticed that no matter what way they go to the ground, they will pass a pub.

The very funny comedian Dominic Holland (sorry, Spiderman's dad*) told me that the pub thing is a bit annoying, but it's easier to be glass-half-full supporters when there are so many glasses readily adjacent. He also told me why he supported them: 'Growing up in Ealing, I faced a choice of Brentford, QPR, Fulham or Chelsea; and because you want to support a club with proud traditions who other football fans quite like, I chose Brentford.' I'm still trying to persuade him to get Tom Holland to say that, it would be straight on the front of the book.

Even worse for Brentford fans is that the second thing anyone will say is 'Oh, didn't Bradley Walsh play for you?' He did. Sort of. And one of

---

* He does have other children. Their names are, oh hang on, he's never told me *their* names.

my favourite things recently was watching him trying to tell an anecdote about Bill Dodgin to a roomful of young comedians. And, to be fair, even after I'd explained that Bill Dodgin was their manager in the early seventies, it still wasn't a brilliant anecdote. But Bradley did tell me what it was like at Brentford in those days: 'It had a pub on every corner, Kev'.

Palace fans know what it's like to be overlooked in the great scheme of London football things, but there's no doubt that Brentford had it worse. Adjacent as they are to Fulham, Chelsea and QPR, they rarely even made it on to our regional football programme, and all those clubs had or are still having periods of success and glamour while Brentford, well, didn't. Actually, it's given them a sort of fierce, microcosmic regional pride, and trips to Brentford could get quite lairy. A pre-season visit there just a few years back turned proper old-school, which is going to happen when you have a pub on every corner.

'Actually, it's given them a sort of fierce, microcosmic regional pride, and trips to Brentford could get quite lairy.'

Brentford's history is sort of arse-about-face. Normally a team is started then looks for somewhere to play. But in 1889, when Brentford, to the far-west of London, was still semi-rural, when the local council built a recreation ground they decided that someone should be playing something on it. So off they went to the local pub (just the one?) and took a vote. Rugby got five votes, football got eight and Brentford FC were born. Incidentally, Chelsea also started the wrong way round, maybe it's a west London thing?

Unfortunately, negotiations for them to actually use the recreation ground broke down – probably because the Council Chairman was a rugby fan – so they carried on regardless, presumably using top hats for goalposts on any spare patch of grass. Until they found a new ground: Griffin Park. And I sincerely hope that was because they were having a kick-about one afternoon when someone came running up and said, 'Lads, what would you say if I told you I've found a park with a pub on every corner?'

After the First World War came a golden period under Secretary/ Manager Harry Curtis. I don't know what his shorthand was like or whether he typed the team sheets, but as a manager he was pretty good because they went from Division Three South straight through the Second Division and into the First where they finished fifth, the highest of any London club, regularly playing in front of 25,000 people (that's 6,250 per pub!).

The Second World War wasn't kind to Brentford. Although maybe I should rephrase that, considering what the Second World War did to the rest of London. The Bees bounced slowly up and down the bottom divisions, losing money hand over fist. To such an extent that in January 1967, news broke that their chairman had made a secret deal to wind up the club and sell their ground to QPR. Luckily, a group of local businessmen bought the club and saved them.

They continued to bounce slowly up and down the divisions, but at least they weren't skint. Except they were. Because the club had been saved with a massive loan and that had to be repaid. So, reserve and youth teams were scrapped, and if the ball went out of the ground someone went and fetched it.*

These days, however, the club, having been stabilised by a period of fan ownership, is in safe hands. They are comfortable in the Championship and about to move into that lovely new ground. But I shall miss trips to Griffin Park. It felt like a different London. No, scratch that. It felt like a different London *and* it felt like Selhurst Park. Raucous, slightly bolshie, very proud. And with a pub on every corner.

But even the lure of a brand-new ground may not make them attractive to younger fans. Dominic Holland has four sons, but, he says sadly, 'None of them support the mighty Brentford'. Well, I suppose it was always unlikely that Spiderman would support the Bees.

Why You Shouldn't Support Them

▪ A pub on every corner and away fans not being allowed into any of them.
▪ Bradley, we know. You used to play for Brentford. Get on with *The Chase*.
▪ Their new 'stadium campus' will be part of an 'urban quarter' and will include '300 cycle spaces'. It's a football ground not an art school.

---

* According to Bradley Walsh. Could well be bollocks then.

BRIGHTON AND HOVE ALBION

'Dear old Sussex by the sea.'

The world's most twee football song

'The famous Alan Mullery went to Rome to see the Pope, and this is what he said: "fuck off".'

Much better football song

Well, this is going to be awkward. When Bloomsbury first begged me to write this book.† I agreed, but only if I didn't have to write about Brighton. My plan was that I would copy the 1956 autobiography of Sunderland goal-machine Len Shackleton, in which the chapter entitled 'The Average Director's Knowledge of Football' was a blank page. Matt, my editor, thought that would be childish, so instead I suggested that I write about my Sunday football career with Venn Street, Dynamo Sabre and Coyd City, who were all actually the same team.

Again, Matt objected because apparently we're all grown-ups here and I had to write about Brighton for the simple reason that they were one of the 92 bloody Football League clubs. Although I suspect the real reason is that Brighton and Hove have a lot of independent bookshops. Mainly visited by middle-class, cockapoo-walking, craft-beer-drinking hipster Brighton fans. I suppose that's childish as well is it, Matt?

Palace and Brighton is one of the furthest, newest and strangest derbies, and has probably the most specific reason for starting, but it is one of the fiercest. Some of the worst violence I have seen at football has been at these games, and neither of us have ever had a reputation for crowd trouble. But before we get on to that, I suppose we should pay the most cursory of visits to Brighton's history before they started

---

† Other versions of that are available.

to define themselves purely by their rivalry to us by nicking songs, badges and nicknames.

They were formed in 1901. Right, on to why we hate them.

What? How is that childish?! Oh, FFS.*

They were formed in 1901 and in truth much of their early history mirrored ours, playing lower-league football for many years at shabby stadiums in front of crowds much bigger than either club deserved. Although, their stadium was shabbier than ours, obviously.

In fact, in the 69 years between 1920 and 1989 we were in the same division as them for near enough all of them, mainly the Third Division South. For 56 of those years they were just another club, so what happened?

In November 1976, with both sides doing well in Division Three, Palace and Brighton were drawn against each other in the first round of the FA Cup. We drew 2-2 away in the first game, and 1-1 at home in the replay. In those days that meant a second replay at a neutral venue, so off we trooped (me included) to Stamford Bridge on a very rainy night in early December. The first two games had been feisty, but nothing to write home about. The third one was brutal.

Brighton were managed by Alan Mullery, and us by Terry Venables. They had been teammates together at Spurs in the sixties but apparently hated each other, with both thinking the team should be built round them. Whatever, that night the players clearly took out the managers' beef on each other.

We won 1-0 with a controversial penalty and at the end of the game, an enraged Mullery marched towards the Palace fans and tossed a handful of coins at us. In the press conference he then tore up a five-pound note and said that was all Palace and its fans were worth. That might have been the end of it, but over the next two and a half seasons we were both promoted twice to end up in Division One. So, every game was important and the atmosphere got edgier and edgier as each one went by.

And there were other factors. Prior to a game down there in 1977, the Palace fans chants of 'Eagles' were met by the ironic chanting of 'Seagulls' from their fans. They and the club thought it was so clever it was adopted as their official nickname, and a seagull replaced a dolphin on their Tesco carrier-bag of a shirt. That was cheeky. But the eagle is a majestic bird of prey, while the seagull is a chip-stealing rat, so they're welcome to it.

---

* That will make sense in a paragraph or three's time.

To make matters worse, after a couple of disastrous seasons that had seen us go from the top of the First Division to near the bottom of the Second Division, our owner Ron Noades decided that Alan Mullery was just the man to get us out of trouble. Mullery was booed on in his first game, and every one that followed. Not that there were many of us left to boo: 51,000 saw the game that got us promoted to the First Division in 1979, while 5,038 watched Mullery's last game in 1984.

We consolidated well enough after Mullery, but Brighton went on a disastrous run of football and finances that saw them nearly relegated from the League altogether. For years we were in a different league to them both literally and metaphorically. While that was happening they lost their spiritual home at the Goldstone ground and ended up playing home games 70 miles away at Gillingham before moving back to Brighton to rent a tiny little athletic track called the Withdean. I wouldn't wish that on my worst enemy; and it's a mark of how football is ultimately more important than rivalries that I willingly agreed to a fundraiser for them when they were searching for a proper ground.

They've got one now alright. Although I'm pleased to say we were the first team to beat them there with the winning goal scored by ex-Brighton hero Glenn Murray. Leading to a clip that went viral of a Brighton fan shouting 'For fuck's sake Murray'.

Both teams are currently in the Premier League, but old habits die hard. In 2016, we played Spurs away in the FA Cup. It was live on BT Sport and Alan Mullery was an obvious choice for a half-time interview. Unfortunately, or fortunately, depending on whether you have an eagle or a flying rat on your shirt, they decided to interview him in front of the Palace fans. Did he think as he walked towards 5,000 puzzled but increasingly expectant Palace fans that enough time had elapsed to let bygones be bygones? I haven't enjoyed myself so much in ages.†

Why You Shouldn't Support Them

▪ Where do I start? The being despicable thing is enough surely?
▪ Brian Clough was their manager for a few weeks. I hate that.
But he hated them, so that's alright.
▪ In the first draft, every time I mentioned them, I wrote 'brighton'.
Matt made me change them all to 'Brighton'. I think he secretly supports them, like the rest of the media.

---

† I don't believe in throwing anything at anybody, but I did laugh as an older Palace fan threw a lighter at him and shouted: 'You fucking started it, Mullery'.

BRISTOL CITY

'I can't understand a word yum saying ow bis.'
'Translation: "I can't understand what you're saying."'

Bristollive.com teaching us how to speak like a native (I have never heard anyone in Bristol speak like this)

'South of the river tend to be Shitheads and north of the river tend to be Gasheads.'

MARK OLVER comedian and Bristol City fan

Mark Olver is the finest TV warm-up man in the business and was telling me all this during the recording of a TV show. So Bristol City fans are happy to embrace being Shitheads?

'Of course, better than Gasheads, ain't it?'

Sometimes in the course of writing this book, I have felt like an anthropologist, but I was fascinated to hear of the strange cultural ways of a faraway town, because I think I may have some spurious connection to Bristol City. Turns out that Ali's gran's best friend was the sister of a man who used to have a stand named after him at Ashton Gate.*

His name was Billy Wedlock. He played for them between 1905 and 1921, and made 405 appearances. His nickname was 'Fatty'. That's nice, ain't it? All those years of loyal service and his reward was to be fat-shamed. Next time someone tells you they were kinder, gentler times, just remember old Fatty Wedlock. I'm surprised they didn't go the whole hog and call it the 'Chubster Stand' just to really rub it in. Who knows, maybe 'the whole hog' was another of his nicknames.† As it happens, the Wedlock Stand was demolished recently so I have no connection with Bristol City at all, which I'm quite relieved about actually because I've always found them to be some of the chippiest fans in the country.

I don't know why. Bristol is a great city with a flourishing comedy and music scene but clearly that isn't enough to soothe the savage brow

---

* I told you it was spurious.
† Do you get the feeling that a certain someone writing a book may be a bit worried about his weight?

of some of its residents. It's in the West Country as well. Everything's delightful in the West Country, ain't it? Gentle rolling countryside, gentle rolling accent, gentle rolling scones and so on, but Bristol seems to play by different rules.

Every club has its share of fans who are borderline feral. Yes, I admit it, even Palace. But I speak their language so I can handle them. City fans are a different matter. In the same way that lion tamers can't do tigers.‡

I was convinced they have a particular problem with Palace, but after a quick search of the internet it turns out, no – it just seems to be the rest of football in general that's annoying them. Possibly because it's no fun being the top dog in a city rivalry where neither dog is winning Crufts any time soon. I thought it was reasonable to assume they didn't like us, because some of their fans attacked our manager on the pitch after they had won a play-off semi-final against us. After they'd *won*! But, as one of my mates said at the time, our manager was Neil Warnock and fans of about 25 other clubs would probably have done the same thing.

Bristol have been City since 1897 and have occupied Ashton Gate since 1904. They were formed as Bristol South End in 1894 and originally played at St John's Lane. That ground was overlooked by a hill, and as their success grew they had to erect giant canvas screens to stop people overlooking the game from the overlooking hill. And as proof that it's not just modern football clubs that try to make money out of everything, they sold advertising space on the canvas screens as well. I'm just surprised that no one came up with the idea of rotating the canvas every five minutes so they could fit more adverts in.

'Next time someone tells you they were kinder, gentler times, just remember old Fatty Wedlock.'

They've been wearing red pretty much since 1904 as well, being yet another team going by the nickname of the Robins. Seriously, come on lads, I know Edwardian times were in black and white but there must have been something else that was red, surely? Why aren't any of these teams nicknamed the Measles? Or the Dog's Dick? Or the British Army Between 1645 and 1905? Alright, bit of a mouthful that last one, but you get my drift.§

With an even worse lack of imagination, legend has it that one of their first nicknames was the Red Shirts. If I was a Bristol City fan, I'd tell legend to keep out of it. Although there is a glimmer of hope. That same legend also claims they were known for a time as the Garibaldians,

‡ Well-known pub fact.
§ No need to check, for a leftie pacifist I have a strange fascination for military history.

named after Giuseppe Garibaldi, the general who helped unify Italy with his red-shirted army. I wish I didn't have to explain that but it may save a lot of you from wondering why they were named after a biscuit.

A city the size of Bristol really should have a Premier League football club. It's never going to be Rovers so maybe City fans feel the pressure of those expectations. Because apart from a few brief seasons in the seventies, City have spent too much of their life in the lower divisions. Good news for them is that they are challenging for promotion as I write. And even better is that after a consultation with fans, the robin is back on their home kit, no doubt spreading fear among their opponents.

Thinking about it, though, the robin redbreast is a normally friendly little bird who can be very aggressive if territorially challenged, so maybe it's a more appropriate nickname than I thought.

Why You Shouldn't Support Them

- They called their goalkeeper Fatty.
- Attacking our manager on the pitch, even if it was Neil Warnock.
- It's not the accent I can't understand, it's why their fans are throwing things at me.

BRISTOL ROVERS

'Since 1883 the club has enjoyed limited success on the field and a turbulent history off it.'

BristolRovers.fandom.com – a refreshingly honest summary from their own fans

'Goodnight Irene, goodnight Irene, I'll see you in my dreams.'

Bristol Rovers anthem since 1950

If I'd been born in Bristol, like my wife's ancestors, I would almost certainly have ended up as a Rovers fan because, apart from Rovers fans, most people would agree they are the wrong team in the city to support.

Hang on, I'm just going to check something. Yep, it was Bristol, thought so. If Ali ever wanted actual proof that I have the attention span of a kitten who's just licked a sugar lump, it's the fact that I have genuinely had to remind myself of her family's Bristol connections even though I wrote about them in the very last chapter. In my defence, that was a whole day ago and I was at a Palace game last night.

Neither Bristol Rovers nor Bristol City have enjoyed massive success, but it's fair to say that City have at least flirted with the idea of massive success. They've glimpsed it on the horizon. Sniffed it in the air. The only thing Rovers have sniffed is gas.

Until 2001, Bristol Rovers were the only team never to have played in either the top league or the bottom league. That's not a bad run of mediocrity considering they were founded in 1883. To be fair, they have done their best to rectify that record of dullness since 2001, mainly by spending most of the years since in the bottom league. And who knows, they may only be several seasons, and billions of pounds of foreign investment, away from an exciting one-off season in the top league as well.

They were founded in 1883 as the 'Black Arabs'. I pause here, while you spit out your coffee. Try to direct it away from the book, it may affect its eBay value. Yes, the 'Black Arabs'. In 1883, of course, that was fine. The club was founded by five teachers (who wore black robes, so far so innocent) and named after the local rugby side 'The Arabs' (oh, and it was going so well).

Mind you, there is still a rugby club called the Saracens, so called because they admired 'the endurance and the enthusiasm of Saladin's desert warriors of the 12th century', so maybe rugby clubs are more enlightened than I gave them credit for. Or more post-colonial racist.

The Black Arabs changed their name to Bristol Rovers in 1888, and that was pretty much an end to the excitement name-wise, and on the pitch, sadly. There was a bit of excitement when they changed their nickname to the Pirates in the 1930s. Or the forties. Or fifties, sixties and seventies, depending on which fan forum/pub expert you believe. The club's own history said fans wanted a nickname that reflected the city's maritime history. I suppose, given the nature of much of that maritime trade for a couple of centuries, 'Pirate' was the much safer choice.

> 'It's a strange quirk of football that so many testosterone-fuelled young men will happily and loudly sing the gentlest or saddest of songs...'

For me, Rovers stand out for two reasons. The kit and the smell. Since 1973, they have stuck to a kit design that they had flirted with since 1930 (and I much prefer a team that flirts with kits, rather than success). They play in blue and white quarters. Yes, quarters. Not stripes, hoops or even halves – quarters. It is the most raffish kit in football, and I loved it on first sight. I still do. It was why Bristol Rovers had the honour of losing to Palace in every single Subbuteo match I ever played. Well, most of them. Eintracht Frankfurt, Dukla Prague and St Etienne were also regular and unlikely losers to Palace. Maybe not so unlikely since I was always playing on my own.

And the smell? Gas. For most of their history, Rovers played at Eastfield, arguably the tattiest, roundest ground I ever visited. It was tatty because it was old. It was round because greyhounds and motorbikes had raced there (not against each other) and it smelled because it was next to a gasometer. Well, so I'm told. To be honest, it's so long since my one visit there that I can't remember a smell. Maybe the wind was in the wrong direction. It's more likely that by then the smell of gas had given up trying to compete with the smell of football fried onions. I do remember the tattiness, though. It felt like the whole stadium was about to ask if you had some spare change for a cup of tea.

It's an IKEA now.* Rovers left in 1986, beset by financial troubles,

---

* Only a few chapters in and already we have a contender for most depressing sentence in the book.

and began a decade sharing Twerton Park with a rugby club before finally finding a new home at the Memorial Stadium.

But their fans still proudly call themselves 'Gasheads' and they still proudly sing 'Goodnight Irene'.

It's a strange quirk of football that so many testosterone-fuelled young men will happily and loudly sing the gentlest, or saddest, of songs as a gesture of pride and defiance.

'Goodnight Irene' was first recorded in 1933 by American blues singer Lead Belly. It's a plaintive song of love and loss, and even though the Gasheads have known plenty of both, how did it become their anthem? Well, in a very specific piece of historical bickering, most Rovers fans agree *when* it was first sung, but not why. In 1950, as travelling Plymouth fans left the ground early, complaining about a heavy defeat and the smell, Rovers fans began to sing 'Goodnight Argyle' at them. This was either because the song had been played at a charity firework display the night before, or because a Plymouth fan had been playing it on an accordion during the game.

Does it matter? I don't know. Does it matter what colour Henry VIII's hair was? Does it matter what the 'D' stands for in 'D-Day'? Or where Charlie Chaplin was born?† What matters is that Rovers fans still sing it.

Why You Shouldn't Support Them

- That smell was truly terrible. Probably.
- Even if it wasn't, you shouldn't be proud of a smell.
- The song sounds much better in a Louisiana accent than a Bristol one.

---

† His hair was red. 'D' stands for 'Day'. Just up the road from me. And yes, it does matter.

BURNLEY

'I think it was the colours partially, but mainly the atmosphere. I loved it.'

ALASTAIR CAMPBELL Tony Blair's right-hand man, explaining his decision when his dad gave him a choice of Huddersfield, Leeds and Burnley to support

'Endeavour is entrenched at Burnley as ego is absent.'

DNApeople.co.uk

On 6 December 1902, Burnley played Manchester United in a Second Division game at Turf Moor. They lost 2-0 in front of around 2,000 fans. Nothing remarkable about that. Except it was filmed by a newsreel camera, and the film has recently been discovered. It's some of the earliest football footage in existence, and definitely the earliest of Man United.

It's a remarkable 90 seconds or so. I always find old film of young men incredibly poignant, but it's impossible to watch this without casting your mind forward a decade or so when those young men would find themselves on a different kind of muddy field entirely.

And one of the things I love is that you can see exactly why Burnley's ground is called Turf Moor. In the first shots you see a tiny stand on one side, the front of the roof entirely covered with a slogan ordering you to smoke Bulldog Flake Tobacco. Behind it, you can clearly see the chimneys of an industrial town. Then the camera turns ... and there it is. A low wooden fence, with a scattering of young men leaning on it, and behind them the vast expanse of moor dotted with skeletal trees.

We go to games week in, week out with barely a thought as to why the ground is called Selhurst Park or Old Trafford or Ashton Gate,* but in those fleeting few black-and-white seconds we see Turf Moor in all its glory. For someone who is writing about football history, it's wonderful to actually see it. And to imagine those supporters in flat caps and boaters going to the pub afterwards to moan about how bad Burnley had been and how cold the wind was coming off that bloody moor.

---

* Although, sadly, we know exactly why we are going to the Amex or the Etihad or the Emirates. Not everyone is as romantic about football as me.

And they couldn't even look forward to seeing it later that night in the picture-house. They decided a home defeat to Man United wouldn't be good box office and it was never shown in Burnley. A level of pessimism that would never enter the mind of TV producers today, when you can watch your defeat on a phone within seconds of it happening. Without, of course, the advert ordering you to smoke any sort of tobacco.

It still baffles my son that there was a time when the only place you could see goals again was in your mind. A time when you only knew you would be on telly that night when you turned up to the game and saw the cameras, because the FA assumed if people knew beforehand that five minutes of it would be available in black and white on a tiny TV set they wouldn't bother to actually go. You can look through that window into 1902 on the BFI website. I'm not ashamed to say that my eyes go as misty as the film every time I see it.

It's impossible to see any sign of 1902 as you approach the ground now. Although, to be fair, last time I was there, I had other things on my mind. It was the annual Ladies' Day and rumour had reached me that it could be an 'interesting' day.

Now, I'd been to Burnley before as an away fan. I like it. It reminds me a bit of Palace – we are a London club but we're not Chelsea London or Arsenal London, we're real London. And Burnley feels the same. It's not that far from Manchester but it feels a long way away, lacking the infrastructure and resources of the big city because of years of under-investment and austerity.

This probably sounds hopelessly naïve but I genuinely think football fans have a slightly different perspective on things because at least we get to see different places and the effect that austerity has had on them. Your average London opera lover ain't getting many chances to go to Burnley, Ipswich or Sunderland, is he?

However, judging by the glamour on show that Ladies Day, austerity had very clearly decided it was having the week off. My guess is that one or two local make-up retailers were probably able to retire on the profits. It was designed to emulate Ladies Day at Royal Ascot, so women who supported Burnley and women who just wanted a jolly were encouraged to look their best and turn up in the morning for brunch and a free glass of prosecco while they browsed various stalls selling make-up and very small lacy items that I think were meant to be underwear.†

---

† If they were, they certainly wouldn't keep you warm during a midweek game in January.

Match of the Day 2 thought it would be fun for me to pop along with a camera crew and I was really looking forward to it – until the night before when I met them in a hotel. It was the same film crew as at the Blackpool game; I worked with them a lot and I was looking forward to seeing them in the hotel the night before. But when I did, they seemed anxious. In fact, they both had a look that I have only seen in films where innocent young men are about to go over the top in 1916.

'Alright lads, this should be fun.'

'No, Kev, it won't be', said the cameraman. The soundman nodded in agreement. They rarely speak.

'How do you know?'

'We were here last year.' I was intrigued; this was like hearing Chris Packham say he hadn't enjoyed a visit to an otter sanctuary.

'What was it like?'

'Carnage.'

I thought they were exaggerating for comic effect,* but we arrived early to set up in the function room and around 9.30 a.m. we became aware of a distant sound and noticed the stewards were starting to twitch.

Then we saw them. Approaching was what I can only describe as a glamorous gorgeous-smelling army of mischief. They'd clearly had their free glass of prosecco and more; they were already leaving empty bottles in their wake like a hot-air balloon throwing off ballast.

Now the stewards were sweating like the trumpeter in Zulu, and then they were upon us. Within an hour my face was more lipstick than skin and with the amount of boozy kisses I was getting I may just as well have had vodka rather than cornflakes for breakfast. Then into this heady mix was thrown Alastair Campbell, Labour Party press secretary and Burnley fan. I don't know if you've ever tried to interview Tony Blair's spin doctor about football while a lady asks you whether her husband would prefer the black knickers or the red, but take my word for it – not easy. Alastair, though, was a professional and spoke passionately about his love for the club, pausing only to tell the lady 'any colour other than blue'.

> 'Approaching was what I can only describe as a glamorous gorgeous-smelling army of mischief.'

Post-game, I caught up with some of the ladies and got their views on what had been a useful point in a one-all draw against Stoke, but then a

---

* Some of us do that for a living.

club official looked at his watch, went a bit pale and suggested we leave immediately.

'What's the hurry?'

'The male strippers are here.'

'That's a relief, I thought they were actual firemen.'

'Seriously, we need to go.'

We managed to get out just in time, losing only our dignity and my tie. I say 'we'. I'm not ashamed to say that the soundman was too slow. Last I saw he was shouting 'I'll never make it, leave me, save yourselves', which, ironically, was a remarkably long sentence for a soundman.

For the record: famous old club. They've won everything that could be won and they've been all the way to the bottom of the League and back again. And all the while watched by men in flat caps smoking tobacco and ladies in high heels drinking prosecco.

Why You Shouldn't Support Them

- I really miss that tie. And the soundman.
- Some of the lipstick wouldn't come off. Ali was not happy.
- I don't care what DNApeople.co.uk says, there's only so much 'endeavour' you can watch in 90 minutes.

BURTON ALBION

'Ali, I can't find any Burton quotes.'

'Try looking at a brewery website.'

Conversation between myself and Ali, 2019

'Burton-on-Trent – the world's most important beer town.'

All About Beer magazine, volume 28, issue 1 – thanks Ali

For some reason, I always knew this was going to be the hardest chapter to write. Fate has never seen fit to send me to Burton-on-Trent, not even to visit the National Brewing Centre or Claymills Pumping Station (bless you, Wikipedia). Palace have never played them, and they are one of those clubs I know many of us look out for in the FA Cup draw just to tick a new ground off the list.* Although it turns out I would have been late for kick-off because they are about 25 miles further north than I thought – who knew the River Trent was so long?

Obviously, I knew about the brewing thing. I've been in enough pubs to have picked that up by osmosis; and any historian of London will tell you that the brewers of Burton were partly responsible for one of the finest railway stations in the world, when they needed somewhere to store the beer brought to London by the new railway lines in the 1860s.

Indeed, if you get the Eurostar from St Pancras International to Paris you will be leaving from vaults made to the same plan as a beer warehouse, in units of measurement based on English barrel sizes. And we're not in the EU any more so none of those pesky foreigners will ever be able to make us change to measuring things in sherry casks. Take that, Europe!

Burton Albion's history doesn't stretch that far back,† but their nickname and their badge reflect that heritage. The nickname, I love: the Brewers. Unfortunately, the badge is arguably one of the worst in football. It consists of a rather pompous-looking stick man containing a

---

* Even I admit that this is not a game the rest of football is hoping for.

† Sadly. It may have been easier to write.

stylised B and A linked together. I'm sure it was cutting-edge graphics at some stage, now it just looks like a pregnant Eiffel Tower.‡

Brewing is also a handy way of celebrating and commemorating those rare occasions when the club made headlines. In 2006, after an unlikely FA Cup draw with Alex Ferguson's mighty Man U side, Marston's produced a beer called 'Fergie's Fury'. Sadly, Fergie was a wine man, so perhaps a nice bottle of red made from sour grapes would have been more appropriate.

Burton Albion were founded in 1950 as a replacement for four Burton teams that existed before the war. Burton United, Burton Town, Burton Wanderers and Burton Swifts. They seem to like their swifts in the Midlands, as you'll see when you get to Walsall (the chapter, not the town). One report says that the club was formed by 'popular demand', but if four clubs had disappeared from the town already that would indicate whatever the opposite of 'popular demand' was, wouldn't it? Having said that, 5,000 people did turn up to their first game, but having said *that*, that's roughly the amount of people who turn up now. So, that's the end of that.

> '5,000 people did turn up to their first game, but having said *that*, that's roughly the amount of people who turn up now.'

By the way, if you think my geographical knowledge is hazy, I'm not the only one. Having started in the Birmingham League, they were then shifted to the Southern League before being shunted to the Northern Premier League, then shifted again to the Southern League because there were too many teams for the north to handle, only for them to be sent back to the Northern Premier League, presumably because somebody in authority looked at a map and realised, like I did, that they were way further north than they thought.

Luckily, they put an end to all the regional confusion by getting promoted to the Conference and then to the League proper. And for a team that's only been in the League proper for 10 years they've done alright for themselves, reaching the Championship for a bit and having some tasty cup runs.

They may not be a big club, but they have certainly been associated with some big names, having been managed by the likes of Peter Taylor (who went on to be Brian Clough's right-hand man), Neil Warnock, Jimmy Floyd Hasselbaink and, more famously, by the son of Brian

---

‡ Whatever I was expecting in this chapter, two references to Paris wasn't included.

Clough himself, Nigel, who has had spells at the club lasting more than 14 years.

Oh, and that's the chapter on Burton Albion done! I thought it would be much harder than that. Apologies if it's not extensive, it would take an actual fan to write that book. But, if it's any consolation, your town is known for two things: football and beer. If it wasn't for you, we'd have nothing to do in a pub on a Monday night. Thank you!

Why You Shouldn't Support Them

- Almost impossible to find a reason to hate them. That makes me suspicious; what are they up to?
- According to Wikipedia, their main rivalry is a 'friendly' one with Derby County. I do not approve of 'friendly' rivalries.
- Truly, that badge is a disgrace.

CAMBRIDGE UNITED

'Laughing at the absurdity of it all is the only way to get through supporting a club like Cambridge United. And that is why I love it.'

MAX RUSHDEN talkSPORT presenter

'Kev, you'd better stop celebrating, you've got a gig tonight.'
'S'alright. I'll sober up in the car back to London.'
'We're already in London.'

Conversation between myself and friends

None of which would have been a problem if I was doing a regular 20-minute circuit gig somewhere, but I was meant to be compering the Comedy Store, which meant being awake and funny for two whole shows between 8 p.m. and 2 a.m., so I was currently being marched/persuaded/cajoled round Leicester Square while they threw water in my face and coffee in my mouth. Luckily, it worked and I sparkled on stage for several hours, pausing only once to throw up in the dressing-room sink. And, yes, I know that sounds gross, but trust me, a lot of things worse than that happened to that poor sink.

I still blame Cambridge United for that now, because none of it would have happened if they'd had a bigger ground. Well, it wasn't *my* fault, was it?

It was 10 March 1990. We were back in the First Division after a long absence, but not doing very well – and were loitering just above the relegation zone, but an unusual thing was happening elsewhere. We were on a cup run. We'd had one before when we reached the semi-final in 1976 but we've been playing football since 1905, so a second one in just 85 years was definitely something to enjoy while it lasted.

And it was lasting. The balls in the bag had fallen nicely and the quarter-final against Cambridge away was our fourth game in a row against lower league opposition. We travelled in hope. Mainly in the hope of getting a ticket. They had a terrible tiny ground and the away end had sold out in minutes, long before we got to the front of the queue. I say 'we'; 'we' sent Chirpy, which was a triumph of optimism over experience. I still love him to bits but I still don't understand why we always asked the world's most unreliable man to sort things out for us.

Not a problem, though. We'd get a ticket down there easily enough and Cambridge would be yet another pushover on our inevitable march to Wembley glory. But there was trouble ahead on both fronts. Several thousand other Palace fans had the same laissez-faire ticket idea; and Cambridge United were a team on the up. I would say they were a club with a modest history, but I'm worried that the word 'modest' might be in touch to complain. Let's say 'unspectacular' then.

They started as an ambitious amateur club called Abbey United in 1919,* but Cambridge United has only existed as a professional football club since 1951. Their first manager was Bill Whittaker, an ex-Palace player. He was 28 years old, but his hair had turned white during his time as a rear-gunner flying bombing missions in the war. A fact I try to remember every time I'm furious about having to wait five whole minutes for an Uber.

They didn't reach the Football League until 1970 and apart from a couple of seasons under a young Ron Atkinson they had pretty much been trying to get back out of it again for 20 years. Until now, that is. Most Palace fans will tell you that it is typical of our luck that we were about to play a bang-average Fourth Division team just a couple of months after they'd brought in the manager that was about to take them on the ride of their life.

The mere mention of the name John Beck will make purists like Glenn Hoddle shudder even now. It wasn't just that he played the longest of long ball games (some teams widen the pitch for their wingers, he would have lengthened it if he could), it was that he played the mindest of mind games as well. He moved the away dugout so their coaches got a lopsided view of the game. He had the grass grow longer round the corner flags so the ball would slow down when it was hoofed in that general direction. He took the kettle out of the away dressing room. He used to throw ice-cold water over his own players as a pre-match motivational technique.

In short, he did a lot of things designed to make his own fans love him and everyone else hate him. And it worked. He got them promoted that season. And the season after that and very nearly the season after that.

---

* There had been other incarnations before then, but that's the year usually taken as their first.

So when we played them that day, they were a team in form and were straining at the leash to get at the Fancy Dan First Division team while the Fancy Dan First Division team were presumably straining at the leash to get a cup of tea. As it happened, it was a terrible game on a terrible pitch and Palace won 1-0 with a fantastic shot from our captain Geoff Thomas. Or, as Max Rushden puts it: 'We were robbed by a mis-hit shot from Geoff Thomas, the only time he ever kicked a ball with his right foot ever.'

Sadly, I saw none of this. In general, football fans hate ticket touts. But what they hate even more is no ticket touts. As we approached the ground we met many people we knew who told us there was nothing available. But sharing the optimism of most idiots we just said 'yeah, nothing available to you, mate'. We, however, had the look of lads who could pay top-dollar and we were convinced a shady individual would approach us any minute offering us four together in the directors' box.

It didn't happen. If there were any ticket touts in Cambridge they were obviously off selling tickets for a hot Stephen Hawking lecture because we couldn't get a ticket for love nor money. And believe me, I would have offered love if necessary.

So, with about three hundred others we listened to the game on the radio in a pub because, believe it or not kids, there was a time when not every game was on telly. The pub was very close to the ground so we could have actually listened to the match from outside the away end. But then we wouldn't have been in a nice warm pub that sold nice warm beer.

And we wouldn't have had one of the best indoor celebrations ever when our goal went in. To be fair, we did apologise to the staff and offered to pay to clean the beer off the carpet, but the landlord was already down the travel agent booking a holiday on the money he'd made, so he wasn't bothered.

Why You Shouldn't Support Them

- You should at least try and win football games with a football, not a kettle.
- Max Rushden is still bloody moaning about Geoff's wonder goal even now.
- I may only have thrown up once, but it was for a long time. Luckily the act on stage had a very loud guitar so no one could hear me. Except the other acts in the dressing room, of course.

CARDIFF CITY

'The scariest place I ever played'

RIO FERDINAND

'Ground's down that way, you Cockney twats.'
'Mae'r stadiwm i lawr y ffordd rydych chi'n twt cocni.'

Police officer at Cardiff Railway Station

That cheery welcome to Wales was met with an equally cheery response:
  'South London twats actually, Sherlock.'
  'Is Tom Jones still shagging your mum?'
  'Nice helmet, mate.'
  'Baa-aah.'
All hilarious stuff, but indicative of the attitude of the travelling London football fan, which is basically bemusement that anyone would actually want to live anywhere else in the country.
  Roy, however, was puzzled: 'How did he know we're from London?'
  'Because our clothes match and we smell nice,' said Gaz. 'And,' I said, 'because we've just got off the train from Paddington.'
  Following a high-level midweek planning session during a pub lock-in, we had decided to get a normal real-people scheduled train to Cardiff rather than a special, mainly because the game had 'tasty' written all over it. This was a pleasant change because it meant we could use an actual toilet and visit an actual buffet bar. And because it was the eighties, and everyone was terrified of football fans, we'd been left with an entire compartment to ourselves – even though we were the nicest boys you could actually wish to meet.* Loud, yes. Drunk, yes. Flash and cocky, a little. But nice. If you wanted a kitten rescued from a tree or an old lady escorted across a road, we were the lads for the job.
  But it meant we were running late, and we were in the middle of Cardiff, which was home to a group of fans with a reputation for trouble

---

* Sadly, all middle-aged boys now. Roy's actually retired, FFS.

and violence that was right up there with Leeds and Millwall, and trust me, that is *right* up there.

Hence my good-natured enquiry to young PC Friendly: 'Any chance of a lift?'

'No,' he said. 'Walk it. And I hope you get your fucking head kicked in.'†

Now, I'm not going to let one copper's attitude tarnish my approach to this book, so of course I will give you the usual potted history, but I'll keep it very potted because I'm sure you'll want to know we all got home safely. They were formed as Riverside FC in 1899, mainly as a way to keep the grass on the cricket pitch flat during the winter. When Cardiff got upgraded from a town to a city, so did Riverside FC, becoming Cardiff City in 1908.

The Bluebirds, of course, are the only club ever to take the FA Cup out of England, beating Arsenal 1-0 in 1927 and thus earning the thanks of the rest of Britain ever since. They are nicknamed the Bluebirds because, in 1911, a play called *The Blue Bird* was a roaring success in Cardiff's New Theatre and the team had just changed their shirts from orange and chocolate brown to plain old blue.

I checked that, by the way, and it seems to be true, which is a shame because *Fanny's First Play* by George Bernard Shaw was also on tour that year. What a nickname that would have made!

A more recent kit change was met with less approval. If by 'less approval' you mean a series of angry confrontations. In 2012 their new Malaysian owner, Vincent Tan, decided he would change their kit from blue to red, because in his culture red was a strong and lucky colour. Vincent was a strong and lucky man to survive that mistake, because it brought howls of protest from Cardiff fans until he rectified the error a season later. To be fair to Vincent, he probably hadn't been there long enough to realise that 'howls of protest' is pretty much the resting face for most Cardiff fans.

'I'll say one thing for Welsh buses. They make them sturdy.'

Which brings us back to that fateful day in the eighties. It was a vital relegation match for Cardiff. If we beat them, they were going down to the Third Division (now League One). Games like that are impossible to enjoy. Not because the football was so bad, we were used to that, but because of the gathering tension and the sense that thousands of young

† His actual words. To members of the public. Except on a Saturday, when we were reclassified as football fans.

Welshmen were watching you rather than the game. And they were just the ones you could see. We were convinced there were many more of them concealed somewhere, creeping silently to a vantage point ready to attack. We'd probably all seen *Zulu* too many times.

Unfortunately, we won. Which meant some very angry fans were angrier than usual and looking to vent that anger on someone else, preferably English, and if they wore matching clothes and smelt nice then so much the better.

We were kept in the ground, as usual, till long after the final whistle (which just gave Cardiff fans more time to fashion rudimentary weapons), but then, not as usual, a senior police officer announced with a megaphone that the expected police escort to the station had been called away, or, more likely, had checked the numbers and legged it.

But, not to worry. They had laid on buses to get us to the station. Which they had. And very kindly they had actually put home-made placards saying 'Crystal Palace' on the actual side of the actual bloody bus. Trust me, promising the NHS £350 million a week is only the second most idiotic thing written on a bus in recent years. The kindest thing I can say about the journey is that it was 'interesting'. But I'll say one thing for Welsh buses. They make them sturdy. It was hit by everything from a brick to a dustbin, but it kept going.

And so did the driver. Fair play to him, the 'code of the bus'* had obviously kicked in and his honour seemed to rest on getting us to the station. If we hadn't been so keen to get on the train we may have stopped to shake his hand and give him a tip.

The station was eerily quiet. And as we'd had the common

'A more recent kit change was met with less approval, if by "less approval" you mean a series of angry confrontations.'

sense to be wearing civilian clothes, we styled it out and headed for the buffet. We had just started playing the fruit machine when we heard an almighty roar. Followed by the unsettling sight of 200 Palace fans running down the railway line. Not alongside the railway line. On it.

This was followed by the even more unsettling sight of 500 Cardiff fans chasing them. On the railway line. After a brief discussion, we decided that six of us joining in wasn't going to affect the odds either way, so we

---

* 1. The bus must get through. 2. You cannot talk to the driver, not even to shout 'Can you go any faster, mate? We're are going to die!' 3. No standing upstairs. Especially not with dustbins flying about.

shrugged, offered up a brief prayer and nudged the melon to win a tenner.

Thirty-odd seconds later there was another roar. Followed by the 500 Cardiff fans running back along the railway line. They were then followed by the 200 Palace fans. This looked like a resounding and unexpected victory until we noticed that the Palace fans were being followed by a train. A real train. Just like in the cartoons, except, did I mention this was a REAL TRAIN!

Luckily, it was *our* real train. A real, human, bought-a-normal-ticket train, not a travelling pig-pen special, and glory be, the bar was open. So we stocked up and had quite a pleasant journey home, during which we were polite and friendly to everyone and helped an old lady off the train after we'd rescued a kitten stuck in a suitcase.

There was also a last stroke of luck. One of the coppers now sulkily guarding the Palace fans waiting for the special was our old friend PC Friendly. So, as the train pulled away, we leaned out of the window, waved him goodbye and sent our best wishes to his family.

Why You Shouldn't Support Them

- It seems funnier now than it was then.
- How can they sing so nicely and be so aggressive?
- PC Friendly could have been 99% of coppers at football matches in those days.

CARLISLE UNITED

'Carlisle United's promotion to the First Division is the greatest feat in the history of the game.'

BILL SHANKLY in 1974, talking about the first club he ever managed

'D'ye ken John Peel?'

Not the legendary alternative music DJ, it turns out

You don't know what cold is like until you've stood on the terraces for 90 minutes at Brunton Park, the home of Carlisle United. We are talking proper cold. Seriously, polar bears would have stuck out a paw then decided to snuggle in for a duvet day until it warmed up a bit. Scott of the Antarctic would have said 'I tell you what boys, let's leave it a while'. We were actually scared to wee at half-time in case it came out as an icicle.

And this was in September. Christ knows what it's like in the winter. And we lost 4-1. It's a bloody long way from Carlisle to Streatham when you've lost 4-1.*

I learnt two things that day. First: always wear more than a T-shirt north of Watford, even if it is a rather fetching New Order one. And second: the phrase 'hairy-arsed Cumbrian'. As in the bloke who tried to keep himself warm by jumping up and down and shouting 'how on earth are we losing to these hairy-arsed Cumbrian chappies?' every five minutes. I'm paraphrasing slightly but I've been very fond of that expression ever since. And jealous of the hairy arses. I imagine they come in very useful for insulation purposes, although to be fair I could just about feel sensation in my buttocks again by the time we reached Manchester.

In 1905, Carlisle United beat Carlisle Red Rose in the FA Cup. It's possible there may also have been a side bet on the game because Red Rose went bust shortly after, leaving United comfortably ahead in the one-horse race to become Cumbria's biggest team.

---

* 321.5 miles actually. Whether you've lost or not.

Indeed, just so we never forget who the biggest team in Cumbria is, Carlisle's nickname is the Cumbrians. Come on now, Carlisle, let it go. Or be honest and change it to The Hairy-Arsed Cumbrians.

Like many teams in this book, Carlisle haven't made many headlines, but they do have two very interesting things on their CV. They were the first team to be managed by the legendary Bill Shankly. And, they had one glorious and terrible season in the top division. Oh, also, a man called 'Twinkletoes' used to carry a dead fox on to the pitch before every game but, curiously, the club's history doesn't linger on that.

In 1949, a 35-year-old Bill Shankly reluctantly gave up his playing career and accepted the job as joint manager and masseur of Carlisle United, who were then languishing in the doldrums of the Third Division North. To be fair, when he left in 1951, they were languishing only slightly higher in the doldrums, but it was a fun two years. Freezing, but fun.

The first thing Bill did was gather the players together and point out that they had no excuse for losing home games because the opposition would be knackered after travelling so far. Fair point. Presumably they didn't work out it worked the other way round as well. And, instead of writing programme notes, Bill would go on the tannoy 15 minutes before kick-off to announce the team to the fans, and explain why he had picked it. He would also throw in a couple of jokes and some caustic comments about the other team. Modesty was never a Shankly virtue, and as he said, 'the fans lapped it up'. I bet they did – it probably took their minds off the weather.

The fans also lapped up his style of football, breaking their record for season ticket sales in his second year. Unfortunately, that was also 'She lived there happily for many years until she snuffed it and they stuffed her.' his last season because he fell out with the board of directors and moved on to entertain the fans of Grimsby (he was obviously a big fan of a chilly town).

Luckily, Carlisle had just 23 short years to wait before the fun times returned and we were all treated to the gloriously unlikely sight of Carlisle United appearing on our screens every week, playing some of the biggest teams in the world. Carlisle was the town with the smallest population ever to reach the First Division, so it was bound to end in tears. But they beat Chelsea away in their first game on a gloriously sunny day (so that was two firsts for a lot of their fans) and two games later they were top of the table. Sadly, 39 games later they were rock-bottom and relegated but it was fun while it lasted and my bet is it will never, ever happen again.*

And Twinkletoes? Well, Cumbria was a hotbed of fox-hunting back in the day,† and in 1912 one Colonel Salkeld donated a tame fox, called Olga, to the club. The club were delighted. Although, I imagine, not half as delighted as Olga. She lived there happily for many years until she snuffed it and they stuffed her.

Then, for no apparent reason, a man called George 'Twinkletoes' Baxter began carrying the stuffed Olga on to the pitch before games wearing a blue and white tailcoat, to the bemusement of all those people watching Carlisle on telly during that one season in the top flight. Even after George died,‡ it's a tradition they continued on and off until just a couple of seasons ago. It makes no sense. But nothing in football really makes sense, and that's one of the reasons I love it so much.

Incidentally, the club's current mascot is a fox called 'Olga', but they tell the kids it's an anagram of 'goal' in case the whole dead animal thing upsets them. My guess is they will be too cold to care.

Why You Shouldn't Support Them

- Colder than a witch's heart.
- They actually placed a dead fox on to the centre-spot before every home game, that's all a bit Wicker Man, ain't it?
- No one likes a smart-arse, or a hairy one.

---

* You never know, Carlisle fans, a consortium of Siberian millionaires may be looking to buy a club somewhere warm.

† John Peel was a Cumbrian farmer and fox-hunter of some renown. It's interesting that quite a few clubs, Leicester City in particular, are not shy of retaining their links to fox-hunting at a time when it is (rightly) so frowned upon.

‡ I'm amazed they didn't stuff *him*.

CHARLTON ATHLETIC

Palace and Charlton are supposed to be rivals, but it's very half-hearted, despite what our elegant and witty riposte to that song would have you believe. Some of their fans call us 'Pal-arse' and some of our fans call them 'Clownton' – it's hardly 'Bloods' and 'Crips', is it?

Truth is we haven't often been in the same division as them (a lot of the time because they were above us to be fair) and all our energy goes on hating Brighton, and I'm sure all theirs goes on hating whoever it is they hate. I can't be arsed to check, that's how half-hearted our rivalry is. It is true that a bolt was thrown at my head there once, but the Charlton fan who threw it actually came over and apologised, said he was only throwing it in my general direction and was glad it missed. Like I said, half-hearted.

We are probably a bigger club than they are now, but time was when we were nowhere near. They were not only the biggest club in south-east London, they were one of the biggest in the country. But it's a bit of a miracle they still exist at all, if you count the amazing efforts of a dedicated group of fans as a miracle.

More of that to come, and hopefully some light on possibly the worst reason for a nickname ever. I genuinely hesitate to do any proper research in case it's true. But let's not get ahead of ourselves.

Charlton's history is almost unique.§ No cricket teams getting fit for summer, no factory lads looking for a laugh, no pub team getting lucky. Instead, a group of teenagers who used to kick a ball about on the street decided to make it a bit more organised. I like to think that they were all

---

§ I know, something is either unique or it isn't. It's artistic licence.

dressed like the Artful Dodger or Bill Sykes, because that's how young men in that part of south London dress now; only they do it ironically and brew craft beer, which they drink from jam jars.

Basically a glorified Sunday League team, they bounced around various local leagues and local grounds (including a brief spell at an early version of The Valley) before they merged briefly with Catford Southend. Very briefly. Probably something to do with away fans not knowing whether to travel to Catford or Southend. They were back in Charlton by 1924, and in the Football League, which is not bad going for a Sunday team, glorified or not. In the last three seasons before the war, they finished second, fourth and third in the First Division. They were runners-up in the first FA Cup final after the war, and winners in the second. And they did this in front of huge crowds at The Valley: 60,000 to 70,000 a week watched their home games in a vast bowl of a ground.

By the time I went there as a Palace fan, it was still a vast bowl of a ground, but much of it was empty and derelict. Great swathes of terracing were now occupied only by nettles and memories. The sixties and seventies weren't kind to Charlton. Success faded away; fans drifted away. Good money was thrown after bad in an attempt to lure back the good times and the people, but by 1984 the club were in administration, and The Valley wasn't fit for purpose. The year after, Charlton were back under new ownership but in a different location – the start of a long and unhappy ground share at Selhurst Park, my second home. According to Ron Noades, then Palace owner, it was beneficial to both teams but it didn't feel like it, especially when, miraculously, they got promoted and we didn't.

At the time, our rivalry did intensify, but a group of their fans, as unhappy to be there as we were to have them, decided to do something about it. But before they could, we did. The ground share ended. Great for us, not for them. They went to West Ham instead. Which obviously made Charlton fans even more unhappy.

Then, in 1989, the club announced their plans to return to The Valley and thousands of Charlton fans swarmed the place to clear the rubbish and burn the litter that had accumulated while it lay empty like some secret garden of football. Unfortunately, the club hadn't checked whether it was actually okay to go back to The Valley and Greenwich Council invited the wrath of every right-thinking football fan in the country by refusing them permission. End of story. Oh no!

Fans set up the Valley Party, a political party that was to contest all 36 wards in the upcoming local election. They had only one item on their manifesto: a return to The Valley. They ran a brilliant campaign and clearly had some PR geniuses among their number, as images such as a small boy on his dad's shoulder with the slogan 'If you don't support us, who is he going to support?' began to appear everywhere.

Nearly 15,000 people voted for them; not enough to win, but enough to persuade the council that they should be allowed to return. And on 5 December 1992, they did, with a 1-0 win against Portsmouth. It was a victory for them, and for every football fan, I think. It's our game, not yours. And if you try to take it away from us, then, like those weeds on the terrace, we will keep trying to come back. We may not always succeed, but we will keep trying.

So, that nickname. Officially, they've been the Robins (why do teams called that never wear brown shirts with a red front?) or the Valiants*. But, unofficially, for a long, long time, they have been the Addicks. There are a few options as to why. It could be a corruption of 'addicts' because their fans were so passionate. It could be a corruption of 'Athletic', in the same way Oldham Athletic are the 'Latics'. And, dear God, it could be this: in East Street, where the urchins first had their kick-about, there was apparently a fish and chip shop owned by one Arthur Bryan. Being a generous soul, he used to supply post-match grub to both teams in the form of haddock and chips. This became such a tradition that he began to attend matches with a haddock on a stick to advertise the fact. And as the club's official history puts it: 'with South London linguistics coming into play, that became "addick and chips" and thus the nickname was born.'

Firstly, yes, we drop the 'h' down here. It's endearing, ain't it? 'Owever, I have tried this out on many South Londoners, and all of them drop the 'h' but don't turn the 'o' into an 'i'. ''Addock', yes, 'Addick', no.

Secondly, who the bleedin' 'ell wants to be named after a battered fish in the first place?

I love history but sometimes it's bollocks.

Why You Shouldn't Support Them

- Half-hearted or not, it's still a rivalry. Bastard threw a bolt at my head!
- No gratitude when we graciously allowed them to share our ground. I mean, we didn't expect flowers or anything but a thank you would have been nice.
- Haddock on a stick, my arse.

---

* Chosen by a competition in 1964.

CHELSEA

'Blue is the colour, football is our game, we're all together
and winning is our aim.'

Opening line of possibly the worst football song ever, recorded by the squad in 1972, and
still sung by fans today (there are other contenders – yes, you, Norwich and Brighton)

'Peter Taylor takes Chelsea apart.'

JOHN MOTSON BBC commentator, apparently unaware their fans were doing the same to us

A friend of mine once became convinced his dad was having an affair after
many happy years of marriage. There was no logic to this. His dad just
wasn't the type, for a start, and he was never an energetic man, but there
was no shaking my mate and he went full on, with private detectives, the
lot. His dad wasn't having an affair but did see a psychiatrist because of
an increasing paranoia that he was being followed.

I now know how my mate felt, because I'm beginning to suspect that
my dad may, for years, have been a secret Chelsea fan. As you'll discover,
I don't support Palace because of him, he supports them because of me.
Actually, when I was a very young kid he was never that interested in
football, although he quite liked QPR (which is still a fairly accurate
description of a lot of QPR fans now).

He definitely wants Palace to win. One of my greatest pleasures in
life is phoning him from Selhurst to tell him we've just won; and if we
haven't won, he will sigh and say what he always says: 'We just can't
score a bloody goal.' He said that after I'd told him we'd just drawn 3-3
with Liverpool.

But there are just these little signs. If we're playing Chelsea he will say
'let's hope it's a draw', but not in a way that suggests a draw would be a
good result. If Palace are on telly he will look up from his *Daily Mirror* if
he thinks something is happening, but when he watches Chelsea he kicks
every ball.

I can't get a private detective to follow him because he lives with
me, but I need to do something to reassure myself he's still a Palace fan.
I don't want to have to kick him out. A few days ago, I was in the kitchen

cooking and listening to football on the radio, when he came positively galloping in from the front room to tell me Chelsea had scored. I said, 'I know Dad, I heard it, I'm delighted for you.' That led to two discussions: one about whether I was being sarcastic (yep) and then one about how come I heard it on the radio before he saw it on the telly and whether there was enough of a gap to put a bet on.

I genuinely worry about how enthusiastic he is for a team from an area that he has always dismissed as posh. And the area may be posh, Dad, but that is not a word you would ever have associated with the football club when I was growing up. Even now, awash with Russian billions though they are, there are still enough old-school 'Chels' fans to remind me of what a thoroughly well-planned exercise a trip to Stamford Bridge had to be back in the day.

Like all the best clubs, Chelsea, darlings of the King's Road, were founded in 1905.* However, unlike most clubs, who start a team then find a ground, businessman Gus Mears had the ground and needed a team to fill it. It had been an athletic stadium, but he bought it, and spent a fortune converting it, convinced that an existing football club, namely Fulham, would take it off his hands at a massive profit despite not actually informing Fulham of his plan.

Luckily, Gus had a mate called Frederick Parker. 'Gus, you plonker,' he said (in my imagination), 'let's start our own team.' So, on 10 March 1905, in an upstairs room at the Rising Sun pub, was formed Chelsea FC. You can guess who two of the directors were, but one of the others was Alfred Janes, the publican. So either Alfred gave them the room for nothing or his beer was very, very good.

Fulham's part in this story is not over. Chelsea applied to join the Southern League, but their west London neighbours objected. Instead, Gus and Fred tried their luck, flashed their cash and applied to join the actual, proper Football League. Whether because of the luck, or the cash, they were accepted into the League without ever having kicked a ball before. By 1906, they were playing Manchester United in front of 67,000 people; and by 1907, they were in the First Division. So within two years of that meeting in the pub, Stamford Bridge was home to a team in blue, playing in the top flight of English football, in front of massive

---

* Their official history has a wonderful photo of their first ever team, and Bristol City fans may like to check out their 23-stone goalkeeper, William Foulkes – he was called 'Fatty' for a reason. (That will make no sense if you are a Chelsea fan starting the book at this chapter.) And as you will soon discover, it turns out that 1905 may *not* have been the best year to found a club after all.

crowds. They were nicknamed the Pensioners because of the home for old soldiers just up the road.

To be strictly accurate, the shirts were a much lighter shade then, called 'Eton Blue', the horse-racing colours of their first president; and the nickname was dropped in the 1950s by manager Ted Drake who considered it old-fashioned and as he won them their first ever League title, who are we to argue?

Their association with the Chelsea Hospital still continues, though, with the red-coated pensioners receiving eight free tickets a game to this day. And I won't say hats off to billionaire owner Roman Abramovich for that in case Dad thinks I'm being sarcastic.

To be fair to my dear old dad, even I can't deny that there has always been a glamour and charisma about a team that is now one of the most successful in Europe. So, I want to talk about two Chelsea games that happened only decades ago, although looking at Chelsea and Stamford Bridge now it seems more like light years.

In 1970, Chelsea, the archetypal soft southern twats, played Leeds, the archetypal dirty northern bastards, in the FA Cup final at Wembley. It's an indication of how rough football was then that Chelsea were considered soft despite the fact one of their players was nicknamed 'Chopper'. The game ended 2-2, leading to a midweek replay, which for logistical reasons was played at Old Trafford. The 28 million people who watched it live on the BBC witnessed possibly the dirtiest game of football in English history, described as 90 minutes of 'seething malevolence', and Chelsea striker Ian Hutchison explained why: 'They hated us and we hated them.' On the night, the referee booked only one player, but a Premier League referee watching it back recently said he would have red-carded six of them and shown yellow to 14! Chelsea eventually won it 2-1 after extra time but also won the grudging respect of many London football fans for busting a lot of the Fancy Dan metropolitan stereotypes. And I know my dad watched it on telly because he always mentions it when a player is sent off simply for breaking an opponent's leg. 'The game's gone, son.'

'The 28 million people who watched it live on the BBC witnessed possibly the dirtiest game of football in English history.'

But Chelsea have suffered the slings and arrows of outrageous fortune as much as any other club, and that glamour has lured in many an unsuspecting fan. The comedian and writer David Baddiel, presenter of one of the greatest football fan shows ever, told me that he started supporting Chelsea after watching that replay on the black-and-white telly: 'I was too young to understand what was going on, but it was very exciting anyway and I remember us all jumping up and down when David Webb scored the winner. But,' he added, 'it was a poisoned chalice. By the time I was old enough to stand in the Shed, we had gone from being a flair side that won trophies to a Micky-Droy-dominated team of donkeys. Pat Nevin was the only flair player we had. Still, I can't imagine supporting anyone else.'

'... I'm beginning to suspect that my dad may for years, have been a secret Chelsea fan.'

Pat Nevin was pleased when I told him Dave was a big fan, but I wanted to ask Pat whether players ever knew as much about the club that they were joining as fans did: 'Well, there are as many answers to that as there are players. But in general, no. I liked to know enough. So, I knew from TV that Chelsea were a cool and hip team, and I knew some of their players, but you'll always lose out to a fan in a quiz. There were exceptions: John Terry read every Chelsea book and watched every Chelsea video there is. He's a Chelsea nut. Still buys loads of memorabilia. If you're skint, paint something blue, and put it on eBay.'

Pat said the sort of player he really didn't like were the ones who became experts after they retired. 'There was nothing worse than hearing an ex-player telling fans the current team were shit. It's doubly annoying because if I tried to claim my Chelsea team were better than this one, everyone would laugh at me!'

In 1976, Palace were drawn away at Chelsea in the fifth round of the FA Cup. We were in the Third Division; they were having one of their occasional spells slumming it in the Second Division.

As a very fine Palace fan site rednbluearmy.co.uk puts it, with just a hint of poetic licence: 'It was a battle in the stands that day, but it was a massacre on the field.'

Despite the terrible tweeness of that song, 'winning' wasn't the only aim of Chelsea fans in the seventies and eighties. On that February afternoon in 1976, Steve's dad* decided to take us into the Shed End where the home fans congregated, because in those days, even for an important game, you could just turn up, queue, and pay cash to get in anywhere in the ground. Apart from the directors' box and the team baths.

---

* One of the many people you'll meet in the Palace chapter.

Stamford Bridge was dominated by a brand-new stand on one side, but Gus and Fred would have recognised the rest of the ground as their own. I've tried every thesaurus I could find for an alternative word to describe it, but there isn't one. Three-quarters of Stamford Bridge was a shit-hole. The old stand was ramshackle and the two ends were essentially both uncovered because the infamous 'Shed' was basically a corrugated iron roof perched precariously on some rusty iron girders.

Any anxiety we had about being in the home end disappeared when we rather foolishly scored. Even as the ball hit the net, what seemed like a giant blue human arrow of skinheads hit the away end like, erm, a sideways avalanche. And the same thing happened the next two times we scored as well, to beat them 3-2.

It's not often that football fans are reduced to yelling 'stop fucking scoring' at their team, but that was definitely one of them. I wouldn't mind, but I'd had exactly the same experience in the fourth bloody round as well (see chapter on Leeds United for details). And, when I got home, did my dad put a consoling arm around me? No, he just said it was a shame it wasn't a draw.

The signs were always there.

Why You Shouldn't Support Them

- Horrible place back in the day.
- Horrible smug place today.
- Blackburn tried to steal my son's affections and Chelsea are trying to steal my dad's. Shameful.

CHELTENHAM TOWN

'The world's greatest racecourse.'

The Racing Post, 2019

'Any quotes about the football ground?'

ME 2019

I have had many happy times broadcasting from Cheltenham. For 12 years running I was part of the BBC radio team that broadcast the Cheltenham Festival from the racecourse. During the day, my job was to wander the course providing 'colour pieces', meeting punters and representing the casual listener by asking the basic racing questions they may ask. In other words, as racing correspondent Cornelius Lysaght liked to remind me, I was a 'professional idiot'.

The highlight, although not from my perspective, was when yet another eager producer decided I should stand just outside the sauna to interview some jockeys who were just *inside* the sauna trying to make the weight for their next race. The jockeys took exception to this idea and decided it would be much more efficient (and funny) if they dragged me inside the small boiling-hot box.

Jockeys are strong little buggers so I was left with no choice and the likes of Ruby Walsh and Tony McCoy couldn't believe their luck that a slightly overweight chap in a suit was actually broadcasting live to the nation in there with them. If it's possible to lose weight by laughing, they would have shed kilos that afternoon.

During the night, my job was to drink too much wine and still not be able to sleep. The entire team, including Cornelius, Clare Balding and John Inverdale, stayed in a remote, supposedly haunted farmhouse in the countryside. And the entire team knew that I wasn't bothered by ghosts but I was terrified of the countryside, especially at night. It's a petrifying combination of silence and screams that completely unnerves me. So, naturally, the entire team thought it was hilarious to scratch on my window and make owl noises. Although, with hindsight, that could have been actual owls.

Sadly, the only time I have been to the football ground in Cheltenham was to broadcast live from a Monday night festival preview, where I managed to get into a disagreement with Geoffrey Boycott, ex-professional cricket player and current professional wind-up merchant. In my defence, that's not difficult. He divides opinion. You either really like him, or you've met him.

Palace have never played at Whaddon Road, but I walked round the pitch that Monday night, so I count that as having been there. I don't really, but I just want to annoy members of the 92 Club. They are a group of men (well, mainly men) who have been to every ground in the Football League. They are the football equivalent of real-ale fans, very nice people but you find yourself edging towards the door after 15 minutes or so. And they are constantly bickering about whether you have only 'done the 92' if you did it in alphabetical order or taunting people like me who have only been in about 65 grounds.

'Geoffrey Boycott divides opinion. You either really like him, or you've met him.'

Cheltenham are the only football team in a place that is world famous for another sport. Which is why they were able to recently rename Whaddon Road as the 'Jonny-Rocks Stadium' without anyone making the fuss they jolly well should have done. They've been competing with the gee-gees for some time because, officially, Cheltenham FC have been around since 1892, playing in local leagues at various grounds before settling on Whaddon Road in 1932. That's Whaddon Road, not the Bert Jones Bespoke Taxicab Hire Stadium. Please note, however, the club have claimed that new evidence recently emerged suggesting they may actually have been founded in 1887. I'm sticking with 1892, and I suggest they should too. When not much has happened in your history, I wouldn't give yourself an extra five years for it to not happen in.

And you've probably guessed that not much has happened. I wouldn't throw in a story about me in a sauna if Cheltenham's history had been a roller-coaster of promotion and relegation, with the occasional trophy and a dog on the pitch for good measure. I mean, obviously all those things have happened,* but mainly at a local level at a rather sedate pace.

Their initial nickname was The Rubies because of the colour of their shirts, but a change to red and white saw them become yet another team nicknamed the Robins. I suppose I could check exactly how many Robins there actually are. Hang on again. I was right. There are loads.

---

* They've been around for 128 (or 133 years) – statistically, there must have been a dog on the pitch at some time. Or a horse.

They spent most of their life in the Southern League, only reaching the Football League proper in 1999 then bouncing around the lower leagues until being relegated back to non-league football. But like a horse recovering from a fall, they weren't down long and in April 2016, according to the club's website 'they lifted the National League trophy in front of 5,000+ Cheltenham fans. The following day many more lined the streets for the open-top bus tour round the town.' I'm not sure how 'many more' actually lined the streets but it's absolutely right that they should be proud of the numbers.

The men will never attract the same crowds as the horses, but if only 5,000 people and many more think Cheltenham is the home of football, then that's good enough for me.

Why You Shouldn't Support Them

- The Jonny-Rocks Stadium? In Cheltenham? The game's gone, mate. You can't ask for two tickets in the away end at the Jonny-Rocks.
- They never seemed to play during the Festival. Some evenings during the Festival I'd have killed to go to football rather than have another meal in a haunted farmhouse.
- I still have bizarre Geoff-Boycott-in-a-sauna dreams.

COLCHESTER UNITED

'I played for England. I won the title with Ipswich. I scored more than 200 goals. And still I'm known as the player who scored two goals against Leeds.'

RAY CRAWFORD Colchester striker, 1971

'Ray Crawford. You lucky bastard.'

JACK CHARLTON Leeds defender, 1971, in a note to Ray Crawford many years later

Colchester United fans will hate me, but most of this chapter is about *that* game. The U's have played many games, but *that* game is the one we still remember. So please forgive me as I retell the story of that amazing day in 1971 when you won the Watney's Cup final.

But first, let's have a quick look at that other game in 1971. Oh, come on, what else am I going to talk about? Your nickname? Your nickname is the U's, it's a terrible nickname. You were part of possibly the most amazing day in FA Cup history. Own it. Or, win something so we can talk about that instead.

The FA have turned their own Cup into a pointless vanity project won only by uncaring big teams to whom it is a distraction from the Premier League and shown across four days on TV by a broadcaster who can't afford the Premier League, to an audience who don't really care for anything that isn't the Premier League.

But time was, my friends, when we would gather round a radio to hear the draw made and every game kicked off at 3 p.m. on a Saturday and *every* football fan cared because *every* football club could win it. Yes, a radio. And not one on a phone. An actual radio, that we gathered round at school with someone given the job of writing down the teams as the balls came out of the bag. Allowing a slight pause, of course, while 13-year-old boys piss themselves at balls coming out of a bag.

With hindsight, we took an enormous amount on trust. On TV you can actually see the numbers being poured into the bowl, even though my dad insists that someone warms up Man United's ball so they can feel for it and give them a home draw. In the radio days we just took their word for it. For all we know, the balls in the bag could have been a sound effect and they just looked at the League table and thought they'd send Spurs to Arsenal or Southampton to Northampton just for shits and giggles.

But what stories that draw threw up. From Hereford to Sutton to Wrexham, top teams were toppled on terrible pitches to spark joyous pitch invasions from thousands of kids in flares and platform shoes.

And arguably the biggest of them all happened on 13 February 1971 at Layer Road when the United of Colchester of the Fourth Division played the United of Leeds.

Colchester is the oldest recorded town in England, but Colchester United are one of the youngest teams in the League. They weren't formed till 1937 and weren't elected to the League until 1950. Since then, as befits a team from an army town, they have mainly spent their time in the bottom two divisions, marching up to the top of the League then marching back down again. But if the League has brought them only bread and butter, the FA Cup brought them caviar.

That Saturday afternoon was one day before Valentine's, and two days before the nation went decimal, but no one in Colchester was thinking about love nor money. Dirty Leeds* were one of the most efficient and most unloved teams in English football. They walked on the pitch with every chance of winning the domestic treble, Colchester walked on the pitch with an outside chance of promotion to the Fourth Division. Most of the Leeds players were full internationals. Most of the Colchester players were over 30,† leading one tabloid to dub them 'Grandad's Army'. Colchester may have had the good wishes of the nation behind them, but in front of them they had a football machine that they couldn't possibly beat.

'You were part of possibly the most amazing day in FA Cup history. Own it. Or, win something so we can talk about that instead.'

Except. Except this was the FA Cup. And this may be the time for a spoiler alert. If you don't already know the result, look away now. Don Revie, manager of dirty Leeds, was a complicated human being. He was conservative in appearance and attitude but radical in his approach to the game. He was obsessed with detailed analysis of the opposition and neurotically superstitious about his match day routine. He rarely showed respect for opponents but expected complete respect from them.

---

* See the chapter on dirty Leeds for more context.
† That was one-foot-in-the-grave old in 1971.

That morning, Don was not a happy man. Far from showing respect, Colchester manager Dick Graham had been publicly stating he had spotted weaknesses in their opponents' playing style. Which is a little like saying he had spotted a dodgy water-lily in a Monet. Worse still, Don and his back-room team hadn't bothered with the usual meticulous dossier on Colchester's players and tactics. It was Colchester, who needs a dossier? He was also unsettled by the travel arrangements. They had arrived at the ground via a flight to Southend Airport, which was way out of the usual match day routine he normally clung to like the Pope clings to his rosary. And as if to prove that fate does not like being tempted, star striker Allan Clarke declared he was feeling unwell but agreed to play despite having a temperature of 106 degrees.

Whatever the reason, Don wasn't thinking straight. Looking at the state of the pitch, and feeling the strength of the wind, he decided to abandon their usual passing game and basically directed some of the best players in Europe to 'hoof it'. As it happened, Colchester hoofed it better, and for a reason. Turns out, there was a dodgy water-lily in the Monet and that was Leeds goalkeeper Gary Sprake. Dick Graham told his players that Sprake would come to the edge of the six-yard box for a header and no further. In the 18th minute, coming to collect a long-ball into the area, he did exactly that and Crawford scored with a header, unmarked by defenders who assumed Sprake would catch it.

Six minutes later, Sprake came out again, went back again, then failed to react when Crawford's header rebounded off a defender and he toe-poked it home.

Whatever Don Revie said at half-time, it didn't work. Possibly because the players couldn't hear him over the sound of Allan Clarke being sick. Yet another long ball saw a mix-up between a defender and the keeper. Dave Simmonds nipped in between them to head the ball home.

'Sometimes you can achieve more glory in 90 minutes than you can in a hundred years.'

Leeds did respond but the final whistle brought a 3-2 win and pandemonium. A furious Don Revie couldn't bring himself to exchange the usual pleasantries with the opposition manager and he ordered his players to be changed and on the coach within 15 minutes.

Back in Yorkshire, Allan Clarke was diagnosed with pleurisy. Back in the real world, Colchester lost 5-0 to Everton in the next round.

But they did win the Watney's Cup in August. That was a short-lived pre-season trophy for the two highest teams in each league who hadn't been promoted or qualified for Europe. They drew 4-4 away at West Brom and then won on penalties. The first trophy in England ever to be won that way.

That euphoria soon wore off. They finished mid-table in the Fourth Division that season, then rather bizarrely, and inspired by Leeds, they abandoned their traditional blue and white stripes for an all-white kit worn with red boots. And inspired by Rome, they changed their badge to a Legionary standard and their nickname to the Eagles.*

But remember, as Don Revie found out, fate won't be tempted. Halfway through the season, bottom of the table, in a desperate attempt to find a solution that didn't involve playing better football, they went back to blue shorts and socks. Fate wasn't impressed. They stayed bottom of the table. The following season they went back to blue and white shirts and became the U's once more.

You may think it odd to reduce a team's history to just one game. But sometimes you can achieve more glory in 90 minutes than you can in a hundred years. Colchester did that in what used to be the greatest cup competition in the history of the world.

Marvellous.

Why You Shouldn't Support Them

▪ Only a properly big team can call themselves something like the Eagles.
▪ What did they think? Copying the Leeds kit like that. It's football, not voodoo.
▪ My first ever out-of-town gig was in Colchester. I got booed off by squaddies.

---

* Sounds like a great idea to me.

COVENTRY CITY

'As true as Coventry blue.'

Medieval tribute to the dyers of Coventry

'Hunt. Oh. Well they don't come much better than that.
Right out of the book and on the first line too.'

BARRY DAVIES BBC commentator

On 3 October 1970, Coventry player Willie Carr took a free kick just outside the box. With one foot on each side of the ball, he jumped in the air and flicked it to Ernie Hunt, who volleyed it home. No one had ever seen anything like it, and to make sure that no one ever would again, the 'donkey kick' was promptly banned by the Football League. It was also the first ever goal seen in colour on *Match of the Day*.

It was appropriate that Coventry were involved in those two firsts because they had always been a team of innovators, particularly under the imaginative management of Jimmy Hill, the long-chinned, long-bearded, slightly pompous, pipe-smoking player and manager who had more ideas in a day than the FA have had corporate dinners.

Ian, my delightful father-in-law, although a very proud Geordie by birth, was brought up in Coventry after his father was sent there to manage a local bank just before the war. 'A bit like Captain Mainwaring in *Dad's Army*', he said. Yeah, a bit, Ian, except Walmington-on-Sea didn't get bombed to shit by the Luftwaffe. My words, not his. If pushed, he may have admitted that Coventry got knocked about a bit in the Blitz, but he was as modest as most of his generation about what they lived through. If anything, he's more angry about the post-war rebuild that replaced what was left of a beautiful city with a giant concrete Tetris. And the only reason I mention any of that is that, lately, Coventry's owners have done to the club what Hitler did to the city. And that's a shame, because I have had some blinding Saturdays there. Mainly, as in they caused a blinding headache on the Sunday.

Back in the day, for fans of any London team, I would recommend Coventry as the perfect place for a child's first proper away game, because it was very definitely 'away' but it was only an hour on the train and you could walk to the ground. Plus, if you had a kid with you, you may actually get a smile from the West Midlands constabulary, who normally had the same attitude to away fans that Elmer Fudd had to rabbits.

Even better, there was the Rocket. A huge pub that was not only child-friendly, it was adult-friendly, away-fan-friendly, dog-friendly and for all I know, cat-, parrot- and donkey-friendly as well. Friendly, but dangerous. The beer was cheap and it was very close to the railway station. The Rocket tempted you to be late for kick-off and late home again. Naughty Rocket.

Like 5.30 p.m. one Saturday, when 'let's have a pint, there's a train every half-hour' suddenly turned into 10.30 p.m. and 'shit, drink up there's only one train left'. The last train to Euston that night was guarded by Cedric, a Jamaican Jehovah's Witness, who decided that the amiable idiots who had just piled on clearly needed some spiritual guidance, so he checked our tickets, commiserated with us for losing, then asked if he could join us for a chat. He started the 'chat' by expressing his disapproval of our drinking cans of beer, not because it was alcohol, but because it was cheap alcohol. Cedric said if we wanted hairs on our chest, we should try some proper Jamaican rum. This interested Roy, who actually did want hairs on his chest, but discovering free rum wasn't available, he fell asleep instead. Nothing daunted, Cedric began his attempt to save the rest of our souls.

We explained to Cedric that we loved him the way that only a group of pissed blokes can love an interesting stranger, but that didn't stop him. Then we explained that we were all Catholics, so if anyone was going to hell it was him, but that didn't stop Cedric either. Luckily, we had one more trick up our sleeves. Or rather, four more cans of trick up our sleeves. He may have been able to hold his rum but two Special Brews was beyond him and somewhere between Rugby and Watford Junction he fell asleep. Don't worry, we tucked our tickets in his cap band.

Growing up, Coventry were a club I took for granted because I assumed that they had always been a top-flight side and had always worn light blue. But it was very much not so. Their early history matches their latter, with fans being the victims of financial decisions made by people that should never have been allowed to run a football club.* They are currently locked out of the stadium they used to rent because of a dispute between the owners of the ground and the owners of the club. As I write,

---

* I ran this paragraph past a lawyer friend of mine. Let's just say it's a lot shorter now than it was.

they are playing their home games at Birmingham City's stadium. They were founded in 1883 as Singers FC by workers of the bicycle factory of that name, changing it to Coventry City in 1898. They had a good spell in the 1930s but for the most part they bounced around the lower leagues, idly toying with kits and nicknames. Black and red, red and green, dark blue and white, light blue and white, all white – these were the boom times for rosette makers in Coventry. And they were known first as The Little Blackbirds, then The Peeping Toms (hopefully, in honour of Lady Godiva riding naked through the town) and finally The Bantams.

'In short, he made football fun for the people of Coventry and the people of Coventry flocked to the colours.'

And then, drum roll please, along came Jimmy Hill in 1961. He had been a useful player and had been the splendidly bolshie head of the Professional Footballers Association. In that capacity he had just overseen the scrapping of the maximum wage, the £20 a week limit on players' earnings imposed by the Football League. It revolutionised football and Jimmy was about to do the same to Coventry. He introduced the new sky-blue kit, along with the nickname of, ahem, the Sky Blues. The 'ahem' is mine.

He introduced pre-match entertainment. He laid on trains to away games and they had entertainment too. He insisted on renovations to the ground, introduced English football's first electronic scoreboard and wanted an all-seater stadium – partly so fans could watch the game in comfort and partly because, as he said, 'you can't be a hooligan sitting down'. There was an obvious flaw in that argument because it was easy enough for hooligans to stand up *and* he'd given them something to rip out and throw, but the sentiment was there.

In short, he made football fun for the people of Coventry and the people of Coventry flocked to the colours. He got them promotion to the Second Division, and then, glory be, to the First. And then … he left. Lured away to ITV for a career in broadcasting. Many of us only know him as an opinionated TV 'character', but he was a true innovator,* and my God, Coventry City could use him now.

They went on to become the first club to try to adopt subliminal sponsorship when they agreed to change their name to Coventry Talbot to advertise a local car maker. The League refused, so Coventry simply incorporated a full-size letter T to the front of their kit (the brown away

---

* Three points for a win was his idea.

version still makes me shudder). Sadly, the BBC refused to show them on TV wearing that kit, which defeated the object a bit.

Jimmy's dream was fulfilled when they had the first ever all-seater stadium in 1981. They won the FA Cup, they got into the Premier League. And now they are in League One, playing at someone else's ground. My lawyer friend suggests I stop here.

Why You Shouldn't Support Them

- Always had a hangover after games there.
- At the time, coppers in Coventry were the least friendly of the West Midlands Police, and that took some doing.
- The brown away kit really wasn't nice. My guess is that Lady Godiva was naked because that shirt was the only other option.

CRAWLEY TOWN

'Every day in Crawley is a day lost in my life.'

RONNIE O'SULLIVAN snooker star

'I will always have a great affection for the place and keep across how the team is doing.'

ROMESH RANGANATHAN comedian, TV presenter and Arsenal fan, born in Crawley

Obviously, being a mate, Romesh is aware of my belief that when a baby's birth is registered, its local football team should be too, and the baby should be made to support said team. But Romesh's dad moved the family to north London at a young age and 'fell completely in love with Arsenal, and I wanted to be like him', so I have decided to forgive him.

Being the fan of a Fancy Dan Premier League team myself (well, for the moment anyway*), I don't get many opportunities to go to the Broadfield Stadium, which is currently known for sponsorship reasons as the People's Pension Stadium, and was until recently the Checkatrade. com Stadium. As you know, I'm not a fan of companies naming a stadium. I'm just waiting for a company called Stadium to sponsor the Stadium Stadium to know that the game has really gone.

The club was formed in 1896, when it was apparently a pretty little market town rather than what now appears to be a suburb of Gatwick Airport. It had an unremarkable time in various local leagues before turning professional in 2005 and climbing the pyramid to actual League football in 2011. That was just a few months after, still a non-league team, they reached the fifth round of the FA Cup where Man United struggled to beat them 1-0.

They've survived in League Two quite comfortably for a club their size, and that stadium of theirs is very nice. Unfortunately, they've tainted it a bit by allowing Brighton's youth teams to play there, but I thoroughly enjoyed ticking it off my list recently. Palace have never played there, but a couple of years back, my cousin Tom† was living with

---

* I mean they are in the Premier League at the moment. I'm not about to support anyone else.

† Last seen in the office at Blackburn Rovers.

us while he was in goal for a Conference South team called Whitehawk, who are the other team in Brighton. They were drawn away to Crawley in the Sussex Senior Cup‡ so a car dangerously full of members of my extended Irish family set off on the short journey down the M23 armed only with enough miniature bottles of whisky to get us to Glasgow and back. In our defence, it was freezing. Not Carlisle freezing, but really cold, with that snidey sort of sleet that creeps up on you and gets in your ears. There are only two ways of dealing with weather like that. You can wear a big coat, or you can drink whisky. And if we'd gone for the big coat option we wouldn't all have fitted in the car. By the way, rest assured, the driver was not drinking. We're not that irresponsible. Besides, he wasn't old enough to drink.§

> 'When a baby's birth is registered, its local football team should be too.'

Anyhoo, after a short, but surprisingly pleasant journey, we found a car park with a handy pub attached, topped up on antifreeze and made our way to the Whateveritwascalledatthetime Stadium.

For me, there is something magical about going to a ground where a low-level cup competition is happening.

The club-shop window was glistening with frost and shone like a star in the gloom. Yes, I said 'window', singular. It was tiny. And it seemed to pretty much only sell shirts and scarves, which was a refreshing change when even a club like Palace will sell you red and blue garden gnomes or teapots shaped like an eagle (I may have made the teapot up; I've got three of the gnomes).

The crowd was also tiny and actually fitted quite comfortably into the bar. Yes, of course that was the first place we headed. And even though the ground only holds 6,000 fans, three parts of it were closed so fans of both clubs sat comfortably together. The small bunch of Whitehawk fans were an eclectic and hipster lot (from Brighton, remember) who looked suspiciously like they might drink cocktails out of jam jars and brew their own tofu, but they were very friendly, especially when they discovered why we were there. In fact, I'm still in touch with two of them.

I can't remember much about the game (really? You amaze me) but I remember the night as a brilliant reminder of how much actual fun you can have at a football match when you're with good people who love their clubs, and you can hear each and every insult hurled at the referee.

---

‡ You'd imagine that Crawley could have won that more than the four times they have, but to be fair, it is played by teams in the *whole* of Sussex.
§ Don't email to complain. He was neither drinking nor 12.

Sadly, Whitehawk lost, but it wasn't Tom's fault so even he was quite happy when we squeezed him into the car (took some doing, he's 6'3") and headed home for a nightcap.

And that's Crawley for you. When one of your claims to fame is that a snooker player hates you, it must be reassuring to know that there is a little jewel of a football club just down the road.

Why You Shouldn't Support Them

- Allowing Brighton teams to play there.
- Worse hangover than Coventry.
- I like Ronnie O'Sullivan. Stop annoying him.

CREWE ALEXANDRA

'Oh Mr Porter, what shall I do? I want to go to Birmingham and they've taken me on to Crewe.'

First sung in 1892 by music-hall star Marie Lloyd

'In 1838 Crewe became the first railway station in the world to have an adjacent hotel.'

UK Transport Wiki

It's not a good sign, is it, that the most interesting quotes you can find about a football team are about the nearest railway station? I'm guessing though, that for those of you over 40, even now, if you hear the word 'Crewe' you either complete it in your head with the word 'Alexandra' or with that song. Unless you live there, obviously, in which case the word 'home' is probably the first thing that comes to mind.

As a kid hearing that song, I used to wonder if it annoyed people from Crewe that, somehow, being there instead of Birmingham was considered such a problem. Apparently not. Some of them embrace it. Richard Hoiles, ITV's brilliant horse-racing commentator, is a passionate Crewe fan. He told me: 'You might as well be famous for something, and we are best known for the fact everyone changes at Crewe.' Sadly, Richard, this is a book about football, not trains, so it doesn't really help. And, as it happens, that song may not even be about trains.

When I accidentally became a stand-up comedian, I became nearly as fascinated with the history of working-class popular entertainment as I am with the working-class history of football. Nearly. So, I learnt that the song may have been a music-hall artiste worried about being late for a performance* or it may have been about a young lady who only wanted to flirt but ended up doing much more. And as the world of Marie Lloyd was much more raunchy than you probably imagine, it could have been either, or indeed, both.

You know who Marie Lloyd was, don't you? Yes, you do, she was one

---

* There was a huge network of theatres and concert halls along which hundreds of performers and shows would travel every week. Crewe was the main railway junction in the north-west.

of the biggest music-hall stars ever, the purveyor of some seriously saucy songs; but who was Alexandra? Why, Princess Alexandra Caroline Marie Charlotte Louise Julia, of course, daughter of the King of Denmark and wife of Edward, heir of Victoria and, one imagines, the purveyor of very few saucy songs. She was Princess of Wales from 1863 till 1901, when she became the Queen and Empress Consort of India. If you're a royal expert and I have any of those details wrong, I don't care.

She was obviously popular, though, or the members of Crewe Cricket Club were all after knighthoods, because when they formed a football team in 1877 they named it straight after her. Although there is still the lingering hope that they may have named it after a pub that was named after her, but knowing cricket players, I doubt it. If they *did* name it after a pub then that means that all pub quizzes are off because there will be no teams actually named after a person (see the chapter on Accrington Stanley).

Now, you would imagine that a club with such a distinguished name may have a distinguished history, but your imagination has let you down. They do have a rightly deserved reputation for developing young players, but they tend to move on to bigger clubs, leaving senior players behind to not win very much, although in all honesty, 'not winning very much' could have been their motto for a long time. (That's not a bad idea, actually: 'Non Multum Lucri' would look quite handsome under a badge. And if you're a Latin expert and I've translated that wrongly, see my royal note above.)

Richard Hoiles told me about the reality of being an Alex fan: 'We produce good players and we live within our means'. And? 'Er, that's it. Actually, because we produce technically good players we often get beaten by more physical teams.' That's what I love about football. Even the good things can turn out bad.

And, as Richard found out, your football team can find a variety of ways to let you down:

> Our regular penalty taker was out for one game and I heard through a source that the players had a competition to see who would replace him. The winner was a defender who had never scored but I had a big bet that we would win and he would score a penalty. As I was commentating a live race I got a notification that we had won 1:0 with a very late penalty. I was still celebrating when I got the call to say it was our second pen of the game. And someone else had taken it because my man missed one in the first half!

Football giveth and football taketh away. I think even a loyal Alex fan like Richard would admit that if your official history includes one of your players being the fastest ever to get a red card in League history then quite a lot of the rest of it won't be talking about trophies.

Caps off to goalkeeper Mark Smith, though: getting sent off after 19 seconds is a decent effort. What's even better (or worse) is that in the official history it comes immediately after the proud boast that in 1993, Crewe Alexandra won the Bobby Moore trophy for having the best disciplinary record!

In more bad news for Crewe, it's not the fastest any more. In 2000, another goalkeeper, Kevin Pressman, was sent off just 13 seconds after kick-off.

And he was beaten by Walter Boyd of Swansea and Keith Gillespie of Sheffield United, who were technically sent off after no seconds when they got red cards for throwing punches while they waited to come on as substitutes (in separate games, you'd have heard about it if it was the same game).

So another unremarkable club out of the 92 then? No, there's no such thing. They share a storyline that will become familiar as you go through this book – cricket club starts a football club to keep fit in winter, then it forgets cricket and becomes a football club that is a focal point of identity for a town or an industry.

In Crewe's case, that industry was the railway that 'Oh Mr Porter' worked for, and what's remarkable about Crewe Alexandra is not their name, or their achievements; it's that 153 years after they first kicked a ball, they are still doing it, and Mr Porter is still going to watch them.

Why You Shouldn't Support Them

▪ Naming your football team after a member of the Royal Family? Come now.
▪ Crewe fans calling their club 'Alex'. It's confusing.
▪ Bringing Richard Hoiles joy and despair in the same minute. That's Crystal Palace's job.

CRYSTAL PALACE

'All I really want is for Crystal Palace to win every game from now until the end of time, that's all.'

EDDIE IZZARD comedian and Palace fan

'We may be the oldest club in the world.'

STEVE PARISH chairman and Palace fan

And so we come to Crystal Palace, Crystal Palace FC, by far the greatest team the world has ever seen.

That's a fact. Have Liverpool and Barcelona won the Third Division and the Zenith Data Systems Trophy? They have not. I rest my case.

It's always amused me that you will hear fans of League Two clubs sing that *they* are by far the greatest team the world has ever seen. I've even heard Brighton fans sing it, which is truly remarkable – imagine that, Brighton fans actually singing.

Liverpool fans could just about get away with it, but for the rest of us that song represents a cheery, ironic defiance and a simple statement of fact: to all of us, our team is the greatest in the world. To us. It's not just a team, or a club, or a place to be visited occasionally for entertainment or disappointment. It's part of who we are. I know I'm preaching to the choir here, but you, reading this, will now be thinking about your own team. What it means to you. Your first game. Your mates. That night in the pub when you thought you'd explode with joy after a big win. The wonderful Jo Brand went to her first Palace game in 1979 with a group of student nurses and was immediately hooked: 'We started going to every home game. The Railway Telegraph for drinks before the game then the curry house across the road after the game. I just thought Palace fans were very funny and I appreciated the art of creative swearing.' I am glad to report that the Railway Telegraph and the curry house across the road are both still there. I walk past them on my way home. Well, I don't always walk past them. I may occasionally pop in to say hello.

Top football journalist Dominic Fifield has spent most of his working life writing about the game for the *Guardian* and now, *The Athletic*. He has the best reason ever for becoming a Palace fan: 'As a kid I became fiercely proud of all things South Norwood, largely because all my mates came from posh places like Purley, where the council were happy to clean up dog poo from the pavement. I actually did a school project counting dog turds around Croydon to prove my point. And, of course, the biggest thing in South Norwood is Selhurst Park.'

'So, Dom,' I said, 'supporting Palace was a faeces-based gesture of working-class defiance?!' 'Yup.'

Obviously it's not easy being a journalist and a Palace fan. One of the greatest nights in our recent history came at Selhurst Park. With about 15 minutes to go, we were 3-0 down against a rampant Liverpool side looking to eat into the goal difference separating them from Man City at the top of the Premier League. We scored a deflected consolation goal and then something magical happened. We turned into Barcelona, and swarmed all over a shell-shocked Liverpool to come back and draw 3-3. It was glorious mayhem. Except for Dom: 'I'd just pressed "send" on my *Guardian* match report about an easy win for the visitors.' Typical Palace.

Eddie Izzard's reasons for supporting Palace are more poetic, as you might expect from a comedian who creates such wonderful flights of fancy. 'Romance is the love of a beautiful thing and football is the beautiful game so, for me, Palace is romance. I have been in love with them since I walked out of Auntie Bea's house and into my first game.'

Auntie Bea, it turns out, lived on Whitehorse Lane, which is where the away entrance at Selhurst Park was. Imagine that, actually living on the same road as the best football ground in the world! I was instantly retroactively jealous when Eddie told me that. He continued: 'Loving Palace has been tough, but I still dream of the next act of the story when everything starts to go amazingly right. Is that possible? Yes, because football is romance!'

'Have Liverpool and Barcelona won the Third Division and the Zenith Data Systems Trophy? They have not.'

I'd never actually thought of Palace as a romantic entity before, but I've started sending them flowers every week now, and I may write a sonnet. Thanks, Eddie!

I'm an intelligent and articulate man,* but as soon as I stop thinking about work, or art, or politics, thoughts of Palace will rush in. Are we

---

* Am so.

staying up, have we signed anybody, who's injured, what do we talk about on the pod this week? Don't worry, we always find something – last week we discussed whether Pete the Eagle would beat an actual eagle in a fight.

If you offered me the choice of never seeing Palace again or never seeing my wife, of course it would be an easy choice, but she would know why I was getting tearful at around midday on a Saturday when I should be getting my first pint in the Pawsons Arms, after, of course, always entering by the same door. The other two doors are unlucky. For a tiny pub, it has a lot of doors.

'I was raised in a nondescript part of south London difficult to point out on a map. My football club is my identity.'

I have been a Palace fan since my first day of primary school when I was sat next to a kid who was so much taller than me, I thought I'd been put in the wrong class and started crying. He put his arm around me, and I sobbed into the brilliant claret and blue striped woolly Palace jumper his mum had knitted him. Five decades later I am still going to Palace with Steve and his four brothers and his many cousins and all the friends we collected on the way; and five and a half decades later he still point-blank denies that any of the details in that touching story are correct.

So how do you write the history of a club when nobody you know can agree on facts about the bits of the history you actually shared together? I don't even know who took me to my first game. Dad insists he took me to see us play Man U in 1969, but I don't remember, and Mum says he didn't. She reckons Bill the greengrocer (not the same as Uncle Bill) took me to a game a year later, and Steve reckons it was his dad who took me the season after that. Why the local greengrocer would be taking me to a game I do not know, so I have decided that, as with Brighton, I shall be grown-up about this chapter and attempt to treat Crystal Palace FC as just another club.*

The Crystal Palace was a huge† glass and iron structure built to house the Great Exhibition of 1851. It was a symbol of the high-water mark of Victorian confidence and, as well as displaying wonders from all over the world, it was a place of popular entertainment and carnival. It was 'The People's Palace'. Although it wasn't to everyone's taste: Colonel Charles

---

* Even though they are clearly the most special football team in the world.
† 1,848 feet long and 408 feet wide. Or, for Remainers, 563 by 124 metres. Sounds longer in feet. You can still see the concrete footprint now. My nan used to describe to me 'watching the sky on fire' the night it burnt down in 1936.

de Laet Waldo Sibthorpe MP described it as 'a transparent humbug and bauble' and it was that attitude that led the resistance by local gentry to making the Palace permanent. God forbid you should have your back garden full of 'people' wanting to be 'entertained'.

So, Joseph Paxton, who built it, had the idea of moving the whole thing to Penge, then a beautiful park in the countryside, which it sure as hell ain't now. In 1854, Paxton's 'Winter Park and Garden Under Glass' was reopened by Queen Victoria after stupendous efforts by thousands of construction workers, and more importantly, glaziers.

Which brings us to Steve Parish's extraordinary claim. Those glaziers retained at the site to maintain and repair the acres of glass definitely formed a football team called Crystal Palace and were definitely represented at the inaugural meeting of the FA at the Freemasons Tavern in Covent Garden in 1863. They definitely took part in the FA Cup in 1871,‡ but then disappeared from the records in 1876 and, as that fine website historicalkits.co.uk states, 'it must be assumed that they closed down. There is no connection with the present-day club which was founded in 1905.'

It has long been thought that when the FA decided that the Crystal Palace park should host the FA Cup final, they also decided that would give an unfair advantage to Crystal Palace, and rather unfairly decided that the club should disband. That theory, however, conveniently overlooks the fact that the first final didn't take place there until 1895.

And it was thought that the huge crowds attracted to the Cup final encouraged businessmen to believe that a local football team would thrive, a view shared by our old friend from Aston Villa, William McGregor, the father of the Football League. 'I believe', he wrote in a letter to *The Football Star* in 1904, 'that a really good team at the Crystal Palace would be a tremendous draw.' If only they had founded a really good team. Instead, in 1905, they founded a mediocre one that faffed around the lower leagues until nineteen sixty bloody nine.

But here's the thing: Steve Parish has been shown documents that seem to show the original team weren't disbanded in 1876, and the team of 1905 wasn't founded, it was revived. So far, the FA don't agree, mainly I suspect because it would involve a lot of reprinting, but Steve is convinced, so watch this space.

Imagine how much more proud I would be of being a Palace fan if it does turn out that we are the oldest football club in the world. Although

---

‡ No, we didn't win it. Don't be daft.

for some supporters, every silver lining has a cloud. 'It just means we've gone even longer without winning a trophy,' said one.

And that's where I want to finish this chapter. I could tell you about our brilliant kits, our brilliant, and woeful, players. I could tell you about the Malcolm Allison years when he put us on the map and relegated us two years running. I could tell you about being relegated with the highest points total ever. I could tell you a thousand things that make my club unique. You could tell me the same about yours. You'd be wrong, but I'd smile politely. Instead, I just want to say that being known as a Palace fan makes me immensely proud. I was raised in a nondescript part of south London difficult to point out on a map. My football club is my identity.

Like most people raised in the Catholic faith, I veer from atheism to devout faith on an almost daily basis. What I do know is, if there is a Heaven, then of course all my departed loved ones and cats will be there. But it will always be the Saturday before Christmas, it will always be the back bar of the Pawsons Arms, it will always be full of all the boys and girls I have grown up with and genuinely love. It will be a sea of red and blue, and, of course, we'll be singing 'Glad All Over' because we've just beaten Brighton 5-0.

Why You Shouldn't Support Them*

▪ We have enough fans already, thank you, and they are all brilliant. Try Charlton, I believe they have vacancies.

▪ You should support your local team. If that happens to be Palace, tough, you should already support them.

▪ Our kit is only a 9.5. Claret and light blue stripes was a 10.

---

* Have to admit, was not expecting them to make me do this for Palace.

DERBY COUNTY

'Make that two pints and we'll be friends again.'

TINY boss of the Palace 'firm', at the Baseball Ground

'Clough was Derby – the flesh and bone and breath of its football.'

FourFourTwo magazine

Outside of Brighton games, Palace never really had a reputation for fan violence. For the most part they would stand their ground, but if any of the serious firms came a-calling they would generally melt away, or leg it down the nearest convenient railway line like they did in Cardiff.

We've always had a big away support, but none of them particularly went looking for trouble, which is not to say trouble never happened, but it was sort of stumbled upon, rather than actively sought out. And for the most part it was easily avoidable. Regular away fans knew which people, which pubs and which alleyways to avoid – and if you were going to a new ground you just headed for the floodlights and ignored anyone who asked you the time, that being the traditional method by which away fans were flushed out.

I don't know if it ever worked. I doubt it, because I don't know of any London football fan who would be daft enough to check their expensive Rolex and say 'of course, me old China, it's a deep-sea dive past Big Ben'.†

Our firm was called the Wilton, named after the pub they drank in. We knew them to nod at and knew to swerve them if we wanted to miss the tear-up, which we did. Their leader was called Tiny, because, of course, he was fucking massive. Football is full of nicknames that can normally be cracked without the aid of Bletchley Park boffins. They nearly always refer to the blindingly obvious, or its opposite. Someone called 'Lightning' will be a slow drinker. Someone called 'Lanky' will be short or tall, or from Lancashire; someone called Donkey Head will either have

---

† Five past ten in made-up Cockney rhyming slang. Which it all is.

a head like a donkey or be very handsome, or in *A Midsummer Night's Dream*. And someone called Fireplace Jack will either sell fireplaces for a living or will have claimed to have had sex in a chimney. They are all real examples.

There are exceptions: my dear mate Gaz is called that because he doesn't look like an ex-Villa player called Gary Shaw. Barry is called Frank because he speaks his mind. Neil the Fish drinks a lot and has a seven-second memory span. Evil John is the nicest bloke you'll meet. You get the drift.

So on a trip to Derby we were standing at the back of the terrace, minding our own business and drinking the first pint of the game. Not the day, the game. In some ways the eighties was a terrible decade, but quite a few away ends would sell you beer. In plastic glasses, of course, they weren't idiots. We were marvelling at the state of the pitch and generally being superior about the surroundings when Roy, making some sort of grand sweeping gesture as always, managed to knock Tiny's pint over.

Roy was handsome. Still is, the bastard. He'd once been mistaken for Donnie Osmond by an Italian tourist, which he mentioned once or twice, in just about every conversation. He was also a complete liability when he was drunk, mainly because he was very good at pool but was a terrible winner. We had to bail him out of a lot of pubs.

This time he was on his own. The entire ground seemed to go quiet, which must have been a coincidence because most of them wouldn't even have noticed, surely? We certainly went quiet. Roy because he was worried and the rest of us because we were wondering how best to avoid helping Roy. I was mentally working out how long I could wait until I asked his mum for his record collection and that coat I really liked.

Luckily, Tiny was of the opinion that as he was in a town full of Brummies that wanted battering, he wasn't going to waste energy on Roy, as long as he replaced the beer, twice. And we weren't going to waste energy telling Tiny they weren't Brummies.

Now, most football fans of my generation will say two things when you mention Derby County. First they'll say 'the pitch', then they'll say 'Brian Clough'.

The club were formed in 1884 when Derbyshire County Cricket Club noticed that more people were watching football than cricket and wanted in on the financial action. They were originally called Derbyshire County Football Club but the cricket authorities objected so the 'shire' was dropped. At first, they played on a racecourse, but in 1895 they decided that a cricket club's football team playing on a racecourse was too confusing so they moved to the Baseball Ground. That had been built by Sir Francis Ley, who had wanted to bring his beloved sport of baseball to England. Of course, it didn't work, so the Baseball Ground was now vacant and Derby moved in.

The pitch at Derby was a disgrace, even by seventies standards. We were used to pitches having no grass by the end of the season, but Derby's started like that. Whatever the weather and whatever the time of year, it always looked like it had just been ransacked by student archaeologists. Which made it even more of a miracle when their free-flowing football won them the First Division in 1972 for the first time ever.

Mention miracles and the name of one man won't be far behind. Brian Clough. He took a football club who had been living in Doldrum House, Doldrum Street, Doldrumshire for decades and got them promoted, then won them the title. Aided, of course, by his brother-in-arms Peter Taylor.

A year later, they were gone. Derby's board became fed up with Clough's constant media work and his constant criticism of the footballing authorities, especially them. Tens of thousands took to the streets to demonstrate and the players threatened to go on strike, but they stayed sacked. Not to worry, a couple of years later they went to even greater glory down the road at Nottingham Forest.

Ah, it's gone a bit quiet and tense in the East Midlands. Forest and Derby are bitter rivals and both clubs claim him as their own. A lot of clubs have shared managers, even the worst of enemies. Alan Mullery managed us and Brighton. They worship him; we don't, for the simple reason he was the worst manager we ever had.

But Clough took both County and Forest to unprecedented success. So, and I really am sorry Derby fans, for more about Brian, you'll have to read the Forest chapter.

If it's any consolation, I will take the piss out of them a bit on your behalf.

Why You Shouldn't Support Them

- Their fans had a very robust attitude towards people not from Derby.
- Derby sacked Brian Clough. Sacked him. The greatest, most entertaining manager that ever lived.
- They all call you 'duck'. What's that all about?

DONCASTER ROVERS

'You will go to prison for four years.'

JUDGE PETER BAKER QC to ex-club owner Ken Richardson, 1999

'Ronaldo could play for Doncaster Rovers and he would score a hat-trick.'

SIR ALEX FERGUSON

It's a shame they never asked Ronaldo if he was tempted by the idea, because they may have made more of an impression on me otherwise.

I have apparently been to Doncaster, my mates swear I have, but I genuinely can't remember doing so. Maybe they've being seeing other mates behind my back. We played there in the FA Cup last season, but I definitely watched that on telly, because I remember Ali asking me not to shout so much; and we have been in the same division as them a couple of times but that wasn't long ago and I'm fairly certain I didn't travel to the away games.

I've been to Doncaster racecourse. I remember the horses. No, hang on, it may have been York, now I come to think of it.

Doncaster Rovers are one of those clubs who have to shout very loudly to draw attention away from their noisy neighbours, United and Wednesday, just down the road in Sheffield. Sadly, for most of their history, they haven't shouted loudly enough. Although in recent years they have actually yo-yoed between League One and the Championship, which represents massive improvement on decades of regularly bouncing up and down between the bottom leagues.*

Of course, if you're a Donny fan, those lower league titles and play-off wins were very distinguished; but recently the only thing that has made the rest of us take note was in 1999 when their ex-owner was sentenced to four years in prison for trying to burn the ground down.

This book is full of clubs being brought to the brink of financial ruin but his *Coronation Street*-style attempt to prevent his own financial ruin

---

* I really wish there were ways other than yo-yos and roller-coasters to describe ups and downs. Tweet me if you can suggest any. I'll bung them in the paperback.

was particularly shabby. I mean, Peter Barlow has done a lot of bad things in Weatherfield but even he would draw the line there.

Further back in time, it's actually quite hard to pin down when *this* Doncaster Rovers actually began. In 1920, it was decided to revive Doncaster Rovers, which had disbanded in 1916 for obvious reasons.† Technically, the club of 1920 was an entirely new organisation, but no one there seems to care, so neither do I, which means we travel back to 1879 for one of my favourite origin stories of all. The club's official history says that was the year that one Albert Jenkins, a fitter at the local railway works, scratched together a team to play the 'Yorkshire Institute for the Deaf and Dumb'. It was a 4-4 draw, and inspired by the experience, Albert and his mates decided to set up a full-time team. At the first recorded meeting of the club, in 1882, Albert was elected as captain and secretary. I don't know why that was the first recorded meeting of the club. Either they hadn't bothered to record earlier meetings, or they didn't want it recorded because they spent the meeting gossiping, or Albert didn't want anything recording until he became secretary. Who knows? No one, I told you, it wasn't recorded.

In 1888 they lost their first ever FA Cup game 9-1 and they lost most of the subsequent ones as well. In fact, the game I watched on TV last year was their first appearance in the fifth round of the FA Cup for 63 years. Every now and then they go mad and appoint a big name ex-player as manager – like Leeds legend Billy Bremner in 1978. But in general they are among those many clubs who have done their time in non-league football only to bounce back again and find themselves in a lovely new stadium.

So there you are, I'm afraid. Not much of note has happened. But the beauty of football is that it *could* happen any season now. Truthfully, not much has happened to most of the teams in this book, so when it does happen, it's wonderful. And lack of achievement hasn't stopped me loving Palace, so it won't stop Donny fans loving them either.

Why You Shouldn't Support Them

■ If someone genuinely can't remember if he's been to your town or your ground, you need to get yourself a fountain or a statue. Any kind of memorable landmark will do.
■ Doncaster or York, I lost a lot of money.
■ Not having the ambition to see if Ronaldo fancied playing for them.

---

† Not every club stopped for the duration of the war, Blackpool, for instance, but most did.

EVERTON

'I wish I'd bought Everton.'

SYLVESTER STALLONE in the *Liverpool Echo*

'I support them both, but if it comes to the crunch, I'm an Evertonian.'

SIR PAUL McCARTNEY in *Observer Sport*

As a child, I felt a strange affinity with Everton fans. It was that shared feeling that somehow they too had picked the wrong team in the city to support.

Everton fans, even Rocky and a Beatle, have it worse than we do. They are a true giant of a football club, yet any success they have is always viewed through the prism of the team on the other side of Stanley Park. Their biggest rivals are actually named after the city, and outsiders usually make the mistake of assuming that all Scousers will support Liverpool. Although my theory is that the more stereotypical a Scouser looks and sounds, the more likely he will be to support the reds.

And that brings me to something that genuinely used to really annoy me on behalf of Everton fans. As you may have gathered, I love football kits. We got our first colour TV in 1973 – bear with me – a brooding monster of a rented box that permanently smelled as though a forest fire was about to begin. But finally I had the chance to see football on TV in glorious colour, and technology being what it was back then, it was COLOUR. Not the mundane shades of actual real life but vibrant, garish colour, the sort even Walt Disney may find a tad bright. To a generation of children brought up with Brian Moore saying 'for those of you watching in black and white, Leicester City are wearing the slightly darker socks', this was like the actual future arriving in your front room, albeit a future that may contain a small explosion from the back of the telly.

My favourite TV watching position as a kid was horizontal on the carpet with my face about a foot from the screen; left hand available to reach for fizzy drinks, right hand permanently occupied in twiddling my hair. Apparently, I looked really cute.

Less cute is the fact that, even in my fifties, it still is the way I watch television – horizontal on the carpet with my face about a metre from the screen; left hand available to reach for pinot grigio, right hand permanently occupied in twiddling what's left of my hair. I still refuse to accept that my receding hairline and short-sightedness had anything to do with the way I spent most of my childhood.

The TV set was delivered on a Monday afternoon, which meant I had six long days and five long nights to wait before 10 p.m. on Saturday found me lying on the carpet, twiddling my hair, desperately willing *Match of the Day* to come on.

Finally, the moment came, heralded by the second greatest theme tune in the world:* it was time for my first glimpse of TV football in colour, and it was Everton at home. The opponents I don't remember, but the kit I do. It was the most glorious, vivid, royal blue with a white collar, and white shorts.

I loved it. I loved it so much that I became furiously indignant on their behalf whenever a commentator would bang on about Liverpool's famous and traditional all-red kit (which wasn't that traditional; they'd only been wearing it since 1964). Liverpool were always 'resplendent' in their red. No one else got to be 'resplendent'. 'Resplendent' means sumptuous, magnificent through colour, impressive. Just say red, for Christ's sake.

Anyhoo, it didn't seem to bother Evertonians as much as it bothered me because relations between the red and blue were generally very good, or at least they were until the Premier League came along and made winning so much more bloody important.

Apart from the kit, there is something else I … blimey, I nearly said 'like' then … there is something else I don't mind about Everton, and that's Goodison Park. Along with Selhurst Park, it's one of the last proper grounds in the Premier League. And by 'proper', I mean old-fashioned, slightly shabby and worlds away from the identikit corporate stadiums that pass as grounds around the rest of the top division. It's a proper throwback. The stand behind the goal is called the Gwladys Street End, how old-fashioned and badly spelt is that?

Incidentally, fact fans, when that end was opened in 1937, Everton became the first club to have four double-decker stands. It would have happened years earlier but one resident of Gwladys Street, Private William Fraser, refused to leave his house so it could be knocked down.

---

* The first being the theme tune to *The Big Match*.

In the end, Everton bunged him £25 to bugger off, and, amazed by such riches, bugger off he did.

The Toffees have always had a quirky history. The Toffees?! Oh, haven't I mentioned that yet? Like many club nicknames and traditions there are as many versions of how it happened as there are blokes in a pub willing to tell you, but this one seems closest. Around 1890, a sweetshop owner called Old Ma Bushell became famous for inventing Everton Toffees. Her shop was next door to Anfield, where Everton then played, wearing red shirts. The club then moved to Goodison Park, which was good news for Mother Noblett,* who promptly invented Everton Mints as a tribute to their new kit of black and white stripes. Nothing daunted, Old Ma Bushell asked permission from the club to distribute free toffees to fans *inside* the ground before the match started. Which is why her granddaughter began chucking toffees at bemused men who were apparently charmed by the idea of a free sweet in the eye after a week of hard graft in the docks. It's a tradition that persists to this day, unlike the dock, unfortunately.

But there was a day when you could have thrown free cars to fans pre-match and they wouldn't have noticed. On 14 January 2007, amid rumours that he was about to buy the club, Sylvester Stallone was guest of honour at Everton v Reading, and my editor at *Match of the Day 2* decided that was the game I should cover. I objected, because (a) that's my default setting, and (b) I was convinced that the whole Sly/ Rocky thing was old news and that a once-iconic figure would barely raise an eyebrow in more cynical times. And I was right, no one raised an eyebrow. They raised a roof. In fact, they raised all four of them, including Gwladys. Why *do* they spell it like that?

I turned up with my camera crew and a full-size cardboard cut-out of Sylvester Stallone. Now, before the match, his appearance was still only a rumour, but the sight of me prancing around with a cardboard boxer was enough to get a lot of people very excited (dear God, I had to keep a tight grip on that cut-out ... and that's a sentence you don't get to use often).

Despite local excitement, I was still slightly underwhelmed by the whole thing until, taking my place in the press box, the match announcer's voice came over loud and clear: 'Ladies and gentlemen, we have a very special guest here at Goodison Park today', and without saying any more played the opening bars of the *Rocky* theme tune.

---

* They seemed to have a Route 1 attitude to nicknames in those days.

I have never seen a football stadium wobble before, but the ensuing noise was off the scale, as a stocky little real-life, actual Sylvester Stallone appeared. The players stopped kicking about and formed an impromptu guard of honour as he came on the pitch and Sly shadow-punched his way around the stadium to the disbelief and delirium of the entire crowd.

Now this put me in a dilemma. First, I was going to have to tell my editor he was right in the first place, which really annoyed me. Second, I, along with 15 other journalists, had been granted a whole minute with Sylvester and, curmudgeon that I am, my one question was basically going to be how nice it must be for him to get out of the house for a change, so I needed a new one, fast.

Then things got even better, or worse, depending on your perspective. The chairman of Everton at the time was the very nice, very generous Bill Kenwright, and when I interviewed him pre-match, he hinted he had laid on a little surprise for me.

Cut to half-time and I'm in the queue to get my minute with Rocky. Suddenly, out of his entourage loomed a big man. A very big man. Big enough to have his own postcode. In a perfect movie New York accent, he asked if I was Kevin Day. I gulped, then nodded. He beckoned. And I found myself in the company of a real-life version of my cardboard cut-out, albeit about a foot shorter.

Sylvester Stallone himself, sounding exactly like Rocky, said that 'Mr Kenwright' had told him I did features on TV with 'the real blue-collar fans'. I was happy to agree, even though I knew my next feature was going to be in an executive box at Spurs.

'I like that,' said Sly. 'No one talks to the blue-collar fans any more', and then proceeded to give me a perfect eight-minute analysis of the way sport was being priced out of the reach of ordinary working people.

None of the other proper journalists even got to ask a question, and to make it even better, Adrian Chiles was hosting *Match of the Day 2* at the time, so for the first and only time in my life I had a legitimate reason to shout: 'Adri-an'.

Why You Shouldn't Support Them

- One of the buggers stole the cardboard cut-out.
- They can't spell 'Gladys'.
- The new owner is planning to build an identikit corporate stadium.

EXETER CITY

'What's a Grecian urn?'
'About three drachmas a week.'

MORECAMBE AND WISE

'There are two St James's Parks?!'

Every football fan outside of Exeter

Once upon a time, *Match of the Day 2* wanted me to go to Torquay to get a 4 a.m. coach to Old Trafford with some Devon-based Man United fans. They liked putting me on long coach journeys because they knew from experience that at some stage I was likely to fall asleep, and apparently the sight of me, eyes shut, mouth open, with another team's scarf draped round my neck, was 'never not funny'.

This time I was happy to oblige, because it meant I'd have several hours in which to chastise Man U fans for not supporting their local team. Sadly, it turned out the point was not to take the piss out of them but to do the opposite, and celebrate the reasons why they followed the Reds. I was banned from using the phrase 'glory hunters' under any circumstances. The theory was that someone who was willing to get on a coach at 4 a.m. to watch them home and away had to be counted as a proper fan. Spoilsports.

It turned out to be a very pleasant coach journey with some lovely people who all had solid reasons for supporting United, so it has no place in this book.

At the time, the BBC were (and sadly still are) obsessed that the *Daily Mail* may discover that any of its employees were travelling anywhere in comfort, and it turned out the cheapest way to get me to Torquay was by flying to Exeter and getting a cab from there. That sounded dodgy. I would have offered to walk but I was genuinely worried they might actually take me up on it. So Friday afternoon saw me at London City Airport, insisting to a bemused official that not only was there a flight to Exeter, but I had a ticket for it. This clearly came as something of a surprise to him, but he rattled his keyboard and found a plane from somewhere because half an hour later a hardy gaggle of us were walking towards an aircraft that was only marginally bigger than the Airfix ones that used to hang off my bedroom ceiling – and, more worryingly, had similar propellers. And smelt faintly of fresh glue.

The pilot greeted us personally and gave the impression that this was not how he had seen his career going (the photo of Concorde on the dashboard was a clue), and he seemed even more pissed off when it turned out he had to do the safety chat as well. That didn't bother me because I never pay attention to the safety chat; if landing on water is such an unlikely event, why do I need to know what to do? As you can tell, I'm not a nervous flyer – normally. It's just that in general I prefer my flying to be just above clouds, not just above lampposts.

'I've flown to Exeter at a height so low we nearly had to stop at traffic lights.'

I watched a documentary recently about the Dambusters, arguably the most heroic pilots of the Second World War, who flew to Germany at heights of 200 feet. I wasn't impressed. I've flown to Exeter at a height so low we nearly had to stop at traffic lights. Still, at least it meant the landing didn't take long. I wouldn't have minded if the aircraft was small but luxurious, like the ones James Bond gets to fly in, but I've sat on more comfortable seats in accident and emergency wards. And it's very hard to enjoy your complimentary tea when the bloke making it should, in theory, be flying the plane.

If the flight to Exeter leaves a lot to be desired, there is a lot to love about Exeter City: they are owned by their fans, for a start, and they have a poet-in-residence – the Exeter Bard. I approve of both of those things, although I daren't tell my dad about the Bard. He thinks goalkeepers wearing gloves are proof the game's gone soft; an in-club poet would only enrage him further. Mind you, it would be something new to tell the doctor: 'What set this off?' 'Erm, I told him a football club had a poet. Can you give him the usual injection?'

Exeter also have a nicely unusual nickname: the Grecians. Nobody is quite sure why. My favourite theory is that during the 18th century the town re-enacted the siege of Troy with those living inside the city walls being the Trojans, and those just outside being the Greeks. Exeter City emerged from a team called St Sidwell's based in an outlying parish who were, therefore, Grecians.

It's the most likely theory because it seems like absolute bollocks, and they are always the best. But the club subscribe to that theory, and it's certainly better than the other contender, that there was a gang of toughs in Exeter called the 'Greasy 'uns'.

St Sidwell's became Exeter City in 1904, leading to my favourite specifically local historical fact on any official club website ever: 'Having won the East Devon League, City spent a challenging three seasons in the Plymouth and District League.'

Another thing in their favour is that they also really annoy Newcastle fans (never a bad thing) by having a ground of the same name, albeit without the apostrophe, and barely a season passes without a story about a hapless coach driver delivering a bemused group of away fans to the wrong ground.*

Why You Shouldn't Support Them

▪ According to that website, celebrity fans include Uri Geller and Noel Edmonds. You'd keep that quiet, wouldn't you?
▪ 'They've got a bloody poet!' I told my dad about the Bard. He's not stopped shaking his head since.
▪ Struggled in the Plymouth and District League.

---

* Although, as Birmingham fans know, it can happen.

FLEETWOOD TOWN

'I'm always there for the club and I'm always there for the town.'

ALFIE BOE tenor singer and Fleetwood Town fan

'Kevin is my favourite comedian.'

ALFIE BOE – nothing to do with football but I thought you'd like to know

'I had to do a streak once as a forfeit at Fleetwood. I can't remember why.'

JAMIE VARDY

I've never actually been to Fleetwood, but I feel like I know it well because for years, my tax office was based there. I always felt that was odd because, there was a tax office a couple of miles away from me in Sutton. Because, like many freelancers, I earn decent money but not on a regular basis, occasionally I'd eat into my tax fund, secure in the knowledge that a massive amount of money would almost definitely turn up the day before my bill was due. It never did, which is why I spent a lot of time on the phone to some very friendly people in Fleetwood explaining the situation and making promises I really hoped I could keep.

My caseworkers were so friendly that one of them kept hoping Fleetwood would be drawn away to us in the Cup so he could come down for a visit. He also had a theory that HMRC didn't want Sutton dealing with me in case the office was full of Palace fans who wouldn't worry that I still owed them nine hundred quid. Bless him.

The one thing you probably know about Fleetwood is that they play at Highbury and wear red and white, but there the similarity to Arsenal ends. Especially because the Cod Army of Fleetwood fans actually make a lot of noise during games.

There has been a Fleetwood Something since around 1870 (probably; even the club's official history is hazy), but the current story only began in 1997. So, to put that into context, I've got socks older than an EFL team. They're not good socks but they were the first present my son bought when he was little so I can't throw them away, can I? Well, not according to Mrs Day.

Since 1997, Fleetwood Wanderers became Fleetwood Freeport,* then Fleetwood Town. And while they finally decided on a moniker, they were taking part in a phenomenal rise from the very low reaches of non-league football to a place in League One. During which time, so Alfie Boe tells me, it was very cheap to see a match, 'mainly because I used to sneak in through a gap in the fence'.

That phenomenal rise is a great story, but I'm sometimes reluctant to tell tales like it, because somehow it implies that the very low reaches of non-league football are a bad place to be, instead of the gloriously madcap world it often is.

So instead let's take a look at the one name that leaps to mind when any football fan hears the name of Fleetwood. After Alfie Boe, of course, who is genuinely baffled when people ask why he supports Fleetwood. 'It's because I'm from there, Kev!'

The other name, of course, is Jamie Vardy. How can I put this? You don't see Jamie Vardy and think 'ooh, he's got a pleasant demeanour, I'm sure he'll sign this bit of paper for me'. He's probably a lovely bloke, but he has the look of a human seagull who is permanently waiting for you to drop a chip. On the pitch, he looks like the cocky kid that every Sunday football team has. The one who tells defenders he's not bothering to run around because sooner or later they'll make a mistake and he'll score. Then they do, and he does, and he celebrates by taunting them and their family. He's the sort of player you desperately want to see thumped by someone but not as much as you desperately want to see him play for your team.

I love watching him play (except against Palace, obviously) because he scores the sort of goals he shouldn't score. When he gets the ball, he should be holding it while another striker makes a run and he slips him in. Instead, he'll like as not volley it over the keeper from 30 yards or he'll waltz past him and tap into an empty net.

He does that because it wasn't coached out of him as a 12-year-old in a Premier League Academy. He came up the hard way. Vardy started

---

* Freeport being a local company, not a place.

his career with Stockbridge Park Steels, then moved to Halifax Town. For a short while at his first club he had to leave away games after an hour because he was fitted with an electronic tag after being convicted of assault and didn't want to break his curfew.

He moved to Fleetwood, where 34 goals in 42 games brought him to the attention of just about every club outside the Premier League. It was at Fleetwood that he really found himself as a player and as a human being, before moving to Leicester to score the goals that won Leicester City the Premier League. He would never have done that without Stockbridge Park Steels or Halifax Town, or Fleetwood. Remember that, next time you're in a tiny ground shouting 'you big useless lump' at someone who could be playing for England next season.

And remember the Cod Army? They are the ones you can hear singing through every Fleetwood game, and they are living proof that the further down the League you go, the more humour and imagination you'll find. To the tune of 'Anarchy in the UK', they sing:

> I am a Fleetwood fan
> I am from Fleetwood town
> I know what I want and I know how to get it
> I wanna destroy Southport FC
> Cos I wanna be … Cod Army

I doubt if Alfie will ever perform it, but it was released as a single by a California punk band, the Sex Presleys. And the name of their version? 'Never Mind the Pollocks'. I love football.

Why You Shouldn't Support Them

- They were nice people in the tax office, but fuck me they were persistent.
- Jamie Vardy always scores against Palace.
- Red and white shirts and Highbury? Come on, use your imagination.

FOREST GREEN
ROVERS

'The world's greenest and only vegan football club.'

Forest Green FC official website (really? They hardly mention it)

'Forest Green Rovers are among the most disliked teams in League Two.'

GloucestershireLive.com (they don't actually explain why but I'm presuming it was a poll of burger fans)

Forest Green are now only the third newest club in the Football League (sorry Harrogate Town fans, I'll get to you in the paperback edition). But if they are only the third *newest* club in the league, they are definitely the first most-radical club in the league. Or, possibly the first most attention-seeking. We shall see.

I'm going to be honest with you here, Forest Green fans. I've not been, but I'm guessing you're based in some sort of forest, and as your ground is called New Lawn, I'm guessing you're not short of greenery. Mind you, Bethnal Green is mainly concrete so I may be wrong.

Of course, the Green in Forest Green is a big feature, so big that fans call themselves the Green Army. And if you know anything about them at all, it will be that they are the world's only vegan football club. And if you do know that, it's probably because they told you.

Now, I have nothing but respect for the vegan point of view (or so Bloomsbury tell me; turns out vegans have a lot of disposable income), but I wouldn't want my son to marry one, if only because I wouldn't fancy the food at the reception.

I have to admit that I am unreconstructed carnivore, albeit a middle-class one that likes to know where his meat was born and went to school. Not at football, obviously. Nothing good awaits anyone who asks where the meat in a football pie comes from, even though they are, in general, the food of the Gods, albeit only within a very specific time frame.

I once accidentally really upset Gordon Ramsay* when I suggested to him that, yes, his food was divine; but context is everything, and nothing he had ever cooked could taste as nice as a burger eaten on the way from Selhurst Park to the pub after Palace had won. The irony being that any actual meat content in that burger is probably accidental.

The team was founded by the very aptly named Reverend Peach in 1889 and I guess it didn't contain many vegans. He was minister of the church in the hamlet of Forest Green, which was on a hill overlooking the small town of Nailsworth. Heard of anywhere yet? They're both in Gloucestershire. England.

Until 1975 they were essentially a glorified village team playing in glorified village leagues, although rumour has it they may once have played as far away as Stroud. And they must have enjoyed it because they changed their name to Stroud FC in 1989 for a few seasons to try and attract support from wider Gloucestershire, only to lose their traditional support from greater Nailsworth. Yes, I am from London.

They inched their way to the Conference in the following years, until, in 2010, on the verge of financial ruin, they were taken over by Dale Vince, the founder of Ecotricity. Dale and Vince are both cool names and he is a cool guy: an ex-new age traveller who made a fortune in green energy. He made the club a wholly owned subsidiary of Ecotricity and began a quiet revolution. Well, not quiet as such. He's as good at generating headlines as he is at generating power.

'Nothing good awaits anyone who asks where the meat in a football pie comes from.'

The pitch is entirely organic. Much of the club's electricity is from solar panels. The kit is 50% bamboo. And the catering for players, staff and fans is entirely vegan. The players don't have to be vegan, but they do when they are playing and training, and with elite athletes like Lewis Hamilton and the Williams sisters switching to a plant-based diet, why not?

As it turns out, I'm not an elite athlete. I do genuinely think we should all eat less meat and what meat we do eat should be far more ethically reared. I do understand the vegan argument. I don't agree with all of it but I do understand it. Just not on a Saturday afternoon. For me,

---

* I've accidentally upset a lot of people. Elton John, Joan Collins, Chris Packham, Neil Warnock, Michael Owen, Sir Bobby Charlton, David Moyes and many more. Ali doesn't even ask me for details any more. I get home from somewhere, she raises an eyebrow, I give her a name, she sighs and goes to bed.

football is still the escape from real life that it has been for generations of working-class men and women, and beer, burgers and pies are a big part of the fun. Especially warm beer, rubbery burgers and indeterminate meat pies that you wouldn't touch on any other day of the week.

Mind you, come to think of it, onions are vegan so at least we'll never lose that smell.

Why You Shouldn't Support Them

- I'll say to them what I say to vegan friends. Well done. But *my* vegan option is that you please stop banging on about it.
- Taking bamboo out of the mouths of cute panda bears.
- Green 'Army' is pushing it a bit. They were a Sunday league team not long ago.

FULHAM

'There's Only One F in Fulham'

Best fanzine name ever

'If I could pay you more than 20 quid a week, Johnny, you
know I would.'

TOMMY TRINDER Fulham chairman and music-hall comedian to Johnny Haynes, shortly
before the abolition of the maximum wage saw a rise to a hundred quid

Going to a game at Fulham is a bit like time travel. If you want a feel
for how Saturday afternoons were in the decades after the war, then
approach Craven Cottage through Bishop's Park and follow the black
and white scarves until you see the floodlights emerge from streets of
terraced houses. On an autumn evening, the mist from the river even
gives you the sense of smoke from a thousand Woodbines.

They may have a brand-spanking-new stand on the banks of the river
(giving a lovely view for all those lovely people paying lovely money for
their lovely food in the lovely hospitality suites), but the rest of the ground
is reassuringly old-school and you can still see traces of old adverts and
match prices painted on patches of brickwork, although whether that's
because of a deliberate policy of preserving the past or they just have
careless cleaners, I don't know.

And, of course, there is the cottage itself. An actual cottage,
nestling snugly in the corner; and no matter how often you see it,
there is always a sense of wonder that no one has found an excuse to
knock it down.

Although, sadly, for fans of romance, it isn't an 'actual' cottage. It's a
pavilion-cum-changing-rooms-cum-offices built by that prolific football
architect Archibald Leitch, in 1905. And the reason no one has found an
excuse to knock it down is it's a listed building and they can't. Have you
seen property prices round there? If that cottage wasn't listed, Fulham
would have been playing at Craven Apartment Block long ago.

The trouble with growing old is that you actually remember the time
that younger fans are getting nostalgic for; and to be perfectly honest,

visiting Craven Cottage in my day actually made you wish for the future, when you might actually be able to watch football on a terrace that had a proper roof and actual toilets, not a foul-smelling latrine that a medieval peasant would have complained about.

Mind you, one glorious consolation of watching football there was that magnificent view of the river, you know, the one that the corporate hospitality guests are now paying through the nose for. I remember one game when the football was so bad, the travelling Palace fans actually got engrossed in some rowers having a training race and celebrated wildly when the crew in red and blue crossed the line first. They looked delighted, mainly because they couldn't hear our hilarious jokes about the size of their cox.

Grossly, you could still see that lovely view when you were in the toilet. Those toilets were basic, to say the least. I'm pretty sure there was no actual plumbing involved and we were all peeing straight into the river.

I've been on the river there myself, although you guess correctly that it wasn't in a race. In 2016 some enterprising fans chartered a couple of disco-cruisers and several hundred of us made our first ever journey to an away game by boat. And glory be, it had a bar. Which means the disco floor didn't see much action, but startled tourists were greeted by the sight of many overweight middle-aged men giving it the full *Titanic*. Even better, a lone seagull had the temerity to land on the boat and was met with a full chorus of boos and anti-Brighton chants.

Oddly enough, I think Fulham's beautiful new stand looks oddly out of place at a club with such an illustrious history. Some legendary players have graced their pitch; but despite two of them being Bobby Moore and my idol, George Best, the official club history claims their greatest player ever was one Johnny Haynes.

Haynes was an inside-forward, so basically, an attacking midfield player, who scored 158 goals in 658 games for Fulham in the fifties and sixties, and was captain of England to boot. Like many players of his generation he was quite happy to only play for one team, although 'happy' may not be the right word because he was famous for the bollockings he gave to lesser players who didn't pass to him properly. His nickname was the Maestro, and Pelé described him as 'the greatest passer of a football I have ever seen'. So perhaps even my idol, George Best, would be happy to come second to a player like that.

Speaking of 'happy', one of my happiest moments in broadcasting came at Craven Cottage. George Cohen, another local boy one-club man, and part of England's 1966 World Cup winning team, was opening a hospitality lounge that bore his name and *Match of the Day 2* had sent me along for a chat. The chat quickly turned into a nostalgia fest as I toured the ground with him and listened in raptures to his tales of running up and down the terraces to keep fit and cleaning the toilets to build character, which had been partially successful because the toilets weren't clean but he was *definitely* a character.

At half-time, I spotted a friendly and familiar face, Henning Wehn, German comedian and football nut. By a coincidence of timing that was either unfortunate or mischievous, Henning had been invited to the George Cohen Lounge with a group of German cultural ambassadors. Naturally, Henning loving football, I felt I had to introduce him to George. Because I'm a nice chap. Plus, I'd been made fully aware of George's view of all thing Teutonic.

They shook hands. Henning said hello in his very strong accent and George looked him up and down in some detail. Then, drawing himself up to his full height, which even at 5' 11" was still nowhere near as tall as Henning, he said:

'Oh, ho. German are you?'

For a brief moment I hoped Henning may have the sense to claim to be Austrian, but he agreed with George that he was indeed German. To which George simply said: '1966, mate.' And sat down again.

Henning was a bit taken aback, mainly by how much I was laughing, but valiantly tried to make a game of it: 'But that ball did not cross the line!'

'Well, you're not having my medal back, if that's what you want.'

Then, with a wink at me, he stood and gave Henning a massive hug before telling us what it was like to play in the most famous game in the history of English football.

And if ever there is a place to learn about the history of English football, it's Fulham.

Why You Shouldn't Support Them

▪ You get a sore neck trying to see the river from the away end these days.

▪ I do not approve of a neutral section.

▪ I saw George Best play for Fulham at Selhurst Park. He broke Ian Evans's leg in a terrible challenge. It's the only thing he did that wasn't brilliant.

GILLINGHAM

'Gillingham Football Club provides plenty of reasons to cheer.'

VisitKent.co.uk (official tourist sites are not normally known for irony)

'Brian Moore's Head Looks Uncannily Like London Planetarium'

Title of Gillingham FC fanzine (from the song 'Dickie Davies Eyes' by Half Man Half Biscuit)

Do you ever occasionally hear a word and think it just doesn't sound right? You've probably heard it, and used it, a thousand times before but suddenly it just sounds weird. I was on a bus one day, idly looking out of the window, when the word 'lamppost' suddenly seemed to be the most preposterous word ever. Obviously I'm aware that it is a post with a lamp on top, but it's not really, is it? Bothered me for days, that did.

I've always felt the same way about Gillingham. It just doesn't sound right as a town or a football team. Maybe it's because I was once rejected by a girl called Gillian.* Who knows? All this gives you a small insight into the way my mind works and into the fact I may not have too much to say about Gillingham itself, except that it is a much more robust town and football club than its weird name suggests. Come to think of it, Gillian was quite a robust girl. Freud would have a field day.

Mind you, a semantic discussion on word play was a long way from my mind the last time I was there, mainly because a fair few of their fans were being 'robust' and lobbing missiles into the away end. I don't know why; it wasn't a crucial game or even an important one. It was a Boxing Day but there was a noticeable absence of seasonal goodwill even though both teams were ding-dong merrily in mid-table. We were just bemused that people who must have had the same hangovers that we did could summon the energy to be so chippy. Maybe they didn't get the trainers they wanted from Santa.

Apart from George Best, one of my football heroes was Brian Moore, the presenter and commentator of *The Big Match*, London's football

* In which case, thank goodness I've never been rejected by a girl called Crystal Alice.

highlights show. He was a Gillingham fan, and indeed director, for some time. In his obituary, the *Guardian* described him as 'modest and affable'. They were not words you could apply to some of his fellow fans. 'Angry and determined' would be more accurate.

The comedian and *Test Match Special* cricket pundit Andy Zaltzman is a Gillingham fan too. I like him a lot, because he is clever and funny and tends not to lob missiles at me.

He obviously had no recollection of my most memorable game there, so told me instead about his. A recollection that, in a way, captures the essence of football for most of us. Gillingham played Halifax in the penultimate game of the 1992/3 season, locked together at the bottom of the lowest league in English football. Only a victory could prevent relegation to non-league football. It was 0-0 at half-time, where Andy takes up the story: 'Scientists and theologians have spent disappointingly little time investigating the possibility of provable, unarguable, divine intervention in the second '... there was a noticeable absence of seasonal goodwill even though both teams were ding-dong merrily in mid-table.' half. First, a totally right-footed player scored a 20-yard screamer with his previously unused left foot. Then our un-cultured centre-forward lobbed the 'keeper from 30 yards. Two goals that, in the context of a season of remorseless struggle and persistent uselessness, defied rational explanation. That match remains one of the most intense emotional occurrences of my life, and a classic example of the splendour of lower-profile football, shared by only a few thousand, but reverberating in the soul for ever.' You see, Gillingham fans? You don't have to throw things to get our attention.

As you know, I love history, so imagine my delight when researching for this chapter revealed a fact almost too good to be true in the context of our skirmish at Priestfield. Turns out that the name 'Gillingham' comes from the Anglo-Saxon for 'homestead of Gylla's family', with 'Gylla' translating as 'shouting man' because he was known for the oaths and curses he shouted as he led his men into battle. I had to do some deep research to make sure this was right, and I mean 'deep'. I went at least three websites in. Turns out I needn't have bothered. The club's motto is 'Domus Clamantium', Latin for 'home of the shouting men'.

The original club name was much less fightily appropriate. New Brompton FC were formed in 1893 after a meeting in a pub in Gillingham, possibly the same pub that had so emboldened the urchins attacking us.

They became Gillingham FC in 1913, presumably after away teams kept getting lost because they couldn't find anywhere called New Brompton on the map.

They wore black and white stripes to try to emulate the success of Notts County (it never worked, although these days, to be fair, they are on a just about equal level) and if they didn't think hard about the kit, they didn't think at all about their nickname – the Gills. It's hard to think of less effort being put into a nickname, ain't it? I mean, some clubs, like Arsenal, obviously can't go down that route, but Gillingham have no excuse (and you Swansea, although at least a swan is a bird and not a measurement of spirits).

Gillingham, the town, is famous for being the home of Chatham dockyard and for being invaded by the Dutch navy in 1667.* Gillingham, the football club, isn't really famous for anything (although some of their fans have a remarkably good aim). Like many clubs, they have spent most of their history bouncing around the lower divisions and most of their recent history bouncing in and out of financial difficulties.

They have the honour of being the only Football League club in Kent (Palace being now firmly in London) and if they were to disappear not many people outside Kent would mourn them. But I bloody would. I'd never been to see Bury play, but I cried when they went bankrupt because I know what each and every team means to its supporters.

Of course, there was the whole missile throwing thing, but we expected that sort of thing from fans who were naturally resentful of us glamorous Londoners. And, to be fair, none of those objects they threw actually hit any of us, so forgive and forget eh?

Why You Shouldn't Support Them

- How can you let yourself be invaded by the Dutch?
- Some of them are a touch, how shall we say, unruly.
- No statue of Brian Moore.

---

* We may not have been *successfully* invaded by anyone since 1066, but a lot of people have given it a go. And I bet not many of you know we hated the Dutch as much as the French in the 17th and 18th centuries.

GRIMSBY TOWN

'Grimsby was magical. In a Mad Max dystopian sort of way.'

MARTIN GRITTON Grimsby Town player

'Let us wallow shamelessly in nostalgia.'

Codalmighty.com, Grimsby Town fansite

Can we do something different? I feel I know you well enough to suggest that. Nothing drastic, just a little change of routine, freshen our relationship up a bit, then we can get back to it with a new energy and commitment to each other.

What I'd like to do is tell you a little about Grimsby Town, then I'd like to tell you about my friend Martin Gritton, who played for them. He played for a lot of teams, but he loved his time at Grimsby, and I thought you'd like to know what it's like to play football for a living, away from the madding crowd in the Premier League. Sound good? You sure? Come on then. But first, some context.

It's 1878, you're in Grimsby, and you fancy a pint, so you pop into the Wellington Arms. Unfortunately, it's rammed because yet another bloody cricket team are having a meeting about forming a football club to keep fit in winter. Why they just don't start a football club in the first place is beyond me, because all of them forget about cricket once they start kicking a proper ball.

Anyway, this lot are from Worsley CC and after a quick chat about the wife and kids, they get down to the business of founding Grimsby Pelham FC. Pelham was the family name of the Duke of Yarborough, who owned most of the land thereabouts, and you're probably going to need land for a pitch, so sucking up to the local lord was a good idea. And they chose blue and white hoops for a kit because they were the Pelham family colours – come on lads, have some self-respect.†

They later tried scarlet and blue halves, then salmon pink, before settling, as so many clubs did, for black and white. Probably for the

† They found some a year later when they changed the name to Grimsby Town. Yes, I know it's in Cleethorpes.

best; they may have started as nice polite cricket club lads, but this was Grimsby, after all; 'salmon' pink wouldn't go down that well in a town where men actually risked their lives when they went fishing.

And Grimsby was *the* fishing town. The home of a giant trawler fleet that fed half the country. They say you could walk for miles across the decks. In the 1950s a train ran every hour, *every hour*, carrying nothing but fish to London. Today, there is no direct train at all. Superstition dictated that a trawlerman should not go to sea with money in his pocket, so the docks were packed with kids waiting to catch loose change thrown into the air from departing boats. Not any more. Like so many of the clubs in this book, especially in the north, the industries that nurtured them have more or less gone. There is a sea life centre in Skegness though, so that's alright.

Grimsby played at Clee Park, then Abbey Park, then moved to their current home Blundell Park, taking two stands from Abbey Park with them, and presumably determined never to go back to the days when they had to change in old bathing huts at the side of the Abbey Park pitch.

Grimsby were a First Division team in the 1930s, but to use language the Worsley CC boys would understand, they have never really troubled the scorer when it comes to success, although they did make headlines in 1995 when they signed Ivano Bonetti, who had played for Sampdoria in an actual European Cup final. And they made even bigger headlines in 1996 when manager Brian Laws threw a plate of chicken wings at him in the dressing room after a match.

So what is it like to play for a team like that, when success is unlikely and motivation comes courtesy of Colonel Sanders? Martin Gritton was a big, strong, handsome, Scottish striker, who shamefully never got the Premier League recognition or international caps his talent deserved. All of which is true, but all of which I also promised I'd say if he bought the last round. And he can put that on his Wikipedia page now because someone said it in a book.

I met him through one of the roughly 28 million football podcasts now available and took him for a pint to discuss life, love, the universe and Grimsby. He made 49 appearances for Grimsby Town between 2004 and 2006 and scored 6 goals. It should have been more but the service was shit. My words. Very much not his.

He was signed from Torquay on Christmas Eve 2004 and drove up on the day. 'They put me up in a hotel opposite a frozen golf course. I was virtually the only guest, which would have been fine but I was reading *The Shining* at the time. I had to chuck it in the bin.' He made his debut on a bone-chillingly cold Boxing Day wearing a short-sleeved shirt because they didn't have a long-sleeved one in his size. The kitman said: 'You're Scottish, you're supposed to be tough.' The half-time team talk was interrupted when the left-back's mobile rang and he answered it. 'No one turned a hair.'

He told me so many stories, all of which had my eyebrows marching steadily up my forehead. This is my favourite and also the most printable: 'The season fizzled out and on the Sunday after the last day of the season we were instructed to attend a Family Day on the pitch, the highlight of which was Roy "Chubby" Brown unveiling the world's biggest prawn cocktail.'

That can't be right, Martin. Roy 'Chubby' Brown was a triple X-rated comedian who had never been allowed on TV. And this was Family Day? But it was right. The next day he sent me a link to the *Yorkshire Post* to prove it. 'Afterwards we had our awards night and then went out drinking in town. It was a nightmare. Lads fighting each other, then the locals, then the police were called a few times.'

A few times?

'The manager was furious and we were all called in the next day, bumps, grazes, black eyes and all to run round the pitch as punishment. Trouble is, the giant prawn cocktail was still on the centre-circle and it was a really hot day. We weren't feeling good already, so tasting a bit for a laugh was a serious mistake. I was throwing up for hours.'

That all sounds horrendous.

'No, I loved it there. The club was the focal point of the community and the fans were truly amazing.'

Thank cod for that.

Why You Shouldn't Support Them

■ Visiting fans will definitely not be nostalgic about the train station that was behind the away-end. It was convenient but it meant they saw us coming.
■ An obscene comedian and a giant prawn cocktail. On Family Day?!
■ Cost me a fortune to try and get Martin drunk enough to tell me 'the other stories'. I'm still waiting.

HUDDERSFIELD TOWN

'Team picking is a complicated and scientific matter requiring expert knowledge'

HERBERT CHAPMAN legendary manager of Huddersfield

'There was just something about Huddersfield Town and their amazing history.'

PATRICK STEWART Huddersfield Town fan

Patrick Stewart said that in an interview with the *Huddersfield Examiner*, but I know from experience that a lot of celebrity fans are way more celebrity than fan; so when he hosted *Have I Got News For You*, which I write for, I thought I'd ask him casually who his favourite Huddersfield player was, just to check. I needn't have worried; he is a *proper* fan and we were still chatting half an hour later. Maybe next time we meet he'll pause for breath and I'll get to tell him about my favourite Palace player. And he was absolutely right to talk about their amazing history. Because young people may be surprised to learn that they were once the biggest club in the country, led by a visionary called Herbert Chapman.

I was amazed when I found out. As a kid, I was just bemused that a team called Huddersfield played at Leeds Road. I also knew as a kid that they were The Terriers, except I can't have known that as a very young kid because that only happened in 1969 when the manager decided they needed a scarier nickname than 'the Town'. Not that scary, is it? It was obviously meant to represent fight and tenacity, but to me 'terrier' just sounds like one Terry is a bit more scary than another.

Huddersfield didn't need a nickname to strike fear back in the day. They simply had a very good football team. In an extraordinary few years between 1921 and 1928, Huddersfield Town won the FA Cup, the League Championship three times in a row, then finished runners-up twice. It was an achievement even more remarkable given a previously inauspicious history and a similar lack of achievement since.

Formed in 1908 after another meeting in a pub, it seemed as though the directors stayed in there, drinking, because by 1912 they had gone into liquidation.* They reformed in 1919, but within weeks were at it again and there were plans to move from Leeds Road to actual Leeds, so they could sell the ground to stave off financial problems. Then to use a technical term: blammo! A whole century's worth of success compressed into one astonishing decade, and mainly because of one man.

I'm guessing many of you reading this book have heard of the name Herbert Chapman. But it's only through writing this book that I have come to realise the sheer visionary genius of the man, and I urge you to look at him in more detail than I give you. No great shakes as a player, he managed Northampton Town, Leeds City and Munitions Factory. Sorry, a munitions factory. It was an actual factory during the First World War. Then he was lured back to football by Huddersfield. He had obviously been doing a lot of doodling in that factory office because it was at Huddersfield that his ideas began to blossom.

English football at the time was still basically many variations of kick and rush. Get the ball, chase after it, shoot at goal. But on mainland Europe (and in Scotland) other tactics and formations were being tried, and finally our game began to catch up. Chapman's contribution was huge. Most teams only played with full-backs in defence, relying on a packed midfield to cope with attackers. Herbert introduced the centre-back to mark the opposing centre-forward and encouraged the midfield players inside the wingers (inside-forwards) to play deeper to link the defenders and attackers, in the process, according to NationalFootballMuseum.com, 'effectively inventing the counter-attack'.

'It's hard to resist the temptation to dwell in the past, but who could blame Huddersfield fans when the past is as glorious as theirs?'

He was arguably the first manager to take charge of all aspects of playing and coaching at all levels of a club and he swept all before him in four years at Huddersfield before Arsenal made him the highest-paid manager in the game in 1925. Unfortunately, his insistence on running every level of the club was his undoing. In January 1934, despite suffering from a cold, he insisted on watching a third-team game. The cold turned

---

* No pun intended. Unless my subconscious intended it.

to pneumonia and he died shortly afterwards at the age of 55. Months later, Arsenal won their third successive League title in a row.

Ultimately, his legacy sustained Arsenal far more than it did Huddersfield. They went on to become serial winners and Huddersfield went on to gradually become ordinary once more. They did finish in the top six regularly in the next few seasons and lost the FA Cup final in 1938, causing a man to eat his hat (see chapter on Preston North End). Before that they also lost the 1930 FA Cup final, against – guess who – Herbert Chapman's Arsenal. It's believed that the tradition of both teams walking out at Wembley together started that day at Herbert's request.

After that, their story mirrors so many others: a slow decline punctuated by brief flirtations with success, followed by the inevitable move to a new stadium and recovery from near financial oblivion (again). They are currently back in the Championship after two unlikely seasons in the Premier League. For football fans, it's hard to resist the temptation to dwell in the past, but who could blame Huddersfield fans when the past is as glorious as theirs?

Why You Shouldn't Support Them

▪ They give their fans those dreadful clacker things so they can create an 'atmosphere'.
▪ I once saw a Yorkshire Terrier bark/bounce itself off a table. 'The Terriers' is a terrible nickname.
▪ How can it be fair that a club that size has won all those things when a giant of a club like Palace has won nothing?

HULL CITY

'The most poetic city in Britain.'

PETER PORTER Australian poet

'A place cannot produce good poems; it can only not prevent them and Hull is good at that.'

PHILIP LARKIN poet of Hull

Fittingly for a city of poetry, some of this chapter will be about words, and one word in particular. You probably already know that 'Hull City' is the only team in the 92 that you can't colour in. A suggested name change would have changed all that, but it wasn't the reason Hull fans dug their heels in.

But first, some background. Like many ports, there is a bit of an edge to Hull. A sense of otherness, and their own identity, that comes from pointing outwards as much as in. Despite being 'the King's Town Upon Hull', in 1642 they denied Charles I access to the castle armoury and helped precipitate the Civil War. It was their MP, William Wilberforce, who led the battle to abolish slavery.

Philip Larkin was the librarian at Hull University for 30 years. The first woman to fly solo to Australia, Amy Johnson, was born there, as, of course, was Cosey Fanni Tutti, co-founder of seminal industrial punk band Throbbing Gristle. And, speaking of 'musicians', Hull was also responsible for my least favourite band ever, the Housemartins.

From the mid-1850s to the mid-1980s, Hull was the centre of the country's distant-water fishing industry with its trawlers fishing the seas around Iceland and Norway to bring the fish to add to the chips of a grateful nation. No more, of course. Although there are signs of a mini-revival: one ship is landing fish again. One!

And despite this rich cultural and industrial history, what's the one thing that all football fans say when we go for the first time? 'Fuck me, they *do* have white phone boxes!' Cream, actually. It's no big deal, in 1904 the city set up their own independent phone network and it's remained so ever since. And, look closely: unlike the rest of the country, the phone boxes have no crowns, marking the city's two fingers to Charles I.

All that is by way of context for Hull City FC, a football team who have not only had to cope with a turbulent century of politics and economics, but have also had to fight for attention with two giants of rugby league. Seriously, if you think teams like Tranmere have it tough competing with Liverpool and Everton, spare a thought for City, stuck between Hull and Kingston Rovers.

In fact, several tentative football clubs in Hull had failed to take hold because of the rugby league teams before Hull City formed in 1904* and held on tight until they were admitted to the Football League a year later. Apart from a brief but buccaneering spell in the Premier League, their story mainly took place in the lower divisions, but their recent history contains another civil war of their very own.

On my first trip to Hull for *Match of the Day 2* I found myself on the coach to an away game chatting with two old ladies. Let's call them Elsie and Madge, because I reckon there must be thousands of Elsies and Madges in Hull. And before you think that's patronising, trust me, they ran rings around me.

I like to think I'm good with old ladies. A bit of charm here, a bit of flattery there, topped with a bit of implied flirting and a genuine interest in what I can learn about their history. None of that washed with these two. I learnt some things, and some words, that would make a trawlerman blush. Elsie had only started supporting them in recent years because her grandson's season ticket had become unexpectedly available and 'even when he got time off for good behaviour, I didn't give it back. I've got me own now.' Madge had been supporting them for decades but what was recent was her Tiger tattoo. So recent, it still had the cellophane on it. 'Feisty' doesn't begin to cover their attitude to life; so when that Tiger caused a struggle between the club and its fans a short while later, I wasn't surprised that it was the fans who won.

Hull City fans have put up with a lot over the years. They've seen their team locked out of their own stadium, just minutes from liquidation. They've seen the Football League mainly from the bottom up and they had one of the worst kits in living memory foisted on them in 1992, their traditional yellow and black stripes being replaced by a truly hideous tiger-stripe camouflaged mess.†

But in 2013, they finally dug their heels in. New owner Dr Assem Allam changed the name of the limited company that ran the club to Hull

---

* Clearly a big year in Hull.
† Which they now regard fondly as a retro design classic. Football fans, eh?

Tigers and announced he planned to change the name of the team itself in order to make them a more recognisable brand 'and attract overseas investment'. This caused consternation at the FA, who pointed out that their approval was needed for any such change. And it caused uproar among the fans, and not just because you *can* colour in Hull Tigers.

Now, some of you may be wondering: why all the fuss? They are nicknamed the Tigers and their kit is tiger-coloured, and hey, Hull Tigers is quite a cool name. But that is to miss the point. They have been Hull City since 1904. They have been providing an identity and a focal point for a community since 1904, much of which time was spent in turmoil for the club and the city. Hull City.

Peaceful protests began. Peaceful. Then after the fans spent one whole game chanting 'We're City till we die', Dr Allam responded by saying 'they can die as soon as they want'. Protests became less peaceful. In 2014, and again in 2015, the FA Council refused by a majority of just under 70% to allow the name change. Dr Allam, to his credit, backed down and apologised (sort of).

The Hull City Supporters Trust thanked the FA for 'securing the heritage of Hull City and listening to its supporters'. Because that's what the club owner didn't do. If he had consulted with the fans first, none of it would have happened. Or he may have been able to carry his argument with those fans and get his name change.

Personally, I'd have left him alone with Elsie and Madge for 10 minutes. No contest.

Why You Shouldn't Support Them

- I know it's childish but I really don't like the Housemartins, mainly because of their album *London 0 Hull 4*.
- Cream phone boxes are weird, though.
- I have never been that shocked by two old ladies, and my family is full of hard-drinking potty-mouthed examples.

IPSWICH TOWN

'I hate being called the Tractor Boys. It conjures up images of carrot-crunching yokels.'

JIM MAGILTON ex-manager of Ipswich Town

'They are the English steamroller.'

ROBERT HERBIN coach of St Etienne, after a defeat in 1981

I have no happy memories of my last visit to Portman Road in 2013. As it happens, I have no memories at all because I knocked myself out celebrating a goal and only properly came to my senses on the train home, convinced we had won 1-0, when in fact the 'goal' had been disallowed and we had lost.

My friend Chirpy Chapman had managed somehow to get us tickets in a hospitality box at Ipswich. As you know, Chirpy 'manages' many things for us – except being on time. He was once 24 hours late picking us up for an away game at Reading (that we bloody won 6-1) because, he claimed, he hadn't put his clock forward, which was a pretty feeble excuse because that would only account for an hour of it. And it was September.

At the time Palace were pushing for promotion and tickets for the away game at Ipswich were like gold dust (these days I just phone the chairman and tell him I want to interview him for a book and by the way can I have two tickets for Saturday), so even though the tickets Chirpy had 'just happened to lay his hands on' were in a box, we snapped them up. But before the knockout blow, let me tell you a little about the perpetrators.

If you've ever wondered why Suffolk is not a hotbed of rugby (well, somebody might have), it's because in 1888 the local rugby club merged with the local football club and, like many in this book, quickly realised they had been wasting their time chucking the ball about and drinking post-match aftershave out of a shoe, so began Ipswich Town FC instead.

Then nothing happened until 1936, when the club turned professional, after which a *lot* happened, including winning a European trophy and being managed by Alf Ramsey and Bobby Robson, two men who went on to become the most legendary managers of England. Under Ramsey they won the First Division at their first attempt in 1962, then under Robson in the seventies and eighties they played a beautiful, continental style of play (possibly because two of the players* were from the actual continent), which won them the FA Cup, the UEFA Cup and the admiration of all. Well, most. Norwich City fans wouldn't have been pleased. They really don't like each other. The rest of the country just leaves them to it.

Jim Magilton may not have liked their unofficial nickname of the 'Tractor Boys',† but the fans have fully adopted it, probably because their official nickname is 'the Blues'.

> 'Ipswich are a team who have been in the doldrums for so long they've now got an option to buy.'

I despair. They may as well have just picked 'the Ipswich' for a nickname. 'Tractor Boys' is much better because there is no denying they *are* a rural club. They've got a bleeding great carthorse on their badge for a start. Sorry, they've got a bleeding great Suffolk Punch on their badge (apparently there's a difference).

Sadly, those glory days are long past and Ipswich are a team who have been in the doldrums for so long they've now got an option to buy. They are a small-town club with a big history, so it's a shame to see them languishing because I want to play them again in the Premier League. Not because I actually give a toss about them, you understand, but because of the Drum and Monkey. The Drum and Monkey is the best away pub in the country bar none. It's big, it's friendly, they decorate the bar in your club colours and show DVDs of your club highlights on the TV. It's … WHAT? It's closed?! When did that happen? 2018. Jesus. It's a car park. Bastards. Seriously, bastards. If Fulham's cottage is a listed building, why the fuck wasn't the Drum and Monkey? Oh well, at least I can drop the pretence I want Ipswich to be promoted. I mean, good luck to them and all that, but that's sacrilege.

So, back to the game. There's not much else to do on the train to Ipswich other than drink because the view goes from 'city' to 'flat' in a very short space of time, so we were already in a good mood when we

---

* Dutch duo Frans Thijssen and Arnold Mühren. Overshadowed by the Argentinians Ricky Villa and Ossie Ardiles signing for Spurs from Argentina, but just as influential.

† Legend has it that it came about after disgruntled Leeds fans began singing 'we're losing to a team of tractor drivers', but I've seen disgruntled Leeds fans close up and they're not famous for expressing their emotions through song. Plus, I've asked several musicians and none of them can make 'we're losing to a team of tractor drivers' scan.

got there. A mood that was improved by an hour or so in the Drum and Monkey. I can't believe they've done that. How many car parks does a town full of tractors need?

Then there was the whole box thing. The reason most normal fans don't like being in executive boxes is that you are expected to dress up and behave yourself. But they also offer free alcohol, and 'free alcohol/behave yourself' is a tricky Venn diagram to navigate.

So, Palace are on the attack and score what seems to be a perfectly good goal from a header, whereupon I jump up to celebrate the goal by copying the header. Unfortunately, the glass in the window was convex (the sticky-out kind), so I bounced back a yard or so and collapsed on a table, to the sound of sympathetic hysterical laughter.

The rest is still a blur. I'm told the club staff were very apologetic, and I was charming and witty about the whole thing (as well as anaesthetised by half a day's drinking), but that can't help but taint a town for you, can it?

Why You Shouldn't Support Them

- They tried to kill me. I mean, seriously, who puts convex glass in a window in the first place?
- If someone tried to turn St Edmundsbury Cathedral into a car park there'd be uproar. BBC Radio Suffolk would be all over it.
- It's a carthorse. Get over it. And it's playing football on the sea.

LEEDS UNITED

'We all hate Leeds and Leeds and Leeds, Leeds and Leeds and Leeds, and Leeds, Leeds and Leeds and Leeds, we all fucking hate Leeds.'

Popular football song (well, popular at 91 of the clubs in this book)

'I wouldn't mind if they said: "you were a dirty set of bastards, but you couldn't half play".'

JOHNNY GILES in an interview with the *Guardian* (they were … and they could)

Let's start with one of the strangest insights into a football manager's mind you will ever see. It's freely available on your laptop, in case you think I'm making it up. In 1974 Leeds United were champions of the First Division. They were one of the most famous clubs in England and abroad. They had a team of world-class players, a massive fan base and that beautiful all-white kit. And, by the looks of a Yorkshire TV documentary called 'The Don of Elland Road', a very odd manager.

In just one small segment, Don Revie, the man who had fashioned this success, is seen following his match day routine of walking from the hotel to the traffic lights and back while making sure all his lucky charms are still in his pocket. And they are staying in a hotel because he insisted his players had no distractions the night before a game, by which he presumably meant sex. But if these young men were denied that pleasure, they could at least play bingo. Actually they had no choice. He made them play bingo. All of them. World-class players or not, Friday night was bingo night.

And there's more. In one almost soft-porn moment, he explains how he likes to relax players *while* he is giving a deep and soapy massage to a naked Jackie Charlton. Any sentence containing any combination of the words 'Charlton', 'Jackie', 'massage' and 'soapy' will be weird to anyone of my generation and it's also the worst possible metaphor for a club that I still always refer to as 'dirty Leeds'. Many football fans my age, on hearing the name of Leeds, will automatically add the word 'dirty'. My mate Dave is from Gloucester, so of course he is a massive Leeds fan, home and away. He knows that when he says 'Leeds', I say 'dirty'. We chant it out; it makes him smile. To be fair, most things make Dave smile, except criticism of badgers. Sadly, his frankly disproportionate anger at any criticism of the stripy little bastards is way beyond the remit of this book, but it does explain why we spend so much time in his company criticising badgers.

And, my word, Leeds were dirty. They were very good, but they were properly physical. That legendary Cup battle with Chelsea (see Chelsea chapter for details) was all in a day's work for Leeds.

> 'My word, Leeds were dirty. They were very good, but they were properly physical.'

Yes, the game was more physical then, but the likes of Johnny Giles, Billy Bremner and Norman Hunter were brutal. And whatever that soapy massage did to Jack Charlton, it didn't relax him. He always looked like an amiable, gangly man, right up to the moment he laid out a centre-forward by way of saying hello.

Jack left us recently, but I met him a few times, and he *was* an amiable, gangly man with a lovely chuckle, which you mainly heard as he told you yet another story that involved someone getting stitches. They all shook hands at the end of the game though, so that's alright. Hard but fair, etc. Thing is that you couldn't even say *that* about them. There was an element of spite about Leeds that may well have come from having to play bingo on a Friday night as all red-blooded athletes must love to do.

One Saturday night in March 1972, I was watching *Match of the Day* with my dad. He was, and still is, famously mild-mannered. Nothing used to annoy him, which, incidentally, used to really annoy my mum. But that night he was fuming. On the telly Leeds were beating Southampton 7-0, and on the sofa my dad was doing his nut because Leeds were rubbing it in. They were doing backheels, keepie-uppies, head tennis, the lot, and genuinely toying with their opponents. Dad hated seeing anyone mistreated and he was furious at what he saw as unsporting humiliation. Personally, I quite enjoyed it, and I imagine the crowd did too, but for once in my life I decided to keep quiet and wait till he stopped chuntering. Tuesday it was.

I am, however, nothing if not fair, and I thought it only right that a Leeds fans should have the right to reply. Ardal O'Hanlon is a very fine comedian and actor, still best known to a generation as the idiot/savant priest Father Dougal in the sitcom *Father Ted*. He is also very happy to take up the cudgels on behalf of his beloved team: 'Yes, Leeds were dirty, if by dirty you mean ultra-professional, tactically advanced and really, really good. People often see innovation and success as suspicious or "dirty", but would you rather have Amstrad or Apple? Okay, they weren't angels but they were more sinned against than sinning, the victims of evil forces. I cried when they lost the FA Cup final to Sunderland in 1973, the most-one sided game ever, when surely voodoo was involved. I was outraged when they had the European Cup stolen from them in 1975 by a referee who admitted he had been bribed. Leeds were only dirty in the way a "dirty fried egg" is dirty when it is brilliantly enhanced by being fried in bacon fat.' If there is a better comparison between a football team and an egg, I have yet to hear it.

And if the team were fierce, the fans were too. Elland Road is a big stadium, and it's normally full even when Leeds aren't successful (which is a handy summary of their recent history).

In those days, it was not only full, it was full of passion and crackled with energy and aggression and the regional pride of fans who had always been proud of their team and now had something to be proud of. In January 1976, Third Division Crystal Palace were drawn away at Leeds in the FA Cup. For some reason my mum thought this would be a good excuse to see her sister in Bradford and while she was doing that, my cousin Charlie was instructed to take me to the game, to his horror. And to my horror, he did take me. Then bunged me in the home end and left me there. I was 14, looked 11, and had long wavy hair. I was so obviously not one of them.

> '"Only dirty in the way a 'dirty fried egg' is dirty when it is brilliantly enhanced by being fried in bacon fat."'
>
> **ARDAL O'HANLON**

I decided to style it out, and if any of them did speak to me, I would pretend to be a girl. We won 1-0 and I have never celebrated a goal less. At one stage, as the hardest of hard men, Norman Hunter, was waiting to come on as sub, the crowd sang 'Norman's going to get you'. I was convinced they meant me. It was terrifying. Not in one of those roller-coaster, terrifying-but-exhilarating ways. Just terrifying. I was still rocking silently as the train pulled into King's Cross.

Not long after Jackie Charlton's soapy buttock rub, Don Revie was involved in another remarkable piece of TV. In July 1974, to the astonishment of the football world, Brian Clough was appointed as Leeds manager following Don Revie being made manager of England. Revie and Clough, both from Middlesbrough, disliked each other intensely and

Clough hated Leeds. As manager of Derby he had constantly criticised their tactics and their physicality. On the first day he took training there, he told Don Revie's players that they should throw all their medals in the bin because they had won them all by cheating. Forty-four days later, with Leeds fourth bottom in the table, Clough was sacked.

That very evening, a local TV celebrity called Austin Mitchell somehow persuaded them both to take part in a live interview on his show. It is still wonderful viewing even today. Clough had been sacked hours earlier after a few weeks managing the team that Revie had taken to success after success, yet it was Clough who took the moral high ground with his claim that, given time, he would have emulated everything Revie had done but with more style.

Much as I love Clough, Revie didn't deserve that. As Johnny Giles also said, Revie didn't revitalise Leeds, he created them. It had always been hard to establish a successful football team in a rugby league town. Leeds City gave it a go, then folded, and in 1919 Leeds United were formed to fill the void.

They played in yellow and blue, and they played in lower leagues. Then Revie appeared. He changed the kit to all-white to emulate Real Madrid. That must have seemed hilarious to fans of a mid-table Second Division team, but bugger me, it worked. A decade later Elland Road was full of razzmatazz. The players had neat little tags on their socks, a smiley-face badge, their names on their tracksuits and when they marched on to the pitch they would wave to all four sides of the ground before kicking autographed footballs into the crowd.

They scratched, bit, kicked and soapy massaged their way to titles and cups and were just a few points and goals away from many more. Leeds fans loved it, and the more other fans complained, the more they loved it. There was a bond between the fans, the manager and the player that would have been seriously difficult to replicate. Or, as it turned out, impossible.

Revie's reputation since has been questioned, but let's face it, if Brian Clough can't follow you, you must have been good.

Why You Shouldn't Support Them

- Seriously, Elland Road was terrifying.
- If I thought Roy Hodgson was making Wilfried Zaha play bingo, I would eat my season ticket with embarrassment.
- Dirty, dirty Leeds.

LEICESTER CITY

'As the Fosse is known throughout the land, so the new club will be known to the future.'

FRANK GARDNER co-founder, 1884 – optimistic about the future, and the fame of the Fosse

'I watched Leicester City lose in the 1969 Cup final with my dad and grandad when I was eight and cried all the way home.'

GARY LINEKER

There were mixed emotions when Leicester City won the Premier League in 2016. Euphoria, of course, for Foxes fans. Frustration for fans of the few teams that usually win it these days, and a sort of 'what the fuck just happened?' from the rest of us. How did a decent team with only one or two genuinely top-class players just win the Premier League title? Scratch that. One genuinely top-class player. Jamie Vardy, * who appeared from nowhere to score goal after goal against the best clubs in England. Although as we have seen, fans of Stockbridge Park Steels, Halifax and Fleetwood will know that it wasn't nowhere he had come from.

There was one emotion that was shared by all football fans. That was a mixture of mild fear and disgust as Gary Lineker had promised to present *Match of the Day* in his pants if his home-town club won the League. But as Gary told me, the win meant as much to the city as to the club: 'People were interested in my city. They flocked to see the market and the car park where Richard III was buried, to see the place where this most extraordinary sporting feat had occurred.'

So, without wanting to sound like a local newsreader in 1970, when did this journey to an unlikely title begin? One night in 1884, a group of lads in a Bible class decided to start a football team. Hang on, what? A group of who? Surely you mean a group of lads in a pub? Or a factory? Or a cricket team wanted to get fit over the winter?

Nope. A group of lads in a Bible class. Actual lads too. The average age of the Leicester Fosse team that played in their first game was 16.

---

* If pushed, I might run to Mahrez and Kanté as well.

Wow, that is young. (Sorry, what's a fosse, by the way? That's right, it is a way. The Roman road that went in a straight line through Leicester from the south-west to the north-east. Yes, I did know that already.)

Because they were so young, and because football folk are hilarious, they were landed with the nickname 'The Fossils',* and in 1891 they were landed with a new ground called Filbert Street, where most of their history unfolded, although not the really good bit in 2016.

The young men of the Bible class were obviously quite modest too, because their original kit consisted of a black shirt with a sky-blue sash and white *trousers*. It took some time before they came to wear their famous blue and white via a dashing detour of brown and blue halves.

Leicester became City in 1919, leaving the Fossils a long way behind them and eventually becoming the Foxes because of the county's association with hunting. Amazingly, in these more enlightened times, not only do they not apologise for the fox-hunting link, they play a hunting horn as the teams emerge.

They got themselves another nickname in 1963. The winter of 1962/63 was the worst in living memory, and for 10 weeks barely any football was played anywhere. Halifax Town actually charged people to use their pitch as an ice rink. But Leicester's groundsman had treated his topsoil with a mix of fertiliser and weed-killer, which caused a chemical reaction that kept the frost out just enough that a 'dozen burning braziers' made the pitch playable. After an army of fans had cleared the snow, of course.

I still don't know why that solution didn't work at any other club, but it enabled Leicester to get some games in, and playing a tantalising brand of football that the *Guardian* called 'whirl and switch' they established a healthy lead in the First Division and the title of 'the Ice Kings' in the tabloids. Sadly, it didn't last, and they fell away to finish fourth, and lose the FA Cup final. But it's an indication of what a force they have been in the past, and I bet a lot of you didn't know that, because they are a team and a city that often went unnoticed. As Gary Lineker also told me: 'It's neither up north, nor down south, it's not a big city, it's not a small city and no one outside Leicester could spell it properly.'

The whole world can spell it properly now. In 2002, they moved from Filbert Street to the King Power Stadium, thus causing every away fan in the country to breathe a sigh of relief. Historic the old ground may have been, but only if 'historic' is a euphemism for 'dangerously ramshackle'.

---

* There are some who think it was because of 'Fosse' but as they were also referred to as 'the Ancients', I'm right.

The move didn't lead to success. By 2007 they were in the third tier of English football for the first time ever, but were back in the Championship when they were bought by a Thai-led consortium led by Khun Vichai Srivaddhanaprabha.

English football fans are an insular bunch and tend to be wary of overseas owners – particularly fans like me who don't like the idea of any club being 'owned' – but there's no denying that at Leicester (and Man City) there has been an unusually healthy symbiosis between the owners and their fans, and an unusual understanding of the area from the overseas money men. So the football world shared the genuine grief of the people of Leicester when their chairman was killed (along with four others, lest we forget) when his helicopter crashed leaving the King Power after a game in October 2018.

At least he got to witness the Premier League season of 2015/16, one of the most remarkable in modern times. All the more so because the season before had been pretty special, but for very different reasons. Well adrift at the bottom of the Premier League with nine games to go, they won seven of them and stayed up by the skin of their teeth. So it was with some justification that they went into the new season as 5,000 to 1 outsiders to win the Premier League, even though they were now managed by the likeable but eccentric Claudio Ranieri, who over the course of the season looked on in as much confusion as the rest of us and said 'dilly dilly' a lot for no apparent reason.

Oddly enough for a team with few amazing players, they were, well, an amazing team. They probably got a bit lucky, in that all the usual top six suspects had an off-season, but there was nothing lucky about their wins or their goals.

Gary Lineker calls it 'possibly the greatest miracle in the history of team sport'. I cannot think of any more uplifting words on which to end a chapter.

Why You Shouldn't Support Them

- They sacked Ranieri the season after.
- Gary Lineker is only a little older than me but looks much, much better in his pants.
- They put a car park on top of my favourite king.

LEYTON ORIENT

'A message to all London football fans. You can't have
a second-favourite child or a second-best mate and we
don't want to be your second-favourite football team.'

BOB MILLS comedian, talkSPORT contrarian and Orient fan

'The cello! How can you give up your football team?
You can never give up your football team!'

JULIAN LLOYD-WEBBER world-renowned cellist, on being asked what he would
give up if he had to choose between his livelihood or his football team

I'm a bugger for a bit of classical music, and for me Julian Lloyd-Webber's playing of Elgar's Cello Concerto is right up there with the legendary Jacqueline du Pré.* I like him even more now I found that quote. Especially since in the same interview he was asked about naming his daughter Orienta: 'It's better than being called "Arsenalla" isn't it? That sounds like you've got some bacteria up your bum.' Good man. Proper supporter.

I wonder if he was at this particular game? It's a long time ago now, but one of my happiest away experiences was one of my earliest. It was 5 May 1979, two days after my 18th birthday,† and we were off to Orient for the penultimate game of the season, a game we needed to win to sustain our hopes of promotion back to the First Division (spoiler alert: we did). The official crowd was 19,945 but I'm sure it was more, and in my mind, only about the 945 were Orient fans, and I'm pretty sure none of them had a cello.

The whole of Brisbane Road was a glorious, seething kaleidoscope of red and blue, and at one stage I was seriously worried that we may end up being squeezed like a champagne cork into the gardens of the terraced houses behind. At the time, Orient were an established Second Division team (a very rare thing in their history) but that day, with not a hint of

---

* A discussion I've actually had at a Palace game.
† And two days after Margaret Thatcher became prime minister. So I got to vote on the day
of my 18th birthday. Not for her.

malice or violence, I first fully realised the joy of belonging to a large and boisterous tribe.

My other abiding memory of that day is how long it took us to get there. Something we forgot every time we went back. It's in London, for goodness sake, so what are we doing on a motorway?

It is London's most easterly club, and probably London's most patronised club as well. Growing up, London football was an intricate web of conflicting rivalries that varied in intensity from season to season and decade to decade, but no one ever hated Orient. If anything, the one thing that united fans of all London clubs was that we all wanted them to do well, in a kind of 'aah, ain't they cute' type of way. And chances were that if a London club's best player got old and past it, he'd go to Orient for one last payday. Indeed, Palace legend John Jackson was in goal for Orient that afternoon.

And if Orient are the most easterly and the most patronised club in London, they are also the hardest club in the capital to pin down name-wise. Even why they were called that in the first place is still a bit of a mystery. Being of a poetic, romantic nature, even as a child,‡ I always assumed that they were called Orient because they were so far east, but it seems more likely that an early player worked for the Orient Shipping Line and suggested it as a handy name for them. No one can actually agree who that player was or when he made the suggestion, but the Orient shipping line sailed to the far east, which would make me right as a kid, so let's agree it's true.

And they weren't Leyton Orient right at the start either. They were Glyn Cricket Club when they started a football team in, probably, 1881, changing their name to Orient, in, probably, 1889. I say 'probably' because between playing cricket and running a shipping line they seem to have been too busy to write anything down. In 1898 (definitely) they changed the name to Clapton Orient because Clapton was posh and they wanted to attract a more affluent sort of supporter.

> 'And chances were that if a London club's best player got old and past it, he'd go to Orient for one last payday.'

It didn't work. In 1937 they moved again and officially became Leyton Orient in 1946. In 1966 they decided to drop the Leyton and became Orient again, then in recent years they decided to add the Leyton again. It's quite possible that by the end of this chapter they will be Leyton

---

‡ I can't actually remember being like that, but I am now, so for the sake of argument, go with me.

Orient Athletic. Still, at least they provided regular work for east London signwriters.

They moved grounds a lot too, at one stage in 1930 playing two League games at Wembley because their own pitch was too narrow. They eventually settled at Brisbane Road where they still are, despite a concerted attempt by their chairman to persuade the Mayor of London that if anyone should inherit the 2012 Olympic Stadium as a football home, it should be them.

Kit-wise, they have been just as relaxed. Red, white and green stripes, red and white hoops, white with red chevron, white with blue chevron, red and white checks and a complete meltdown in the 1960s when they went from all blue to all red to all white in the same decade. They obviously thought east London kit manufacturers should be kept in regular work as well.

Rather wonderfully, though, their nickname is the O's. As you know, I don't approve of lazy nicknames, but this one stems partly from their name, and partly because one of those early kits had a massive O emblazoned on the back.

Sadly, their history on the pitch is nowhere near as interesting as their sartorial one off it. The blue kit was worn in their only season in the First Division and they've won a couple of lower league titles since, but a disastrous spell of irresponsible ownership saw near-financial disaster and a drop into the National League in 2017.

Happily they are back now and seem to be in safe financial hands. Which is a relief to their fans. I would say that the rest of us are pleased to see cute, harmless little Orient doing well too, but that would really annoy them.

Why You Shouldn't Support Them

▪ Well, for a start, you'd be patronising them and they don't like that.
▪ Are they actually a London club like they claim? It's bleeding miles away.
▪ Bob Mills is from Chester.

LINCOLN CITY

'You will often hear echoes of Lincoln's RAF past at Sincil Bank as air-raid sirens and the *Dam Busters* [sic] theme are sung by the home support.'

VisitLincoln.com official guide to five things for visiting football fans to do (I don't think you can actually 'sing' a siren)

'The most one-eyed, aggressive and annoying crowd I've sat in for a long time.'

DAVID GUEST author of *A Town of Two Halves,* unofficial guide to visiting football fans (he especially didn't like the siren)

Apart from Cornwall, Lincoln is the only part of the country with which I have no personal relationship. Despite my love of football and history, I have never been to the city or its remarkable cathedral.

Palace, or comedy, have taken me to most places, but the closest I've been to Lincoln is Boston, where, after a gig, a middle-aged couple approached me to say they had enjoyed it very much and, given some of the things I had been talking about, did I know it was apparently the most racist town in England? I said I was sorry to hear that. 'No need to apologise,' the man said. 'No,' said his wife, 'that's why we moved here.'*

Not only have I not been there, I'm not sure I've even seen them play, and there aren't that many clubs I can say that about. I definitely didn't see them when they played Palace in 1961; 1970 was in the League Cup so I was way too young to go to an evening game. Hmm, League game in May 1977, could well have been at that. Three other League Cup games in the nineties. No bells ringing. January 1995, FA Cup. I must have been at that. I reckon.

If it helps, I do know why you are called The Imps, though, because of my love of history and cathedrals. I didn't know any other 11-year-olds who loved football *and* cathedrals. According to legend, sometime

---

* I'm not making that up, sadly.

in the 14th century, Satan got bored and sent some imps down to make mischief. They stopped at Chesterfield to twist the spire of the church there, then hightailed it to Lincoln for some evil merriment, chucking things around, lifting bishops' robes, that sort of thing. These were obviously not Premier League sprites. One took things a bit too far, though, and hid in the roof of the cathedral lobbing rubble at people until a passing angel turned him to stone. And there he still sits, high in the rafters, leering down. The imp became the symbol of the town and the nickname of the football team. And Chesterfield FC took the nickname 'The Crooked Spireites', so the devil and all his works accidentally gave two football teams their nickname. Well done, Satan! And that's high on the list of sentences I wasn't expecting to type today.

'I didn't know any other 11-year-olds who loved football *and* cathedrals.'

The fact that their record crowd, set in 1967, is 23,196 shows that we are not talking about a giant of a club here. Especially as their fiercest rivals, Boston United, aren't even a League team. But, as you know, that doesn't matter. Lincoln City matters as much to the thousands who follow them as Liverpool does to their millions.

There had been earlier versions in Lincoln Rovers and Lincoln Recreation but the current incarnation, City, started as an amateur side in 1884. Unusually, there seems to be no record of who started them. As we know, there is usually a pub, factory, school or cricket team involved somewhere but even their official history makes no reference and I have genuinely researched elsewhere to find the answer.

I suppose I could go to Lincoln to ask a bloke in a pub, but I am becoming stubbornly excited about the fact I have never been there so that won't happen. Also, I don't like the sound of sirens (also high on the list of unexpected sentences) so that would give me the hump. It sounds every time they get a corner.

In 1895 they moved from the splendidly named John O'Gaunt's ground (which had been splendidly donated by a local brewer) to Sincil Bank, where they have remained ever since. In truth, though, since then even the biggest Lincoln fan will admit their history isn't exactly illustrious ... I shall just pause here while irate Lincoln fans shout: 'Well what have Palace bloody won, then, you've never won the Midland Counties League, have you?' Fair point, mate, well made.

But like every club their size, something occasionally erupts and for them it was Graham Taylor, who went on to manage Watford, Villa and England, but his managerial career started there. He was a young ex-Lincoln player, and in the 1975/76 season, a few seasons' worth of groundwork paid off as they erupted out of the Fourth Division with a record number of wins, home wins and points.*

Who knows what could have happened to them if Watford hadn't lured Taylor away? He took them from the Fourth Division to runners-up in the First while Lincoln resumed the everyday life of a smaller club. A couple of promotions, a few relegations, out of the League and back again. Loyally supported by a few, rarely troubled by the TV cameras. Well, until recently.

In 2016, two PE teachers, brothers Danny and Nicky Cowley, were installed as manager and assistant manager, beginning a remarkable few seasons that saw them climb out of the National League, win League Two and reach the quarter-finals of the FA Cup. They played attractive, exciting football and they energised the whole city. Suddenly, they were on telly every second week, they started taking 3,000 fans to away games, *away* games, and the atmosphere at Sincil Bank was back to Graham Taylor days.

Obviously, the same thing happened. Huddersfield Town lured the brothers away to help restore them to the Premier League. That hasn't happened yet, but the Imps are still feeding off the energy that run brought them; and it gave hope to the fans of every struggling club that new life may be just around the corner.

And if it continues, I promise I *will* go to Lincoln to see Palace play in the Premier League.

Why You Shouldn't Support Them

- Sirens and dambusters – come on, chaps, that war's been over a long time.
- Only five things to do for visiting football fans, and one of them is visit an imp.
- One-eyed, aggressive and annoying fans.

---

* If you look it up, remember, it was still only two points for a win in those days.

LIVERPOOL

'The socialism I believe in is everyone working for each other, everyone having a share of the rewards. It's the way I see football, the way I see life.'

BILL SHANKLY Liverpool manager – one of the most famous quotes in football is actually a shortened version of what he really said

'Mind you, I've been here during the bad times too – one year we came second.'

BOB PAISLEY Liverpool manager – one of the least famous quotes in football, as befitting a more modest but equally brilliant manager

As we speak, a Liverpool team who play a wonderful attacking style of football have just won the Premier League for the first time ever. That seems a strange thing to say about one of the most successful clubs in the history of world football, especially for those of us who spent tedious decades watching them win trophies in season after season.

As you know, I'm fairly convinced that Palace are the greatest and most glamorous team in the world, and I lack only actual trophies to back me up on that; but even I am willing to concede that Liverpool are one of the clubs that can almost match us for greatness and glamour. Their history could fill this book, let alone this chapter, so a brief trot down memory lane will have to suffice, starting with a memory that most Liverpool fans will want to suppress.

There has always been a famous Liverpool team playing in an iconic red kit at Anfield, but for six years it was Everton. In 1892, a row broke out between John Houlding and the other members of the Everton board. He was a local brewer who owned the ground and saw no reason why any other local brewer who didn't own the ground should be allowed to sell their beer inside it. Whether it was a comment on the quality of his beer, or his threat to raise the rent, the other directors walked out and took their club with them. Faced with an empty ground and no one to sell his beer to, Houlding did what any self-respecting capitalist did, he started his own club.

And the rest, as they say, is history. Except Scousers don't say that. Mine is a precis of available research, but obviously there are fans of both clubs who can't accept the version of history that doesn't make them look like the kings of Liverpool.

I haven't got a dog in this fight. I'm genuinely not bothered. Although I willingly concede that if Charlton suddenly claimed they were the glaziers who built the Crystal Palace, I'd be furious.

Liverpool's early years were relatively successful, but by the time Bill Shankly became their manager in 1959 they were actually languishing in the middle of the Second Division, playing in front of crowds of around 16,000 people. He changed all that. And despite the fact that the managers that followed him had more actual success, he is still the name that first springs to mind when you think of Liverpool in the sixties and seventies, and recall those images of the Kop* swaying like barley in the breeze to the music of the Beatles, or waving flags and banners like a medieval army on those legendary European nights.

Although the image is slightly tainted by hearing fans of that generation reminiscing fondly about having to piss in people's pockets because it was impossible to get to the toilet. Well, maybe not fondly. Ted Robbins, comedian and cousin of Paul McCartney, told his mate he couldn't possibly piss in his pocket. 'Why not?' came the reply. 'I've just pissed in yours.'

If this book was twice as long, I would devote as much time to Shankly† as I have done to Clough, but I still love watching old film of him and that total bemusement he had that everyone else in the country didn't share his 24/7 passion for football. He understood the importance of football and identity to working-class communities, which made him the perfect fit for Liverpool; and much as supporters of other giant clubs in the north-west may disagree, there was a symbiosis between Shankly and the Reds that has seldom been matched elsewhere. And it was one we could all share, because barely a weekend went by without them being on telly with a commentator telling us the Kop were an extra man who sucked the ball into the net, when they weren't pissing in each other's pockets, obviously.

But, whisper this softly, when times haven't been brilliant, the atmosphere at Anfield could only be described as 'alright', rather than 'breathtaking'. I wasn't at Anfield the night they beat us 9-0 in 1989,

---

* Not the only Kop, by the way. There are around 20 clubs who had a steep terrace at one end, named after a steep hill ('Spion Kop') fought over during the Second Boer War in 1900.

† And to Bob Paisley, Joe Fagin, Kenny Dalglish, Bert Head and many other great managers.

which I am ashamed of because about 25,000 Palace fans claim they were, but I was there two years later when we beat them 2-1 and my abiding memory is that there was barely a peep from the Liverpool fans, even though, for reasons I can't remember, every single Palace fan was wearing a hat.

I was also there on a freezing cold evening in January 2001 for the second leg of the League Cup semi-final when we genuinely thought we had a chance of getting to Wembley, fools that we were. Even though we were a division below them, we'd had the temerity/stupidity to beat them 2-1 in the first leg at Selhurst, and Clinton Morrison, who had scored one of the goals, had the temerity/stupidity to tell the world he'd do the same at Anfield.

The away end was sold out (of course, we're a massive club, remember) but a lot of Palace fans were delayed getting there because of fog, and, in our case, really needing a drink to get over Roy's driving in the fog. So, a lot of us were approaching the ground while on our mobile phones to reassure loved ones that we had got there safely. This absolutely infuriated a female police officer on a horse, who seemed to think that, rather than reassuring loved ones, we were flaunting our phones as a symbol of wealth and southern supremacy. Now, being a gentleman, I make it a rule not to argue with women, and in particular women on horses carrying truncheons,* so I made my excuses and left.

Chirpy, unfortunately, totally overestimating his flirtatious charm, decided to try and work his magic. Turns out that the words 'calm down, love' weren't the soothing balm he'd expected, so he missed the first two goals. Which, of course, they scored. We lost 5-0 eventually. And it says a lot about the mentality of the football fan that, towards the end, we wanted it to be 10-0, so we would have the bragging rights back in Croydon.

Why You Shouldn't Support Them

- I reckon I have about 30 mates and colleagues who support Liverpool; 27 are from Hampstead, one's from Plymouth, one's from Scotland and one's from Tranmere. The Tranmere one should be most ashamed.
- Plenty of other grounds have an atmosphere too. And flags.
- When is it ever alright to piss in someone's pocket?

---

* She was carrying it, not the horse.

LUTON TOWN

'Hats off to Luton.'

Introduction to the Luton Hat Trail, www.Luton.gov.uk (really? You're the government and that's the best you can do?)

'I used to play football in my youth. Then my eyes went bad. That's why I became a referee.'

The peerless Eric Morecambe, comedian and Luton Town fan

Nowadays, every team has a celebrity fan. Tom Hanks and Prince William support Aston Villa; Hugh Grant supports Fulham; Robbie Williams supports Port Vale; Stig from *Top Gear* supports Burton Albion. The list is endless because football is cool and trendy these days and everyone wants to declare their undying love for the team they've supported for ever/been to twice.

But it wasn't always so. When I was young, football rarely made it into popular culture. Occasionally on FA Cup final day, a familiar face from TV would crop up on the pitch, like Freddie Starr dressed as Hitler,† and a ventriloquist called Roger De Courcey had a puppet bear called Nookie who wore a giant Crystal Palace rosette (sometimes I think everyone who was alive in the 1970s should just offer a blanket apology for everything), but for the most part football was only mentioned on TV when football was actually on TV.

The glorious exception was Eric Morecambe. I am, as I'm sure you know, a hard-bitten left-wing stand-up comedian forged in opposition to the casual racism, sexism and self-loathing working-class humour of the sixties and seventies. Hell, one magazine devoted a front cover to myself and Mark Thomas, declaring us the 'third wave of alternative comedy'. Our job was to make you laugh *and* bring down governments (which, to our credit, we always did – eventually).

But no one made me laugh like Morecambe and Wise. Even after hard nights driving another nail into the coffin of capitalism, I would

---

† Jesus, that sentence looks weird now. It was an everyday occurrence then.

come home and put a Morecambe and Wise show on and laugh again at bits I had seen a hundred times. It's hard to explain now what those two meant to an entire generation (they had an injured, yet slightly smutty innocence that seemed to particularly appeal to young people), but our world was a better place when they were on.

And Eric supported Luton Town. He was from Morecambe, but lived in Hertfordshire and supported Luton. Properly. He went to games. And he wasted no opportunity to mention them on the show. And Luton were about as un-showbizzy a football club as you could get. They weren't a bad side. In fact, throughout Eric and Ernie's BBC heyday they were in one of the top two divisions; they just weren't glamorous. And they're still not.

Formed out of an amalgamation of Luton Wanderers and Luton Excelsior in 1885, by 1891 they were the first professional club in the south of England, and in 1897 they joined the Second Division of the League, until all the travelling to northern away games took its toll and they went back to amateur life in the Southern League, although from where I'm standing they are a northern club, obviously.

As their official history puts it, since then 'there's been ups, there's been downs – but it's never, ever, been dull'. Maybe not to a Luton fan, mate, but they've never excited me much. The ups and downs bit is certainly true, though, with the 'ups' including Joe Payne scoring 10 goals* in a 12-0 defeat of Bristol Rovers in 1936, getting to the FA Cup final in 1959 and winning the League Cup final in 1988; and the 'downs' consisting of losing the FA Cup final

'You walk along a terraced street wondering where the bloody hell the ground is and suddenly there's a gap between two houses with a turnstile at the end of it.'

of 1959, losing the League Cup final of 1989 and being relegated out of the League altogether in 2007 after they started the season with a 30-point deduction, which was scandalously given by the FA for financial misdemeanours by *previous* owners of the club.

Scandalous though it was, it has to be said that for many other fans there was little sympathy. In the eighties they had been the first club to introduce plastic pitches, the first to ban away fans and the first to introduce identity cards for their own fans. It may or may not have been a coincidence that their chairman was David Evans, who was also a Tory MP and outspoken supporter of Margaret Thatcher.

---

* Still a record.

In truth, some away fans were probably happy to be banned. It was always an antsy town to visit, which we put down to the fact that they could almost reach out and touch London but they weren't London. Mind you, they hate Watford, so they do have that in their favour.

And that plastic pitch may have looked modern, but it was in a ground you could only describe as weird, or if you were being kind, homely. If your home was weird. And you have to go through someone's home to get into the away end. You walk along a terraced street, wondering where the bloody hell the ground is, and suddenly there's a gap between two houses with a turnstile at the end of it.

Apart from the hating Watford thing, something else in their favour is the nickname. I love a nickname that reflects the industry or culture of a town. At one stage, in the 1930s, the town was producing 70 million hats a year so it was fairly inevitable that they would be called the Hatters.

Or was it? In the 18th and 19th century the area was also the centre of the nation's straw-plaiting industry (you knew that, right?) because local soil conditions produced a type of wheat that was very flexible when it dried.

So, Luton's original nickname was the Straw-Plaiters. What do you think of that, Eric? Rubbish!

Why You Shouldn't Support Them

- No statue of Eric Morecambe outside the ground.
- I hated plastic pitches.
- Officially the worst reviewed ground on Tripadvisor. Although what sort of person rates grounds on Tripadvisor?

MACCLESFIELD
TOWN

'We're the Macc Lads, we were born in a pub, we like us ale and we like us grub.'

THE MACC LADS – punk band, 50% music 50% mayhem

'The Pride of Cheshire.'

DWAYNE 'THE ROCK' JOHNSON

Dwayne 'The Rock' Johnson did actually say that about Macclesfield Town. He does actually support them. During an appearance on the once-glorious *Soccer AM* on Sky Sports, he was assigned them as his English team. Seeming to grasp the whole idea of fan culture, he really got into it, and he still sends them messages of support before big games.

I would give anything to see Dwayne go pint for pint with the Macc Lads after a match, but only if I didn't have to be up early in the morning. Me and early don't get on. I have no issue with, say, 6 a.m., as such. It's only doing its job. After all, without 6 a.m. there'd be no 10 a.m. to have your morning tea and toast at.*

Sometimes I positively love 6 a.m. There used to be a pub in Edinburgh, called the Penny Black, that opened at that hour to serve postal workers coming off the night shift. In that terrible dry hour between Fringe venue bars closing and the Penny Black opening, I was a big fan of 6 a.m.

Also, despite having the Londoner's innate sense of superiority, I have no issue with places in the rest of the country. They are mainly lovely, and without them, we would have nowhere to feel superior about. I do, however, have an issue with Macclesfield at 6 a.m., especially if it also involved waking up in Manchester at 4 a.m.

---

* Yes, I know most of you are up and about long before that. Comedy is the fourth emergency service and, as such, the hours are irregular.

I was there for *Match of the Day* to travel on a coach with Macclesfield fans down to a cup game at Chelsea. Because meeting them when they got off the coach in London would obviously have been too simple. Nobody is at their best at 6 a.m.,† but the lads and lasses I was travelling down with were bright, funny, enthusiastic and very hospitable.

Plus there was the consolation of the best bacon roll I have ever had. I still dream of it sometimes. It was basically about four inches of salty goodness with a crusty bap clinging on for dear life at each end, slathered with actual butter, dotted with ketchup so thick you could stand a spoon in it. The only downside was that I still didn't have room for the gorgeous free food in the Stamford Bridge press room when the game finished some nine hours later.

'It's never seemed fair to me that clubs like Macclesfield are allowed to struggle while just up the road are clubs whose prawn sandwich budget for the year could save them.'

Of course, Macclesfield got hammered by the soft southern millionaires, but they didn't seem to mind. They also didn't seem to mind when the Stamford Bridge PA announcer patronised them dreadfully before the game. As he announced the Chelsea team, he also announced the country each of them played for, pointing out that, of course, he wouldn't be able to do that with the Macclesfield side. Then he wished them a pleasant visit to the capital, but wondered why there were so many of them here when their home crowds were so small. It was crass, and I was glad to hear from my coach crew that many Chelsea fans had apologised to them.

I've been thinking of that crew a lot lately. The club is in massive financial trouble and there is every chance it may not even exist when you read this. And, just as at Bury, it will be entirely through the fault of an irresponsible owner and the complicity of the useless EFL that those dedicated fans will have lost the club they love.

Macclesfield Town was born out of an unlikely amalgamation between an army regiment's football team and a cricket club's football team getting together to play rugby. The 8th Cheshire Rifle Volunteers joined with the Olympic Cricket Club in 1876 and made the sensible decision to swap rugby for football a couple of years after. At the time there were about 120 silk mills in the town, and they have been known as 'the Silkmen' from the start, which is either a rather romantic sort of

---

† Especially not Edinburgh postal workers during the Festival.

name or sounds like an alien race from Dr Who, depending on what sort of mood I'm in.

'Dr, it's the Silkmen!'

'Quick, into the Tardis while we think of a half-arsed late plot twist to foil them.'

Irresponsible business people have dogged the club throughout its history. It was liquidated and re-formed a few times in the early years and in 1946 only survived after local residents donated money and enough ration coupons to get a new kit. And they helped fix up the dilapidated old Moss Rose, the stadium they still play in (assuming, please God, that they have negotiated the financial crisis).

It was as a thank you to those locals that Macclesfield FC changed its name to Macclesfield Town.

In 1975, back in financial trouble again, they agreed to change their blue kit to black and amber for a season, those being the colours of a local business who paid them handsomely for it. Perhaps they would agree to play in skimpy black trunks if The Rock paid them handsomely enough. God knows, they need the money.

And in 2005, under the ownership of Amar Alkhadi, the FA fined them £62,000 and made them repay a £195,000 grant because of financial irregularities. He is still at the club and the finances are still irregular. He hasn't been seen at the ground for years, communicates with staff by WhatsApp and blames Brexit for his recent failure to pay wages to the players and manager, or tax to HMRC. Macclesfield Town currently face three winding-up petitions from all three of those.

It's never seemed fair to me that clubs like Macclesfield are allowed to struggle while just up the road are clubs whose prawn sandwich budget for the year could save them, but I'm not a businessman. Just someone whose heart sinks at the thought of those amiable fans having nowhere to go at 6 a.m. in the morning.

Why You Shouldn't Support Them

- Too nice. They should have invaded the pitch and stuck that PA announcer's mic where the sun don't shine.
- I'm really jealous of those bacon sandwiches.
- Have you seen the price of silk?

MANCHESTER CITY

'Blue moon, you saw me standing alone.'

City fans' anthem

'This time next year, Rodney, we'll be millionaires.'

DEREK TROTTER *Only Fools and Horses* (I know it's set in London – wait and see)

As you'll find out, the vast majority of West Ham fans hate their swanky new stadium, for many reasons. Man City fans share a similar traditional working-class demographic but have long ago made their peace with the move from a 'proper' old football stadium with its old-fashioned 'robust'* atmosphere, because not only are the seats more comfortable but they have had nothing but success since they moved from Maine Road to the Etihad.

Not only that, but Sheikh Mansour and the Abu Dhabi United Group, who own them, have invested millions into regenerating an economically deprived area, while the London Stadium is surrounded mainly by concrete and a couple of craft-beer and posh hot-dog stalls. My guess is that most of the complaints from West Ham fans will disappear when the area is thriving and the team are successful. Don't hold your breath.

Much has been said of the mega-millions of oil money poured into City in pursuit of the Champions League. Yes, it has shattered any romantic notion that the Premier League is a level playing field, and yes, they have tested the definition of Financial Fair Play in their desperate quest to win the Champions League, but unlike many, Sheikh Mansour and the others have shown themselves to be remarkably sympathetic to the context of the club and their responsibilities to the people of the light blue half of the City.

It is undeniable, though, that their ability to lure the best players and coaches in the world has created a mini-billionaires playground at the top of the Premier League; and before we get too romantic about Liverpool's

---

* Proper meaning old, and robust meaning hostile.

sparkling football, let's not forget they spent £596 million on sparkling players to achieve it.

The rest of us can only console ourselves that we support our local team, a team that will scrap, battle and harry for points against the bigger boys while we sing our hearts out so we can at least brag that we have retained our pride and passion.* And, in truth, many City fans say the same thing. For every City fan who has 'Ag ... uer ... ro' as his ring tone, there will be a hundred who tell you that their favourite ever game was the 1999 play-off final at Wembley when they were 2-0 down to Gillingham in the 89th minute and scored twice to take it to a victorious penalty shoot-out. And that was the League One play-off final.

All I can say is that Wembley must have Tardis-like qualities to fit the amount of City fans who claim to have been there that day, because it is a remarkable quality of us all that even as the captain hoists a trophy into the air, some of us will remember the days when we were shit. Although, God knows, I'm hoping not to give the bad old days when Palace were shit a second thought if only one of our captains would hurry up and lift a bloody trophy.

I don't begrudge City a bit, partly because I haven't met a City fan I didn't like, but partly because I don't have to come to terms with the fact that my club is, as journalist Simon Hattenstone said, the 'media-friendly face of repressive government'. But you could argue that their ownership of a football club actually helps to highlight the human rights issues in the UAE. I'm just glad that the only thing I have to face is that the chairman of Crystal Palace supported Brexit. Back to the game.

That play-off final was arguably the first step towards the glory to come, but there had always been a bit of glory about City, a bit of swagger, a bit of otherness that came from not being United. The city of Liverpool still prides itself that their club rivalry is a friendly one – 'we all travelled to the cup final on the same train yadda yadda'. The city of Manchester makes no such pretence. Their games were often marred by violence, none more so than after the last game of the 1973/74 season, when United legend Denis Law was seeing out his career at City, and reluctantly scored the goal against his old club that sealed their relegation. Except it didn't. United would have gone down anyway, but the sight of a forlorn and tearful Denis Law turning away from his celebrating teammates in light blue is still heartbreaking.

There is still very much an edge in Manchester derbies, which is a

---

* Until the glorious day that an oil-rich country buys us, in which case it's hello Champions League and goodbye atmosphere.

little to do with City being the top dogs for once and a lot to do with which is the *real* Manchester club. And if Salford City ever get to the Prem they can fight with United fans about who is the real *Salford* club.

The club that became Man City was St Mark's Church in 1880, and most people agree it was the idea of the curate's wife as a way of keeping kids off the street in a very deprived area. Their kit was all-black with a large white Maltese cross on it. Which, depending who you believe, was because of St Mark, or because of links with local Freemasons. It just proves the usual: football fans will believe any old bollocks rather than accepting that we just don't know!

In 1887, wanting to represent a bigger area, they became Ardwick AFC and in 1894, thinking even bigger, they became Manchester City FC in a bid to represent the whole city. Newton Heath didn't become Manchester United till 1902, so that's one for the bragging rights. In 1904 they won the FA Cup, becoming, as the official club website pointedly puts it, 'the first Manchester side to win a major trophy'. Take that United, another one for the bragging rights.

In truth, and if it was possible to whisper in writing, then I would: United have always had that little more to brag about. But not in crowds: City's have always been massive too. And not in kit: City's light blue† has always been way cooler. But in achievement, United have won just that little more. And while City spent part of the 1990s outside the top flight, United were winning it year after year. Until City win the Champions League a couple of times, they will still be playing catch-up.

But, here's the thing, City fans have always appeared to be having just a bit more fun. They are just that little bit more wry in their humour, more aware that other clubs have history; so far, the City fans I know are still taking their success with a pinch of salt, aware perhaps that money comes and money can go.

'Here's the thing, City fans have always appeared to be having just a bit more fun.'

Fans like Ena, a glamorous lady in her late thirties (we settled on that when I checked it was okay to mention her in the book) who I met when I was filming and has sent me regular anti-United messages ever since. She's properly posh, but she is a City fan home and away, including Europe; and every time they have played at Selhurst since we met, she appears in the Pawsons Arms with her entourage, having made sure I kept her a parking space.

---

† Adopted in 1894, it was officially described as 'Cambridge Blue' so presumably someone, somewhere, had a degree.

On another *Match of the Day 2* trip there I spent the day with Ricky Hatton, former light-welterweight champion of the world, starting at his house, which, as you would expect, is full of the most amazing boxing memorabilia. And, as you may not expect, full of the most amazing *Only Fools And Horses* memorabilia. Ricky is as proud of his original Del Boy cap as he is of his original Muhammad Ali dressing gown. His pride and joy, though, is an actual three-wheeler Trotters Independent Trading Co van used in the series. He offered to drive me to the game in it, until his wife mentioned it wasn't actually insured. It would have been a really quirky way to arrive at a modern, state-of-the-art stadium that still somehow manages to retain a bit of the spirit of the long-gone Maine Road, the site of which, incidentally, Ricky insisted we visit.

Why You Shouldn't Support Them

- Seriously, you can't all have been at Wembley for that play-off game.
- When they moved to the new ground, they didn't name one of the ends after legendary player Colin Bell.
- No one should have a manager as cool as Guardiola. It's not fair.

MANCHESTER
UNITED

'If only one person thinks I'm the best player in the world, that's good enough for me.'

GEORGE BEST

'There is a mystique and romance about United that no other club can match.'

JOSE MOURINHO

'Away from home our fans are fantastic. But at home they have a few drinks and probably the prawn sandwiches ...'

ROY KEANE Man United captain, complaining about quiet fans at Old Trafford

As it happens, Roy, the prawn sandwiches at Old Trafford aren't all that. The Marie-Rose sauce is a bit thin and they are light on cucumber for that contrasting crunch.*

I'll tell you what is *amazing* at Old Trafford: the balti pie. It was the first place I had one, and if I had a hat, I would take it off to the genius who came up with the idea of putting a chicken curry hotter than volcanic lava into a thin pie crust. I'm convinced whoever it was must own a chain of dry cleaners because the first thing you say when you bite into one is 'holy mother, this is good', and the second is 'oh, it's all over my shirt'. And my God, the heat! I'm convinced that's why Man United fans are so quiet at home games, most of them have scalded their tongue on the way in.

So, Manchester United. Look away now, City and Liverpool fans, while I say that Manchester United are still the most famous English

---

* And if that sentence doesn't mark me down as a southerner, I don't know what will.

football club in the world. From their early days (wearing yellow and green) as Newton Heath to the international sympathy over the Munich Air Disaster in 1958, which robbed them of a golden generation of talent, through to being the first English club to win the European Cup in 1968, then winning everything in the 1990s, United have become a truly global brand.

I pause here to acknowledge, on the advice of my cousins in Glasgow, that the first *British* club to win the European Cup were Celtic in 1967. The irony being that not one of that team would actually consider themselves British.

It used to be said of Man United that if an explorer travelled to the deepest depths of the Amazon rainforest and discovered an unknown tribe, the chief would probably greet him by saying, 'How's Bobby Charlton getting on?' Bobby, of course, was not only arguably the most famous player in the world, he was also the most famous bald man in the world – only don't tell him that. He genuinely seemed to think that combing those three strands of hair over his head had us all fooled: 'Ooh, here comes that hippy Bobby Charlton.'

And Bobby was the recipient of what is still my favourite leaving present ever. After 20 years, 758 appearances and 249 goals, he played his last game for Manchester United away at Chelsea in April 1973. Before the game, the Chelsea players lined up to applaud him and handed one of the finest footballers to grace our game – a silver cigarette case. And he was delighted! Turned out that not only did one of the finest footballers to grace our game smoke like a trooper, he also enjoyed a quick fag at half-time. The past really is a different country.

Now, the more observant among you will have noticed, probably to your disappointment, that so far I haven't told you how much I hate Man United. I would guess that for every one Man U fan who loves them, there are a hundred fans of other clubs who really cannot stand them. Maybe because they kept winning things for decades under Sir Alex Ferguson, maybe because a recent lack of success hasn't led to a corresponding lack of media coverage, or maybe because of that global branding they chase so relentlessly. Does your club have an official soft drinks partner in Nigeria? United does. Hello Chivita! Any sign of your team getting an official global mattress partner? Hi there MLily!

I understand that Palace may be negotiating a two-for-one chicken deal with their official Thornton Heath partner branch of Morley's, but

> 'I'll tell you what is *amazing* at Old Trafford: the balti pie.'

we have neither an official coffee partner nor an official hotel loyalty partner. Way to go Mellita and Marriott (I believe Mellita and Marriott were also a famous knife-throwing act in the 1960s).

So, about the not hating them thing. Let me tell you about a recurring dream I have. In this dream I walk slowly and anxiously down a long anonymous corridor. As I pass each door I check the numbers, slowing down as I come to the one I seek but don't wish to enter. I pause, rehearsing the words I need to say out loud to a room full of strangers so I can begin this battle. Through the glass panel I can see a semi-circle of men and women, leaning forward intently to catch the words of the group leader. Suddenly, a middle-aged man stands up and says something I cannot hear. There is applause and he is hugged by everyone. Many of them are in tears.

'I push the door open, take a deep breath and whisper: "Hello, my name is Kevin and I don't hate Man Utd."'

It's now or never. In a moment that will be me accepting the love and sympathy I will need to get through this. I push the door open, take a deep breath and whisper: 'Hello, my name is Kevin and I don't hate Man United.'

Silence. No applause. No hugs. Maybe it was because I whispered. I say it again. 'I don't hate Man United.' Still nothing. Eventually, the group leader looks up awkwardly and says: 'I'm sorry, Kevin, this is AA. You need IDHMU next door.' Subconscious Kevin wonders briefly why I chose AA, then the cat from *Shrek* turns up demanding to play Scrabble and I wake up in a cold sweat.

So, there you have it. God help me. I don't hate Manchester United anywhere enough. 'What?!' I hear you say. 'But you're a Palace fan, you must hate them, what about Eric Cantona?' Well, obviously I hate that overrated twat, but I just can't bring myself to waste valuable energy hating them. Look, I don't *like* United. Of course I don't, I'm a civilised human being, but I just don't despise them as much as some of you do.

In fact, I've always been intrigued by the reasons people choose United over City. I asked top football journalist Jim White why he was a red nut and not a blue one. 'Well, there are traditional red and blue areas of town. United are dominant in Salford and Wythenshawe, whereas City are big in outlying parts like Oldham.' Nice subtle dig, there, Jim. City fans are all from out of town. 'But, it's still largely driven by family. You support who your dad supports. My dad didn't like football but was happy for me to go on my own and, to be honest, I was seduced by the glamour and seeing the Stretford End in full voice. I went to City occasionally with mates, but the Kippax just wasn't as exciting. I was won over by fan culture.'

Tony Wilson would understand. He was a Manchester TV presenter obsessed with his city and responsible for Factory Music and the Hacienda (I just know you're the sort of indie hipster that won't need that explaining). He knew I was a proud Londoner and used to drive me up the wall by holding me up against an actual wall to tell me London was shit and had never produced any decent music. From my position up the wall I would yell 'David Bowie, the Kinks, the Clash, Madness', and he would yell back 'all shit'. But when it came to his theory that Man U were the biggest, most famous football club ever, ever, ever in the whole world, my response was always 'well, yeah, could be.'

> 'Then laugh with glee at the celebration. One man, arm half-raised, standing and smiling at his own temerity.'

My mum supported them, which didn't help. Well, not supported them as such: she mainly fancied Tommy Docherty, their manager in the seventies, and I mean *really* fancied. To such an extent that when I interviewed him years later, I didn't know whether to call him 'Tommy' or 'Dad'. I loved my mum, so as a kid I didn't think it was right to laugh at Man United when they were shit, or hate them when they were good. That took some discipline, but like I say, she was my mum; *and* I hadn't learnt to cook yet.

To make matters worse, when Alex Ferguson took over, she decided she really fancied *him* as well. Which was even more disconcerting, but explains why my actual dad hates Man United as much as my mum liked them.

Obviously, by this time I could cook, but I still loved my mum and decided that if an unrequited love for Fergie was getting her out of bed in the morning, then I'd leave her to her dream that an angry red-faced football manager would one day sweep her off her feet and whisk her away for a scalding hot balti pie. (Yes, we do have weird dreams in our family.)

But it's not because of one brilliant woman that I can't share the absolute hatred they seem to inspire across the world. It's because of one brilliant man. A tiny, glamorous, insecure waif of a man whose sole job, it seemed to me, was to humiliate hard-tackling thugs by gliding past them, through them or over them with the ball tied to his feet by magic. George Best was, still is and forever will be my footballing idol. I adored him.

He played in the first ever Palace game I saw (well, according to my dad; see the chapter on Crystal Palace for that still unresolved mystery) and to this day I remember the low murmur that went round the entire crowd when he got the ball – accompanied by actual screaming from the girls in the crowd. It was genuinely exciting; it was also an early reminder that most of the rest of my life was going to be relatively free of murmuring or screaming. Forget Pelé, forget Eusébio, forget Maradona. I *am* the person who thinks he is the best player in the world.

And, oh, those goal celebrations. Please, just for a moment, put this book down and type 'George Best, lob, Tottenham' into your search engine. Then glory in the chip that somehow eludes eight defenders to find its way into the top corner. Then laugh with glee at the celebration. One man, arm half-raised, standing and smiling at his own temerity.

For me, that represents my childhood love of football – a game that back then was in reality often slow, brutal and tedious – but in my head was that goal, in every game, every Saturday of every week. George played for many clubs, but close your eyes and you can only see him in red. So he, my friends, is why I can't fully cross that bridge from 'don't like' to 'hate'.

Oh, plus Joy Division and the Smiths are still my favourite bands. Really, grandad? You amaze us.

Why You Shouldn't Support Them

- Relentless global expansion.
- Palace have been in two FA Cup finals. We've lost them both. To Man United.
- The roof of my mouth is still missing two layers of skin from that balti pie.

MANSFIELD TOWN

'Won't you be my coo ca choo?'

ALVIN STARDUST (the closest I could find to a celebrity Mansfield fan)

'Sometimes you see potential in something that is so downtrodden, you can make a difference. I fell in love with it.'

CAROLYN RADFORD CEO of Mansfield Town, explaining her involvement with the club

I'm not sure how Mansfield fans would have reacted to Carolyn Radford's admission that she knew nothing about the club when she first went there.*

She should have asked me, or rather, she should have asked the nine-year-old me. If you'd asked 1971 Kevin (not Kev, please) about Mansfield Town, he would have dutifully said: 'The Stags ... yellow shirts, blue shorts ... a stag's head ... Field Mill.' I would probably have been able to tell you the name of the manager and the captain as well ... let me think, Jock Basford was manager and I believe the captain may have been Stuart Boam.† As a nine-year-old I could reel off the vital statistics of every club in England. Most of us could, there wasn't much else to distract us.

I have to admit that I have never been to Mansfield or Field Mill. I've definitely seen Mansfield play, though – on 23 August 1977. Obviously I checked the date, but I remember the game, if only for what happened afterwards. We had just been promoted to the Second Division and it was our first home-game of the season. Selhurst Park was full of optimism and sparkled in the sort of sunlight that only really exists in your memory. We won comfortably, which probably caused the bit I remember best.

There were only about a hundred Mansfield fans left at the end, but at the final whistle they went on a mini-rampage that took as many as

---

* She's made up for it since. Carolyn was League Two's CEO of the year in the 2019 Football Business Awards.

† I'm not a very good actor, am I, even in writing. Of course I looked up the manager but even the internet doesn't seem to know who the captain was. Feel free to inundate Bloomsbury with the answer. I'm sure they check non-Harry Potter correspondence from time to time.

one policeman to stop, but not until about £3.50's worth of damage had been done to the away terrace. It didn't make any headlines the next day.

So this is very much not a personal history of Mansfield Town FC. And to be honest, even among those for whom the history of Mansfield *is* personal, there is some confusion. The official club history, on the official club website, begins with these splendidly snippy words: 'Much has been written of the formation of Mansfield Town Football Club and many dates have been given, however most are apocryphal or at the very least wildly inaccurate.' That's the spirit!

Field Mill has been a football ground since 1861, making it the oldest in the country still in use (I think; that club website has got me paranoid), but it has not always been used by Mansfield Town. Come on, Kevin, you can't let yourself be intimidated by a website, go back in and check …

Yep, it confirms that it is the oldest ground in the EFL and the oldest in the world still to host professional football. Ooh, *and* in 1930, it hosted the first ever competitive match under artificial light. And if you think I'm going to query how competitive the North Notts League Senior Cup final actually was, then you are mistaken.

Remember the Methodists of Aston Villa? Well, in 1897, some lads of a similar non-denominational bent formed Mansfield Wesleyans who were to become Mansfield Town. They wore light blue and brown striped shirts (that sounds a bit flash for Methodists) and drew their first game, against Sherwood Foresters, 2-2.‡

'…their Chairman and Secretary were once banned by the FA for signing a player on the Sabbath, and them Methodists too.'

In 1910, they changed their name to Mansfield Town and … oh, look, if you want to carry on reading a really detailed, and I mean *really* detailed, account of Mansfield's history, I suggest you go to that official club website. You'll find out about their bitter rivalry with Mansfield Mechanics and discover that their chairman and secretary were once banned by the FA for signing a player on the Sabbath Day, and them Methodists too! It's a very entertaining read, but I warn you, have a cup of tea and several biscuits because you'll be there for a while.

If you want a potted history, well, they joined the League, won a couple of titles, got promoted a bit and relegated a bit, fell out of the

---

‡ Presumably the football team of the army regiment of the same name. Whatever, I really hope they played in Lincoln Green shirts.

League and came back again. Not very interesting. Except it is, of course, to their fans. And to those people who dedicate their time and energy to researching that history. And to all of us who are endlessly fascinated by the myths and legends (and occasionally the hard facts) of every single one of our football teams.

Why You Shouldn't Support Them

- Paul and Martin may start throwing questions at you to prove your allegiance.
- The oldest professional football ground in the world is now known as the One Call Stadium. They're tampering with their own history.
- That baffling mini-rampage. It was hilarious but I just know they would have gone home and lied to their mates about how they terrified the cockneys.

MIDDLESBROUGH

'Thank goodness my kids are big Boro fans.'

BOB MORTIMER big Boro fan

'What a sensation!'

FRANK BOUGH BBC commentator on one of the most amazing goals ever seen at Ayresome Park

That missing 'O' always used to bother me as a kid.

My dad taught me to read when I was four because he thought working-class kids needed to be able to communicate with 'posh people' if they wanted to get ahead or bring about permanent revolution, whichever was easier. And I loved reading. By the time I was seven, I had a reading age of 15, to the delight of my primary school headmaster, Mr Collins, who kept the certificate proving it on his office wall. Mr Collins had played in goal for Wimbledon, but was obsessed with all sport and saw no reason why we shouldn't be too, girls and all. He was way ahead of his time. He was the father of Shirley Valentine, sorry, Pauline Collins, and he was the kindest, most caring man a south London primary school could ask for.

I read everything I could get hold of, which really annoyed my mum, who'd much rather I was outside getting the sort of ruddy glow that all my Irish cousins had; and she was fairly certain that none of them had read any 'Just William' books, let alone all of them, twice. I also read a *lot* of football magazines and was convinced that every single one of them had actually misprinted the name Middlesbrough every time they mentioned them.

Obviously, even as a child, it seemed I already had that latent sense of London superiority that made me assume it was *their* spelling mistake and not *my* ignorance that was the problem. And I still don't know why it's not spelt 'Middlesborough', even though I have a friend who is so knowledgeable about the town he could tell you whether a milk bottle was from there just by its shape.*

---

* That sounds impressive, but try spending a car journey with him. He's like Wikipedia you can't switch off.

The other problem is where it is. I mean, I know where it is, but where does it fit in football culture? And while I'm at it, what the bloody hell is a 'parmo'? The first time I went to film there, I was told by everyone that I had to try the press room parmo. It's a snack found only in Middlesbrough, and I reckon there's a reason for that. Apparently it's based on a parmigiana, but this version is flattened pork covered in breadcrumbs then deep-fried and dipped in white sauce and melted cheese. Obviously I tried one, it ticks a lot of my boxes. Meh. It's basically a glorified Findus crispy pancake, which you have to eat really quickly because you can see the cheese congealing at one end even as you're eating the other. But, being polite, I told the catering lady it was delicious. Yes, I did take a second one but only for research purposes.

Too often they are considered a north-east club, but in reality they are in north Yorkshire and they want their big rivals to be Leeds United, not the Geordies and Mackems. They do, however, have a proud, self-deprecating nickname of their own. They call themselves 'Smoggies' after the smoke and fumes that enveloped the town from the giant iron and steel foundries of the Industrial Revolution.

It had the largest Irish immigrant population outside of Liverpool (although I had no cousins there, which makes it pretty much unique) and was the first town bombed by the Germans in the Second World War – well, it's nice to have a claim to fame that isn't 5,000 calories of cheesy pork.

The original amateur Middlesbrough FC, formed in 1876, were yet another cricket club looking for some winter fun, but in 1889, some lads upped sticks to form a professional club called Middlesbrough Ironopolis (maroon and green stripes – I'd have been in Heaven). The club's own official history referred to them as a 'breakaway sect' but my guess is they were working-class lads who were fed up mixing with posh cricket boys. Unfortunately, whoever they were, they had no business sense, because despite that rather cool name, they went bankrupt in 1893 while the amateurs they left behind carried on winning (amateur) things all over the place.

Professionalism followed soon after becoming the town's only club, to the extent that they caused an absolute scandal in 1905 when they paid £1,000 for a striker called Alf Common. I can remember the fuss when Trevor Francis became the first £1 million player, but apparently that was nothing compared to the outrage of furious Edwardians at the first ever four-figure transfer fee, although to be fair, it must have seemed astronomical to a population who mainly earned less than a pound a week.

In 1949, they were at it again; Andy Donaldson was signed from Newcastle for the first ever *five*-figure transfer fee, an enormous sum in a town still largely flattened by the Luftwaffe.

Brian Clough played for them, which is always a plus for me, and, even better, he once scored five goals in one match when they beat Brighton 9-0. In the 1966 World Cup, the whole planet got to wonder about the missing 'o', with Ayresome Park hosting the games of group 4.

It must have come as a bit of a culture shock to the Italian, Chilean, Russian and North Korean fans who managed to find the place, because Boro's current ground is lovely, but Ayresome Park fell squarely on the wrong side of shithole. And worse was to come for Italy: it was the scene of one of the biggest shocks in World Cup history when they lost 1-0 to North Korea. It is very much to the club's credit that the housing estate that replaced Ayresome Park has many memorials, including a plaque on the very spot that the goal was scored from. And it was to the credit of Smoggies everywhere that even though memories of the recent Korean War were very fresh, they took the North Koreans to their hearts.

Twenty years later, the club became one of the biggest in recent history to nearly fold. Floundering under crippling debts, they went into liquidation but were saved at the 11th hour and 59th minute by a local consortium, and a team of youngsters and veterans were allowed to continue playing, albeit at Hartlepool's ground since the gates of Ayresome Park were padlocked.

One of that consortium, Steve Gibson, has been chairman ever since, bringing a degree of stability unmatched by most clubs (especially Ironopolis). On the pitch there have been relegations and European wins and that move to the Riverside Stadium, but Gibson has ensured that they will never be locked out of their own home again – it's a sorry thing to realise that, as for many communities in this book, for the people of Middlesbrough, the football club is the only thing financially secure.

Why You Shouldn't Support Them

- The spelling thing does genuinely annoy me.
- Inexplicable taste in snacks.
- If Leeds, Sunderland and Newcastle don't care about them, why should you?

MILLWALL

'No one likes us, we don't care.'

Millwall fans (I suspect they do, deep down)

'I thought that in general, southerners were less passionate. I learnt so much.'

GEORGE GRAHAM Scottish manager of Millwall between 1983 and 1986

Millwall fans really don't like us. I mean *really* don't. They seem to think we are middle-class. Christ knows why, it must be all those art galleries, independent bookshops and French restaurants around Thornton Heath.* It's particularly annoying considering you can't actually move in Bermondsey these days without tripping over a beard-sculptor or ironic cheesemonger. Nevertheless, that's what they think. They hate us and we're posh. And they assume we hate them so they will no doubt be expecting me to use this chapter to have a go at them.

But I'm going to do something worse. I'm going to treat them like any other team. And then patronise them a bit.

Millwall have always been associated with hooliganism and violence, especially since a notorious *Panorama* documentary on BBC1 in 1977 that took an almost anthropological approach to Millwall firms like the 'F-Troop', the 'Treatment' and the 'Halfway Line'. It wouldn't be fair to say that *Panorama* glorified the troublemakers, but they certainly gave them a voice and hinted that many kids and young men at other clubs aspired to show the same level of violent commitment to their team.

The irony is that *Panorama* had been invited by the club to show that their reputation was exaggerated, only for it to be tarnished for decades. It still is, and no matter how many brilliant things the club does in its community (and they do a huge amount), they still tend to be associated with a dark side of the game. Partly because one of the darkest of the dark days of the eighties was a rampage by Millwall

---

* For those of you not au fait with the area, we have no French restaurants. Nor indeed many restaurants where the food doesn't come in a box. There are art galleries, but round here we call them 'walls'.

fans after a cup tie at Luton in 1985. It nearly changed football forever because Margaret Thatcher, then prime minister, had to be talked out of making fans carry identity cards, eventually accepting the argument that we had civil rights too.

As I said in the chapter on Bradford, I very much subscribe to the *Guardian*-reading loony-left argument that if you treat people like animals they will eventually behave like them, but Millwall fans did sometimes test that theory to extremes. And it wasn't a new phenomenon. In 1906, the *East Ham Echo* reported that 'free fights were plentiful among the crowd' during a game against West Ham, and in later years a Newport goalkeeper was knocked unconscious by fans and a referee was attacked outside the ground.

'You can't actually move in Bermondsey these days without tripping over a beard-sculptor or ironic cheesemonger.'

In the 1930s the club, aware of its image even then, appointed a team of uniformed page-boys to act as mini-commissionaires around the ground. Didn't last long. Putting anyone in uniform around The Den probably wasn't a good idea.

So it won't surprise you that I used to hate away games at The Den. It was a truly intimidating little place, closed in by terraced houses and surrounded by alleyways that were just made for ambushes. And despite the fact we looked like them and sounded like them, they just knew somehow that we *weren't* them.

I remember a particularly terrible incident after one game at The Den when we left what we thought was a friendly pub a couple of hours after a game and Roy got rammed by a car. Although, to be fair to Millwall, the car in question was driven by Ali, who had come to pick us up, and Roy had drunkenly weaved into the road to wave her down. She still claims it was an accident, but I've known her a long time and Roy once criticised her driving, so I'm not convinced.†

The odd thing is that I went to a few non-Palace games there with Barry, a Millwall-supporting mate, and really enjoyed them. Without the actual threat of violence (well, to me anyway) it was a boisterous and raucous place to be, and, like Brentford, seemed to be a very different London to the one that Arsenal and Chelsea lived in.

West Ham fans will disagree but Millwall probably had the most distinct identity of any other London club. The hooligan element were

---

† Of course we still talk about it. We're football fans. Which also means the story gets better every time.

despicable, but they were a club born of dockers, and Barry and his pals resonated with a fierce working-class pride – that's not a bad thing.

Well, the fans may have been dockers. The club was actually formed as Millwall Rovers in 1885 for the workers of a jam and marmalade factory on the Isle of Dogs. Hang on, Isle of Dogs? Rovers? Really? Yes, really, and that may be one of the reasons they became Millwall Athletic shortly after.

And yes, really, a jam and marmalade factory. Not many riveters and welders in that job, are there? Although it does make me wonder if Paddington Bear may be a Millwall fan. In the interests of historical accuracy (and because Barry has quite the temper), I should point out that a lot of boiling sugar is involved in industrial jam-making. And you could get a nasty paper cut off the labels as well.

Many of the factory workers had apparently been recruited from Scotland, and that may have been the reason the team wore dark blue shirts and adopted a lion as their badge, and subsequently their nickname. Obviously, the 'may' and the 'apparently' are doing a lot of work in that sentence, but the history of any football club is hard to pin down. Clearly these teams were not meant to last for centuries and it's very rare that anyone actually bothered to definitively write stuff down for posterity. The early history of football is mostly oral, and for every version that *is* written, there's normally one to contradict it.

'Hang on, Isle of Dogs? Rovers? Really? Yes, really.'

The Isle of Dogs isn't an actual island. It's a marshy peninsula. And in the 1880s it was a strange, desolate place, hostile to outsiders (The Den was exactly the same – sorry, had to be done). Finding a permanent ground there proved difficult because space was often needed for more profitable things like docks and warehouses, and crowd numbers were erratic, so it was decided that a move to Bermondsey, teeming with shipyards and dockers, was the only way to stay afloat (you're welcome) and by 1910 they were safely housed in The Den, even if away fans rarely were.

It would give me great joy to detail in full their relative lack of success as an actual football club and to gloss over their few successes (there was the occasional promotion, I believe, and rumour filtered through of reaching the FA Cup final in 2004, luckily followed by a laughably short run in the UEFA cup), but Millwall are a rare club who can't really be defined by trophies.

Here comes the patronising bit … They continue to be firmly rooted in their relatively small community. Indeed, for some years the shirts were sponsored by the local council. True, the Lion is a slightly different beast since they moved to the anodyne New Den in 1993, but they are, if not unique, definitely different. Their heroes tend not to be glamorous wingers but tough-tackling midfielders like Terry Hurlock and Keith 'Rhino' Stevens (that nickname is a real giveaway, ain't it).

And if you ever want to pacify an angry Millwall fan, just whisper the name Harry Cripps in his ear – it's like putting a baby back on the breast. He played 400 games for them between 1961 and 1974 as a (very) tough-tackling full-back. They adore a full-back. Now, that is different.

Why You Shouldn't Support Them

- Come on lads, it's not the seventies any more. Stop terrifying people.
- And who wears Burberry any more?
- They keep the jam and marmalade bit quiet, don't they?

MILTON KEYNES
DONS

'The footballing equivalent of SClub7, artificial, contrived and admired only by the terminally gullible.'

Post on NorthStandChat.com, a Brighton fansite (oh, the dreadful places I have been to research this book)

'What do Wombles do? They recycle something people don't want. That's us.'

GREG MK Dons fan, interviewed on dreamteamfc.com

It must be difficult being a fan of MK Dons. They are *nobody's* second team and they are a story that should never have been allowed to happen. But it's in the past now (technically, everything in this book is in the past now, including that sentence), and MK Dons fans presumably love their club as much as I love mine, so I suppose they should be treated with the same respect, although you probably won't find many AFC Wimbledon fans that agree.

It seems odd to be talking about the history of a football club when that history only began in 2004 after Wimbledon were, well, I was going to say 'relocated', but AFC fans hate that word: they prefer words like 'shafted' or 'betrayed'. In any case, where they are now is Milton Keynes, a new town incorporated from three towns and 15 villages in Buckinghamshire in 1967. It's actually a pleasant place with good transport links and a thriving cultural scene, but for the purposes of this book it was the scene of a footballing crime so let's ignore anything nice about it.

Right from the start it was considered that a Football League team would be a nice little accessory and it was clear that none of the local amateur teams would be joining the 92 anytime soon, so tentative discussions were had with first Charlton Athletic and then Luton Town, who were at least close by.

Of course, there was the option of growing one of those local amateur teams but that takes time and passion and a level of commitment that commerce is rarely interested in. So ears were pricked when it became clear after the Taylor Report (see chapter on Liverpool) that Wimbledon could neither afford to redevelop Plough Lane as the report demanded, nor build a new stadium (they shared Selhurst Park for a while but couldn't sustain themselves at somebody else's ground). By 1996, Wimbledon's owner, Sam Hammam, in an act of desperation, was actively seeking to move the club to Dublin, despite opposition from, well, everyone, apart, presumably, from one or two exiled Wombles. Frustrated in this, he sold the club to two Norwegians, who then sold Plough Lane to a supermarket chain, meaning Wimbledon would never have a home to go back to.

Enter Pete Winkelman, a pop music promoter who looks like a pop music promoter as imagined by the writer of *Midsomer Murders*. If you promote pop music you need a state-of-the-art concert venue, right? And it may as well have an Asda and an Ikea while you're at it, and hey, here's an idea, how about a football team who can play there too? You could go to a Take That tribute band, a cup game and a furniture sale all on the same day. Then, in 2001, the Norwegians arbitrarily announced that the club would

'To the surprise of no one, the new owner of the club did what he promised he wouldn't.'

go out of business unless it was relocated to a stadium that their mate Pete the Promoter was conveniently planning to build in Milton Keynes – just 56 short miles away from Wimbledon.

The FA, miraculously, said no. The team belonged where the team belonged; but, scandalously, an appeal was allowed and a three-man independent committee (i.e. not football people) allowed the move to go ahead, even though the new stadium wasn't ready, and the only option was a hockey stadium they could rent while they waited.

Obviously, as soon as the move happened, many Wimbledon fans announced they would not travel those 56 short miles; and to the surprise of no one, the new owner of the club did what he promised he wouldn't: he changed the team's name to the Milton Keynes Dons, and changed the kit and the badge.

It was a US-style franchise move in all but name, and it infuriated most right-thinking football fans, who feared that Pandora's Box had been opened to reveal a future of Manchester Mackerels and Chelsea Cheetahs.*

---

* Let's face it, if we wanted to watch teams with shit names like that we'd go to basketball.

Angry Wimbledon fans responded by setting up their own phoenix club, which, guided by the gentle breeze of karma, rose gracefully from a local park to League One.

And yet. And yet. Not every Wimbledon fan bailed out of the MK Dons project, and some still make the journey up the motorway to support them. There are two sides to every story. Even this one. MK Dons have some brilliant community outreach schemes. Pete Winkelman has publicly apologised for what happened and an accord has been signed by both clubs in order to create some harmony.*

I imagine Winkelman thought his new creation would be in the Premier League by now, instead of the same division as AFC Wimbledon, and if anyone is the 'villain' of the piece, it's him, not the fans. But is he a 'villain'? It's a weird one, because I know whose side I'm on. It's not fair that fans are the ones who suffer when an owner takes them to financial disaster, but technically, Wombles fans suffered because Winkelman and the Norwegians were trying to prevent financial disaster. Although, as I said at the start, you probably won't find many AFC Wimbledon fans who agree.

Why You Shouldn't Support Them

- Ask a Wimbledon fan.
- No disrespect to the fans but it's a club that shouldn't exist.
- They had a new club, a new ground, a new name and they chose an all-white kit.

---

* And an element of humour does seem to be creeping in to the fans' acrimonious relationship: MK fans refer to AFC as 'KFC Kingston' and AFC refer to them as 'MkDonalds'.

MORECAMBE

'Allez, allez, allez, allez, oh allez, allez, allez, oh we're
Morecambe FC, we f****n' hate Stanley.'

Morecambefc-supporters.org

'I have always taken a very deep interest in the Morecambe
Football Club, and have been anxious to help it forward.'

JOSEPH BARNES CHRISTIE the wealthy benefactor who kept the club solvent in its early
years and bought Rosebery Park for them, 1927

A lot of clubs have creatures as their badge. Palace have the magnificent
eagle, Brighton have their bin-raiding gull thing, there are a few lions,
a tiger, Coventry have an elephant for no apparent reason, there's a
wolf, a fox and a ram. Morecambe have a shrimp. Just a shrimp. No
Latin inscription or added flourishes. Just the words Morecambe FC
and a shrimp.

I don't know if that's the sign of a club secure and confident in its
own identity or a club that had a quick meeting back in the day and
on a show of hands just decided 'shrimp'. Did someone say 'hang on,
Southend have got a shrimp as well', only for the rest of them to reply
'no problem, they're miles away, the pubs are open, shrimp it is'? As it
happens, Southend do have a shrimp on their shirt but it's surrounded by
a football and some swords so it's quite cool. A lone shrimp is not cool.

I worry that they may lose players over it. A promising young kid flies
over from Portugal and is impressed by the ground and the facilities.
He likes the sound of the deal he's been offered. Then he turns to his
agent and whispers 'isso e um camarao na camisa?'† Five minutes
later, he's in a cab on his way to sign for Accrington Stanley and next
season he scores the winner against Morecambe in the last minute. And
that would be *really* annoying for Morecambe fans because they hate
Accrington. Especially as the only reason he is kissing the badge on
his Accrington shirt is that it's his way of saying he was never going to

---

† Is that a shrimp on the shirt?

kiss a bloody shrimp. It's not a likely scenario, I know, but why would you take the risk?

I wouldn't mind but you used to have a lovely badge, a sailing boat underneath an arch of roses. Lancashire and the sea. Simple. But presumably considered too old-fashioned. Unlike a cutting-edge shrimp.

And your mascot is a cat. Christie the Cat, named after your old ground, which was named after the chap above. If a shrimp won't cut it as a mascot, get it off your shirt! And if he was acting like a proper cat, he'd be licking the shrimp on the badge. Not that I'm advocating mascots should be acting like the real thing.

> 'If a shrimp won't cut it as a mascot, get it off your shirt!'

It would be terrifying to see Pete the Eagle halfway up the floodlight tearing a stolen cat apart to feed his young.

I like Christie, actually; he once had a tear-up with an opposition goalkeeper and got a red card. Shrimpy the Shrimp wouldn't have done that. And I like the fact that Morecambe and Accrington* is a proper rivalry. I don't know if it's a Lancashire thing or a milk thing, and I don't care. I'm just reassured to know that football still weaves its magic and several thousand people in Morecambe don't give a stuff about Liverpool or Chelsea or Real Madrid, they just want to beat Accrington bastard Stanley.

Not that they have done often. Between 2007 and 2015, they failed to beat Accrington in 16 attempts. I blame the shrimp.

It's in the nature of local rivalries that Accrington fans could probably tell you more about Morecambe than I can. Just as, if you want to know the bad stuff about Brighton, come to me. Not that the spoilsport editor would let me put it in the book.

Morecambe were formed in 1920 and have had the same problem as many small clubs in the north-west – just down the road there are teams winning the Premier League and the Champions League on a regular basis. And for all the comparative wealth and media coverage that comes with being a Football League club, it's possible that Morecambe fans enjoyed their many years of non-league success more than the mere 13 years they have had in League Two, where their highest finish by a distance was fourth, and they got hammered 7-2 in the semi-final of the play-offs.

Sadly, as I write this, there is every possibility that they may not even be in the League when you read it. There are currently several clubs

---

* Would Eric and Ernie have been as funny if they were called that?

scrapping for survival at the bottom of League Two and Morecambe are one of them. Even worse, Accrington are mid-table in League One.

Oh, one more thing. At Morecambe's new ground there is a bar called JB's in honour of that estimable chap Joseph Barnes Christie, without whom the fledgling Morecambe FC would almost certainly not have survived. And for those Morecambe fans who don't know, Joseph was born and raised in Accrington.

Why You Shouldn't Support Them

- Mainly the shrimp.
- If the limit of your ambition is hating Accrington, you may have a problem.
- Mr Christie saved your club. There should be a stand named after him, not a bar.

NEWCASTLE UNITED

'It's been the most enduring and infuriating of all relationships. I wouldn't have it any other way.'

GABBY LOGAN TV presenter and Newcastle fan

'Imagine the size of the crowd if we ever won something.'

KEVIN KEEGAN being greeted by thousands on arriving to sign for Newcastle

Sorry, Kevin, Newcastle United are a massive club by every criterion except one – winning things.

They have a huge stadium, a huge fan base, a huge history and a trophy cabinet that has been gathering more dust than Miss Havisham's dining table. The last thing they won was the Fairs Cup in 1969. And the Fairs Cup was a bizarre European tournament, originally open only to cities in which trade fairs had been held. It became a kind of consolation prize for clubs that had not quite won their domestic leagues.

Nevertheless, despite the trophy-less decades, despite actual relegations and despite current mid-table mediocrity, Newcastle fans always tend to behave as though the open-topped bus is only a couple of streets away. And despite the fact that many towns only have one football team; Geordies really do think that they are the only one-club city, and that there is a unique symbiosis between them and their beloved Magpies – and perhaps they are right; after all, 'toon' can refer equally to the city as to the club and its fans. There is something almost Basque-like in their sense of separateness, and if you talk to a Toon fan about the Toon, in the toon, their gaze will almost certainly turn to the stadium on the hill with a faraway look in their eyes, like a pilgrim to Lourdes seeing the statue of the Virgin Mary.

And it's infectious. Gabby Logan is a football child. She wouldn't be here if her dad, Terry Yorath, hadn't been sent across the road every day to get the bacon sandwiches when he was an apprentice at Leeds United. Hopefully managing to dodge a superstitious Don Revie on the way. Terry fell in love with the girl who buttered the bread in the cafe, et voilà: Gabby. He was a very good footballer and a very good manager, and

Gabby told me that she supported whatever team he was at, but fell in love with none of them because she knew that sooner or later dad would be on the move again.

Newcastle changed all that. As a student at Durham University, with a Geordie boyfriend, she started to go regularly because she was offered £10 a time to drive the wife of Cypriot signing Nikki Papavasiliou to games and look after her baby for 90 minutes. Ah, that old chestnut. I have heard many reasons for supporting a football team and baby-sitting wasn't any of them.

Nikki is long gone, but Gabby remains. Shortly after, she was offered a job on Metro Radio, presenting the breakfast show and, even better, being the touchline reporter at St James' Park. And that was it – hooked. And what a time to be on the touchline: 'A revolution was happening, and I wanted to be around it.'

The combination of Sir John Hall's chequebook and Kevin Keegan's gung-ho management was irresistible and the 1995/96 season was one of the best in living memory. Gabby described that team as 'an alluring combination of swagger, long hair and local grit'. They were entertainers, that's for sure, but ... there's always a bloody but. Twelve points clear in January, they lost the title to Manchester United on the final day, not long after Keegan's famous rant live on air: 'I'd love it if we beat them, love it.' Newcastle had spent 212 days on top of the table. That's the longest time any team has ever spent at the top of a league but not won it. Toon fans would probably be proud of that.

The optimistic belief among Newcastle fans that the Champions League must be just around the corner is quite touching actually. But it can go against them too. They are a bit like toddlers. At the start of each game they are *so* excited, but if they're not 3-0 up after an hour, it can go a bit quiet. If they lose, you half expect to see them being carried home exhausted over the shoulder of parents because all that passion has worn them out.

'Newcastle fans always tend to behave as though the open-topped bus is only a couple of streets away.'

Speaking of which, if you've ever wondered what a football pitch looks like to a pigeon then you have never been in the away end at St James' Park. Call me old-fashioned, but you shouldn't need a base camp halfway up the climb to your seat at a football ground. I suspect they did it deliberately so that it takes away fans a good 10 minutes to get their breath back before they can start roaring on their team.

But a full St James' Park is an exhilarating place to be, inside and out. I was there filming when one of their legends, Alan Shearer, returned as manager in an ultimately doomed attempt to save them from relegation. The police had warned against us being there – not in a bad way, just in a mayhem way. I have certainly never experienced anything like it outside a ground. You could barely move, and the passion was such that you half expected Shearer to arrive on a donkey covered in palm leaves.

The Geordies do love a 'legend'. Particularly if he has a 9 on his shirt: Milburn, McDonald, Keegan, Shearer – there will be many Geordies with at least one of those names tattooed on him somewhere.

One consolation for Toon fans lies in the past. But what a consolation it is! They have a history and tradition that I can't do justice to in a few words here. Also, I don't support them, so I don't have to.

> 'Call me old-fashioned, but you shouldn't need a base camp halfway up the climb to your seat at a football ground.'

Newcastle East End FC and Newcastle West End FC* became United in 1892 after a skint West End side asked the East Enders to budge up and let them join their successful side. Initially, the locals were indifferent, to the extent that the club wrote to the local paper to complain that 'the Newcastle public' did not deserve professional football. The Newcastle public sulked a bit for a couple of years and then decided to give the professional football thing a go.

Many, many thousands of them turned up to watch United dominate the first decade of the new century. It's almost like Newcastle United were glad to see the back of Queen Victoria, because in the decade that followed her passing they won three League championships and reached five FA Cup finals (although they only won one).

They won more titles and cups, got relegated a couple of times to give Toon fans something to talk about, then in the 1950s they won three more FA Cups playing in front of crowds that averaged around 60,000. And all the time wearing those famous black and white stripes. I intend to ignore one historian who has suggested that their original kit was red and white stripes because I know what football fans are like. Their eyes would be drawn to that sentence, they'd ignore the rest of the chapter, and I would never be able to perform in Newcastle again.

And then it all sort of ground to a halt. They've had mediocre teams that won nothing. They've had brilliant teams that won nothing. At the

---

* Neil Tennant of The Pet Shop Boys is a Geordie so maybe that put an idea into his head?

moment the limit of their ambition is staying in the Premier League. But still they inspire such passion.

I think most of us understand the mindset of Newcastle fans. After all, we feel about our clubs in exactly the same way but most of us don't have that burden of expectation that history brings. They are like Jacob Marley, weighed down by chains made of old silverware, doomed to walk the earth lamenting until new glory can be found.

We other fans are bemused by it but I suspect that a lot of us secretly, very deep down, wouldn't mind if they won something, unless they beat my team doing it. But for all that most of us were a bit enchanted by the Kevin Keegan season that ended in meltdown and tears, being football fans, most of us also found it a little bit funny as well.

Why You Shouldn't Support Them

- The away end is ludicrous.
- Their absolute inability to accept that other football fans are passionate as well.
- Put a bloody shirt on, man, it's freezing.

NEWPORT COUNTY

'A thirty-year-old club with a hundred-year history.'

Wales Online

'If you google world's unluckiest or least successful professional football club, then I guarantee Newport would come out somewhere on top.'

NEAL HEARD Newport fan and fashion designer responsible for their latest kit

Someone has to be the other something. The one you will be able to answer in a pub quiz, given time: the drummer in the Jam; Zeppo Marx; the third team in Wales. County fans knew where that was going, but sadly it's true. Everyone will get Cardiff and Swansea straight away but there will often be that slight pause before they go … oh, yes, of course, Newport.

It's a shame, because Rodney Parade may be smaller than the Cardiff stadium and the Liberty but it still packs a punch atmosphere-wise. Mind you, I'm only basing that from the telly because Palace have only played there once since 1962 and that was a League Cup match in 1987. I love my club very much but not to the extent that I would travel to Newport for an evening game.*

And Newport, and their fans, the Amber Army, have been on telly quite a lot recently, what with spectacular FA Cup defeats of clubs like Leeds and Leicester City. But it's a miracle that the club, and the Army, exist at all. Or rather, it's a testimony to the stubbornness of football fans, who clung on bitterly to their team as the team itself clung on bitterly in the face of obstacles that would have made Hercules say 'look lads, I'm not sure this is doable'.

Newport County were formed at a meeting in the Tredegar Arms in 1912 as a deliberate attempt to bring football to a rugby town and to tap into the potential fan base of a giant steelworks nearby. Many of the workers there had been moved from Wolverhampton so it's quite

* Which makes no sense because I've been much further for evening games. Not in the League Cup though.

possible that the amber kit may have been chosen deliberately to appeal to Wolves fans among them. Or it may have been chosen because it stood out on the road, because legend has it they were so skint they walked to their first game in Cardiff.† And the ground they were walking from was Somerton Park, which was their home until ... well, let's wait and see, shall we.

For most of my childhood, the glorious *Shoot* football magazine started the season by giving away cardboard League tables with little grooves in to move the cardboard team names up and down. I'm convinced that not one single child was still doing it in January but while we were, Newport were invariably in the bottom half of the Fourth Division. Indeed, they and Workington seemed to exist solely for the purpose of making every other team feel good about themselves.

They did try a bizarre experiment in 1976 by changing their kit to light blue and white stripes like Argentina, in the hope that a bit of South American magic might rub off on them. Sadly, the players mainly being from South Wales, it didn't work; they have been back in the amber ever since.

Imagine being a fan and being asked to design the kit. Neal Heard is a designer and fashion historian (blimey, I thought I had a cool job) who was asked to come up with something new but resolutely amber for this season's home shirt. How did that feel, Neal?

'For good or bad they are my team and I love them but it was semi-surreal to design the shirt and I was worried about doing it justice. But everyone was pleased. The icing on the cake would be to get promoted wearing it.'

Whatever happens while it's being worn, he has done a beautiful job. Especially considering his remit was pretty much: shirt/amber.

Some glamour did follow that blue and white experiment. In 1980, aided by the goals of Liverpool legend-in-waiting John Aldridge, they were promoted to the Third Division *and* they won the Welsh Cup, which meant they qualified for the European Cup Winners' Cup, losing to Carl Zeiss Jena of East Germany in the quarter-final. As any child of that generation will still know, Carl Zeiss Jena were the team from a factory that made optical lenses. Children of that generation really didn't get out much.

That campaign, however, was to be the high-water mark for the old club (spoiler alert). In 1988, after amassing only 25 points back in the

† I think legend may have had it wrong. If you can afford a kit, you can afford a bus fare, surely?

Fourth Division, they were relegated to the Conference but with debts so heavy they couldn't fulfil their fixtures and in February 1989 they were wound up, or as I prefer it, killed.

But it lived in the hearts of fans, and in June the same year, 400 of them formed a new club, Newport AFC. However, the council wouldn't let them play at Somerton Park if they claimed to be the same club that went bust owing them rent and rates, while the FA of Wales decided they had no claim to be the same club and so denied them the right to take part in football in Wales. Thus began what their first chairman called 'a magical mystery tour of the Cotswolds'.

They were offered a place in the Hellenic League of the English FA, a league so far down the pyramid it's not even in sand, and in the absence of a ground played their home games at Moreton-in-the-Marsh, 85 miles away. Which, I imagine, made it impossible to walk to many games.

In 1990, impressed by successive promotions, or perhaps ashamed of their earlier refusal, Newport Council unlocked the gates to a now derelict Somerton Park and jubilant fans swarmed all over it to restore it to glory. Then, the FA of Wales launched the League of Wales and invited/ expected them to join it. When AFC politely declined as they wanted to rise up the English pyramid still further, sanction to play in Wales was once more withdrawn – there are people behaving very churlishly in this story and none of them are Newport fans.

So the club were on their travels again, this time to Gloucester, just 50 miles away so still not walkable. It took legal action that went all the way to the High Court before the FAW relented and Newport returned in triumph to, erm, Newport. Although not to Somerton Park, which was now a housing estate. Ah well, at least it wasn't an Asda.

These days, now happily flourishing back in the Football League, they share Rodney Parade with a local rugby club, which is kind of ironic considering why they started the football club in the first place. And their nickname is no longer the Ironsides. It's the Exiles. Welcome home.

Why You Shouldn't Support Them

- They share a ground with a rugby club.
- And it's called Rodney.
- Didn't ask me to design their kit. I've designed hundreds of kits. I was always getting told off at school for doing it.

NORTHAMPTON TOWN

'The miracle of 1966 was not England winning the World Cup, but Northampton reaching Division 1.'

JOE MERCER manager of Manchester City

'We couldn't believe our luck when it was announced that in the fifth round we would play Manchester United.'

DIXIE McNEIL Northampton striker

You know my thing with George Best. Come on, yes you do. Well, this seems like the ideal place to explain why Northampton fans won't share it. On 7 February 1970, in an FA cup tie at their old County Ground, Manchester United beat Northampton 8-2. George Best scored six of them.

George was returning from a four-week ban for kicking the ball out of a referee's hand. Although I like to think he spent that four weeks with Miss World in a St Tropez hotel, he obviously missed football because he returned that day with a bravura performance during which, in the words of another great Manchester entertainer, Morrissey,* George proceeded to 'tease, torment and tantalise' the bemused Northampton defenders. All his pent-up frustration at a month without football was distilled into something close to football perfection.

Of course, there are two sides to every story. Defender John Clarke said, 'all I kept seeing was George's backside disappearing into the distance'. At least there was some consolation for Dixie McNeil: 'The high spot was I scored against one of the greatest teams in Europe. The low spot was George scoring six.'

Chairman Eric Northover was not as philosophical. He said it was 'disgraceful, unforgivable, we should have put the pride of Northampton

---

* Although I sincerely pray that if he were still with us, George wouldn't also have turned into a deranged nationalist.

first'. And to be fair, there has been plenty to be proud about. Indeed, they were quite the quirky little number and in the early years had a groundbreaking player of their own, although for very different reasons.

First of all, they had a natty kit, and you know me, I was a bugger for a natty kit. White with two maroon hoops on the chest. They've always had some variation of maroon and white but that one was perfect. And they had a strange-looking stadium. The County Ground was a name more associated with cricket and sure enough they shared it with Northamptonshire County Cricket Club. So three sides of it were completely normal but the fourth side was open to reveal an actual cricket field. On the rare occasion you saw them on telly, that was really intriguing. And a little bit sinister, for some reason.

There was controversy with another sport at the very start of the Cobblers' life. Shall we get that nickname over and done with? The town was massively associated with the shoe industry, that's all. Grow up.

The club was founded in 1897 by a group of teachers and one solicitor. The solicitor was handy as the local rugby club objected to the name Northampton Football Club because, as far as they were concerned (wrongly), what they played was also football. It got quite unpleasant until the FA stepped in and made a simple suggestion: change the name to Northampton Town Football Club. Quite why the argument had gone on so long before is baffling, although I suspect the solicitor may well have been spinning it out for expenses.

Now at this stage I could bring you a detailed history, but suffice to say that they have been to the top division and back, are now in a lovely new four-sided stadium and they have the potential to be more than the regular citizens of Leagues One and Two that they have been lately.

Instead, let me introduce you to a player you may vaguely have heard of but who should really be as well known as George Best. Walter Tull was the first black outfield footballer in England (and the second black footballer overall). He was born in 1888 to an English mother and a father from Barbados. Both died when he was very young, and Walter and his siblings were separated, with Walter ending up alone in an orphanage in the East End of London. He excelled as an athlete and was spotted by local amateur side Clapton, from where he signed for Tottenham. It was not a happy experience. In 1909, following a game at Bristol City, one reporter wrote that 'a selection of the crowd made a cowardly attack on him in language lower than Billingsgate'.* The same reporter went on to

---

* The porters of Billingsgate fish market were legendary for their coarse language.

write: 'Let me tell those Bristol hooligans that Tull is so clean in mind and method as to be a model for all white men who play football. Tull was the best forward on the field.'

In 1911 he joined Northampton Town and went on to appear 110 times, until war intervened. Tull volunteered for the Middlesex Regiment, part of the famous 'Footballers' Battalions'. Walter may have been the second black footballer, but he became the first black officer to lead white soldiers into battle. His own commanding officer commended his 'gallantry and coolness' after one night raid into enemy territory.

This story has no happy ending. On 25 March 1918, the Germans launched the last major offensive of the war. Lieutenant Walter Tull was shot and killed attempting to stem the tide. Private Billingham, Leicester's goalkeeper, tried and failed to drag his body back for burial, but a remarkable man lies unknown with many others in the mud of France. There is a beautiful memorial to him close to Sixfields, where Northampton now play.

The *first* black man to play football in England was goalkeeper Arthur Wharton, who signed as a professional for Rotherham in 1889 before moving to Sheffield United. He died a penniless alcoholic in 1930. So far there is no memorial to him. Incidentally, in 1938, Northampton signed John Parris, the first black man to play for Wales.

This is not the right place for me to vent my spleen, but it would be nice to tell the spirits of Walter, Arthur and John that football is now a place free of racial abuse and hatred. However, sadly, the game I love is still periodically blighted by it, and there is a shameful lack of black managers, coaches and directors at all levels. Perhaps teaching people about those remarkable men would help.

Why You Shouldn't Support Them

- The editor thought all my 'cobblers' jokes were childish.
- The shirts are boring plain old maroon now.
- They have a shoe on their badge. Should be a football boot.

NORWICH CITY

'Oh, the affection. The sense of a club being part of a city, a truly local entity, it is so powerful and pleasing.'

STEPHEN FRY Norwich fan, in 2020, after I'd asked him if he could explain the attraction

'Let's be 'aving you. Come on!'

DELIA SMITH Norwich owner, in 2005, after a first half in hospitality

'On the Ball, City' is reputedly the world's oldest football song, having first been belted out at Norwich City's first ever game. It may be old but it doesn't always work, and sometimes even the loudest of fans need a reminder to get behind their team.

Who doesn't love Delia Smith? For four decades and more, the slightly stern but genial TV chef has been teaching us Brits how to boil eggs, roast meat and, for the really adventurous, make a risotto. She is a proper national treasure. And therefore the most unlikely person to be part of one of the most jaw-dropping football moments ever, and one that made us all suspect that if she had made a risotto that evening, none of the wine had gone into the rice.

It's Monday 28 February 2005. Norwich, threatened with relegation from the Premier League, are at home to Man City, who are yet to begin their journey to becoming a juggernaut, but are still a useful team. Norwich raced into an early 2-0 lead, but had been pegged back, and the first half finished 2-2. The game is live on Sky TV, otherwise she might have gotten away with it. And before I describe what 'it' was, I cannot stress enough how nice a person she is, and what she has done for Norwich City Football Club as its joint majority shareholder.

My very first *Match of the Day 2* was at Carrow Road, in a game against Palace, which was very handy. I spent the day with her and she was clever, witty and charming. Which made it all the more annoying when the then chairman of my club, a wannabe wide boy called Simon Jordan, wafted into the boardroom on a wave of expensive aftershave and his own self-importance to say, 'What have you got a trophy cabinet for, you 'aven't won anything', which was not only rude but also indicated he had never seen *our* trophy cabinet, in which somebody allergic to silver could sleep without fear.*

I also learnt that Delia had just had a room at the ground consecrated as a chapel, because she had noticed elderly fans trudging uphill to evensong after a game. That's how nice she is.

So that's how bizarre this was. As the pundits discussed the game, Delia could be seen marching on to the pitch with a microphone in her hand. That was fine, it's her club, she was probably going to give Margaret from accounts a long-service award.

Nope. She stopped in the centre-circle, raised the mic, and said: 'A message for the best football supporters in the world.'

Still not a problem. I mean, she's wrong, but she owns the club, she's hardly going to tell the fans they are possibly the 15th-best supporters south of Newcastle. But then came the fun part: 'We need a twelfth man here. Where are you?' she demanded, belligerently. 'Where are you?! Let's be 'aving you. Come on!'

Then she smirked, dropped the mic into someone's hand and meandered off

'I am firmly of the belief that if you *choose* to live in the countryside, it should be difficult for you to get anywhere.'

the pitch. It was 19 seconds of the best TV I have ever seen. It could only have been better if Stephen Fry had followed her out waving a bottle of champagne and shouting 'one wonders as to your whereabouts' in Latin.

The eerie silence that followed was exactly like the eerie silence that follows when a previously mild-mannered teacher explodes into a rage and throws a desk at you,† but then Carrow Road erupted into a cauldron of noise.

Sadly, it didn't work. What Norwich needed was an *actual* twelfth man. Man City scored late on. Weeks later, Delia's team were toast. Delia, however, was now a legend on the pitch as well as in the kitchen. I'm pleased, because I like her and I've always had nice times there. It's a great ground, Norwich is a great city and so friendly that every pub is an away pub. The only problem with Norwich is getting there.

For such a small island, it really is astonishing how difficult it is to get to some places. On a map, Norwich is only half a thumb away from London (and I've got small hands) but it takes ages getting there. The train takes the scenic route, stopping at places that look too small to have phone boxes, let alone railway stations (like many Londoners, I am

* It's also wrong, They've won the League Cup a couple of times.
† That only happened once. Apparently he couldn't take any more of my insolent grin.

firmly of the belief that if you *choose* to live in the countryside, it should be difficult for you to get anywhere). If you go by car, it's fine until about three-quarters of the way when the road gets modest about having three whole lanes and decides two is enough when it clearly isn't.

Still, it being hard to leave may be one of the reasons why there is such a bond between the city and City. The club has a fierce (but friendly) regional pride that should be the envy of some bigger teams; and while it's not quite the yellow wall of Dortmund in there, it's not far short.

Stephen Fry explained: 'There is a full ironic understanding that we are not, and probably never will be, up there with the giants, and self-knowledge is a calming and beneficent thing.' I know they were his exact words because I had to keep asking him to say it again while I wrote it down.

'Norwich beat Bayern wearing a yellow shirt covered with green splodges that made it look like Kermit the Frog had been sick down the front.'

By the way, City are not known as the Canaries because of their yellow shirts, their shirts are yellow because of the canaries. When Flemish weavers came looking for work in the 19th century, they brought their canaries with them. Presumably on the basis that if they were going to be cooped up all day, some other poor creature was bloody well going to be too. The canaries, ahem, took off as a local hobby, so despite starting their first season in a light blue and white shirt, the yellow was adopted soon after; and the avian connection was well enough established by 1908 that their first proper ground was called The Nest. Shame really, because it was built on a site known as Rump's Hole – only in England would that make a middle-aged man laugh.

It's strange that a simple thing like colour can mean so much to football fans. Stephen Fry elaborated on his love for Norwich:

> Irony is behind it all, which doesn't in any sense mean a lack of love or a desire to win but we're aware that even our colours are slightly amusing. 'Come on you Yellows.' We know how that sounds. And we love it. And when we win, when we defeat Bayern Munich, the joy is quite extraordinary. Maybe I'm talking out of my arse but that's how it feels to be a proud Canary.

They beat Bayern Munich?! Yes, they did. In 1992, in their first ever European campaign, after beating Vitesse Arnhem in the first round of the UEFA Cup, they were drawn against Bayern Munich for the second. On paper it was a complete mismatch and, to be fair, it should have been on grass, too. But Norwich were a useful side and, inspired by a 'country bumpkin'* headline in a local paper, they won 2-1 in Munich thanks to a volley from the not-normally-prolific Jeremy Goss. Even better, Jeremy scored again in a 1-1 draw at Carrow Road, and those proud Canaries had knocked out one of the biggest clubs in the world, never mind Europe.

There were only two downsides. They were knocked out in the next round by Inter Milan. And you may think it would be difficult to muck up a yellow shirt, but you'd be wrong. Norwich beat Bayern wearing a yellow shirt covered with green splodges that made it look like Kermit the Frog had been sick down the front. Even Stephen Fry would struggle to defend that monstrosity.

Why You Shouldn't Support Them

- I've never liked seeing birds in cages.
- 'On the Ball, City' is even worse than 'Blue is the Colour'. I'm all for tradition, but the words 'kick it off, throw it in, have a little scrimmage' should not be sung at a modern football match.
- You shouldn't have to allow yourself a good two days to get there.

---

* Which Bayern insisted they had mistranslated.

NOTTINGHAM FOREST

'The River Trent is lovely; I know because I have walked on it for eighteen years.'

BRIAN HOWARD CLOUGH 21 March 1935 to 20 September 2004

'And he was Forest too – every sinew of him.'

FourFourTwo magazine (see chapter on Derby)

Note to self. Take piss out of Forest fans, as promised to Derby fans.

After football, my big passion is history. So the first time we went to an away game at Forest I suggested to the boys that we get there early so we could visit the castle. A suggestion that was met with a sort of puzzled silence, as though someone had suggested to Prince Charles that he make his own cup of tea.

My friends are all intelligent people, but on match days it seems they are not interested in what happened four pints ago, never mind four centuries ago. And I don't know what I expected when I got there, but there was no Robin Hood and none of the many men who were milling around the station in red shirts were merry. No, they were *way* through merry, had gone past pissed and were now verging on the feral. They seemed to discuss something, but I don't think it was history.

Shame really, because Forest is full of it. And they have one of the few team names I am prepared to admit is on a similar level of cool to Crystal Palace. If you can't have a mighty eagle on your badge, I would happily settle for a stylised tree emerging from a few wavy lines representing the River Trent.

They are a team that claim many firsts. They are definitely the first, and only, football team to emerge from a Shinney team. Shinney was a sort of violent version of hockey,* and in 1865, presumably nursing some injuries, the players had a meeting in a pub and decided that football may be safer. At the same meeting they also decided to order 12 red caps in 'Garibaldi Red', which seemed to be the red of choice for many clubs in those days, although quite why so many English clubs were inspired by the Camicie Rosse, led by a man determined to create a liberal, progressive, united Italy, is a mystery (I really do love history).

Forest played their first match on 22 March 1866, against ... Notts County. Which makes it arguably the first ever local derby. The first reported use of a referee's whistle was at a Forest game in 1868. Before that referees had waved a white flag to indicate a foul which wasn't very efficient but did keep seagulls off their sandwiches. They were the first team to use shin pads, presumably left over from the Shinney; and it's also likely that the first ever crossbars and goal nets were used at a Forest game.†

All that is all very interesting (no, seriously, it is, I'm not being sarcastic); but the more discerning among you will have already guessed the real reason I've been looking forward to writing this chapter: Brian Clough.

My mum had little interest in football (other than that mystifying love for Tommy Docherty) but she hated Clough, 'the cocky little shit'. I loved him. Still do. I so wish I'd met him but I'm also glad I didn't, because for every story that ends in hilarity, there is one that ends with a player hanging from a coat-peg.

Very few people live up to their own hype. He did, even when he was failing. Clough didn't go into big successful clubs and win them trophies, he went into small mediocre clubs and won them trophies. As we've seen, the only time he did go into a big successful club, he was sacked after 44 days at Leeds United.

As a striker for Middlesbrough and Sunderland he scored pretty much a goal a game until 1962, when the injury that eventually ended his career left him a bitter and broken young man. He could never bear to be around injured players, even at the height of his managerial career.

---

* It may surprise you that someone with impeccable working-class credentials like me went to a Catholic boys' grammar school with a hockey team. But I did and I played for the hockey team. We played the next-door Catholic girls' grammar school in a charity match once. *That* was the most violent version of hockey. My nose was broken. I've been to over a thousand football matches and the only time I've been punched in my life was by a 17-year-old St Trinian's lookalike.

† Thank God there was no VAR then. It would have taken forever. Like it does now.

That career started in Hartlepool, where he teamed up for the first time with Peter Taylor and took a tiny club to their first ever promotion. But not before falling out with the chairman several times. Then they took Derby County from the Second Division to the League title in five seasons. And left after falling out with the chairman. There's a theme developing here. A brief and inexplicable spell at Brighton was followed by that 44 days at Leeds, where they fell out with the chairman, the players, the media and most of Yorkshire.

But it was what they did at Forest that was most remarkable. When they took over in 1975, Forest were 13th in the table. In 1980, they won the European Cup. For the second year running.

I've already told you about one of his very many legendary TV appearances in the chapter about Leeds. The last time he appeared on TV as a manager was not legendary. It was in 1993, moments after they had been relegated from the Premier League. He was a pale shadow of himself and it was very difficult to watch.

But if Clough at the end was tragic, the rest was glorious, marvellous. He was a lifelong socialist, which suited his bolshie character. He was funny, sarcastic, disrespectful, unpredictable and irrational. He teased, cajoled and coached team after team of decent players to ridiculous achievements. He had a temper and was unforgiving of disloyalty. There were ugly sides to his character, for sure. But by God, the football his teams played was magical.

Why You Shouldn't Support Them

- They sacked Brian Clough. Yes, I know I said that about Derby.
- When Forest beat Derby in the 1898 FA Cup final, they borrowed Derby's shirts because they showed up better in the photograph. That's an obscure reason for disliking them both.*
- The tree on their badge is quite cool but it needs an eagle in it.

---

* And some people say studying history is a waste of time.

OLDHAM ATHLETIC

'Oldham Athletic. No ups. Only downs.'

CHRIS ENGLAND author, playwright and Oldham fan

'Things Can Only Get Better'

D:REAM song, with keyboards played by physicist and Oldham fan Brian Cox

On 8 April 1990, as Palace fans were leaving Villa Park after beating Liverpool 4-3 in the greatest semi-final in the history of any sport ever, Oldham Athletic were about to kick off against Manchester United in the other FA Cup semi-final. At the time, both clubs were in the First Division and if Man U were favourites, it wasn't by much. The game was almost as exciting as ours, ending in a 3-3 draw. Oldham, cheered on by Palace fans who figured that they may be easier to beat in the final, lost the replay 2-1 on the following Wednesday. United went on to win the Cup. Bastards.

And speaking of bastards: on 1 May 1993, Palace beat Ipswich 3-1 to leave us eight points clear of relegation. Oldham would have to win all three of their last games to have any chance of climbing above us to safety, and they were really difficult games.

To the dismay of most of us, our players went on the most ill-advised lap of honour in the history of sport.† We weren't technically safe, and the avenging gods of football tend to notice these things. And notice they did. They gave Oldham their nine points, we got only one more and we were relegated on goal difference. Technically, you could say that Oldham won their own nine points, but I prefer to think of Palace as a victim of universal forces, not a small town in south-east Lancashire. I hated Oldham then as much as any team I have ever hated, and that's all 91 of them, even though it was our fault not theirs.

In truth, they are a difficult team to hate, if only because they are another of those clubs who have somehow managed to gulp just enough air to survive in the pond that is Greater Manchester football and deserve

---

† That's as official as my claim about our semi-final win, i.e. definitive.

a bit of credit for it. Plus, since they relegated us, our paths have taken very different directions so I can afford to patronise them a bit.

I'm a fully qualified pub historian, but even I struggle to explain why that small corner of the world is so full of football clubs that have managed to survive in the shadows of United and City. Fans of clubs like Blackburn and Burnley will argue that they were the big dogs once, and they are right, but still I'd love to hear the opinions of a real historian as to why other equally industrial conurbations have far fewer clubs surviving. Even the most ardent Oldham fan couldn't argue that they were the big dogs once, because, apart from a brief spell in the nineties, most of their history has been spent bottom-feeding in that big old pond of theirs.*

My mate Chris England co-wrote *An Evening With Gary Lineker*, the world's only funny play about football. I was in it once, so for his sake I want to be kind to them because they've suffered enough. As he told me over a pint: 'We've got the coldest ground in the country, we're owned by a former agent and his dodgy brother and we've got a shonky squad and all our fans have disappeared.' That was a cheery hour in the pub. I didn't have the heart to tell him that I reckon Carlisle is much colder.

Maybe Chris would be happier if Oldham were called Pine Villa, which is how they started. Unfortunately, hardly anyone in Oldham seemed to notice and they went bust in 1899 after a four-year struggle. Or possibly it was a team called Oldham County that went bust, and Pine Villa took over their ground and changed their name to Oldham Athletic. Either way, not sounding like an air-freshener any more seemed to endear them to the locals and the new club took root.

For Chris's sake, I wish I could fill this chapter with tales of domestic derring-do and European excursions but, sadly, I can't. Well, I could, but he would know that I'd invented them.

Mere survival is triumph enough for them; but to be honest, it is for most of us. Eighty-six out of the 92 clubs will almost certainly never win the Premier League title; it's just a question of finding the level you can survive *at*.

They do have one cool thing about them, though, and that's the bird on their badge. I mean, it's not a majestic eagle, but it is a rather handsome owl with an expression on its face that looks he's trying to decide whether to bite you or bring you a mouse.

The owl, of course, is a reminder that their first manager could turn his head almost in a full circle as a party trick.

---

* If I have any advice for aspiring comedians, it's always milk a metaphor.

I wish it was. Apparently, it's a heraldic pun from the coat of arms of local toffs who were called the Oldhams, or the d'Oldhams or the Owldham. Presumably the latter if the pun is going to work at all, which it isn't because puns never do. Trust me, I'm a comedy writer. I've tried.

It's lovely that football historians attach so much significance to things like club crests, but every now and again, when someone asks a question like 'why is Oldham's badge an owl?', I'd like the answer to be 'because the chairman loves owls'.

Working on a TV show recently, while waiting for the kettle to boil,† I was chatting to the archive researcher who is a football-mad West Ham fan, and also one of the nicest people you could meet. Let's call him John Smith, because, poor sod, that is his name. John asked me about the book and what chapter I was writing at the moment. I told him it was this one. Without hesitation, he said, 'I fucking hate Oldham. Plastic pitch ponces.'

Wow, I'd never seen a vehement John Smith before. And I'd totally forgotten the plastic pitch they'd had back then and how unfair an advantage it gave them.‡ I'd also forgotten, until John reminded me, very loudly, that they beat West Ham 6-0 in a League Cup semi-final in 1990 then pipped them to the Second Division title by one point the season after.

Chris laughed when I told him: 'Yeah, we scored a penalty with the last kick of the last game of the season. They'd already engraved West Ham's name on the trophy.'

Just goes to show though, what a strange web of rivalries and lingering dislikes binds all our clubs together.

Why You Shouldn't Support Them

- They relegated us.
- We would have beaten them in the FA Cup final.
- I have never seen John Smith angry before.

---

† It's hard work writing jokes.
‡ UEFA subsequently banned artificial pitches except in countries where there are extreme climactic conditions. In other words, cold. Oldham should count, then. And Carlisle.

OXFORD UNITED

'If anyone has got one of those hats, I would love to put one on again. Mine didn't make it out of Wembley.'

JIM ROSENTHAL TV presenter and Oxford fan, in 2016, recalling the horned hat he wore on air after they won the League Cup final in 1986

'The boys from up the hill.'

Surely the most poetic club nickname ever

For one reason or another I've spent a lot of time in Oxford in the past few years and I love it. And as I've grown older and wiser, the throbbing chip on my shoulder has mellowed enough to allow me to appreciate the glorious facades of those university buildings that hide coyly on every street. But it always makes me chuckle as I get tangled up in yet another phalanx of Japanese tourists in Gryffindor scarves* that none of them realise they are just a short bus-ride away from the home of Oxford United, a football club with a surprisingly feisty working-class fan base.

Mind you, I suppose having historical reminders of educational privilege on every street corner is enough to make anyone feisty (the chip has mellowed, not disappeared). And in 1983, they would need all that feistiness to fight off one of the most bizarre attempts ever to improve the financial fortunes of a football club: make it disappear.

Robert Maxwell was a sort of low-rent pantomime villain version of Rupert Murdoch. He too had invested in newspaper publishing and printing and was reaping the reward as the Thatcher government began to de-regulate and de-unionise those industries in the early eighties. Later, it transpired that he was further subsidising his lavish lifestyle by raiding the pension fund of the *Daily Mirror*, which he owned. However he acquired his money, in 1982 he used it to buy Oxford United and become its chairman. Slightly annoyingly for the chippy narrative of this story, by doing so he saved them from bankruptcy and appeared to be behaving as a responsible and financially prudent benefactor.

* Enterprising locals having created a very canny little earner out of the fact that they have buildings that *look* like the ones in *Harry Potter*.

Until he dropped the bombshell. It turns out that he had also bought shares in Reading, just down the road from Oxford. Reading were Oxford's local rivals. *Fierce* local rivals.

On 16 April 1983, shortly before both clubs kicked off important away games, Maxwell announced that he was about to acquire a controlling interest in Reading and had decided on a radical plan to solve the financial problems of both clubs: he was going to merge them. Oxford United and Reading FC were to disappear, and the 1984/85 season would kick off with a new team called the Thames Valley Royals. Both grounds would be sold and a new one built 'roughly halfway' between them, and the only place that was 'roughly halfway' between them was Didcot,† so now the residents of three towns were unhappy, although the apprehension of Didcot residents was nothing compared with the wrath of Oxford and Reading fans being told that they were soon to be a band of brothers with a new ground, a new kit and presumably some kind of new drug-induced amnesia to make them forget they hated each other.

Yes, I know there will be many football fans reading this and thinking 'Oxford/Reading/hate/fierce?' but trust me, it's true. I made the mistake of saying the same thing to some of the stage crew at the Playhouse.

'Robert Maxwell was a sort of low-rent pantomime villain version of Rupert Murdoch.'

Oxford United were originally formed as Headington in 1893 in what was then a village, not a suburb. Presumably there was a hill between the town and the village, which would explain that lovely nickname. You can't tell for concrete these days, and besides geography is not my strong point.‡

In 1911 the boys from up the hill merged with a team called Headington Quarry to form Headington United. *That* merger was fine. They were basically Sunday league teams in 1911 and besides, I imagine men who work in a quarry are real hard bastards so you're not going to say no if they fancy a quick merge.

United bounced around the amateur Oxfordshire leagues for a while, not doing much; although one newspaper reports that the fans had disrupted one game when they invaded the pitch and 'freely baited the referee'. I told you they were feisty.

In 1949 the club was invited to join the Southern League – one below the Football League proper – and in an attempt to get there decided to raise their profile by changing their name to Oxford United in 1960. Two

† Probably still is.
‡ Seriously, I can't even read maps.

years later they got their reward when they replaced Accrington Stanley in Division Four.

So by the time Maxwell came along they had only been Oxford United for 20 years, and you may say: why all the fuss? If you do say that then I'm amazed you're still reading this, because Mr Maxwell was about to discover something umpteen other club owners have already discovered in this book – if you attempt to change a club's badge, its kit, its nickname or its heritage then fans will want to know why. And if they don't like the answer, you are in for trouble. So imagine the trouble when he tried to magic two football clubs into one.

Club legend Ron Atkinson said at the time: 'Mr Maxwell obviously believes that if you add 6,000 United fans to 6,000 Reading fans you'll get 12,000 supporters of the new club. You won't.' What he did get was 12,000 fans (now, ironically, united) who simply said no. There were protest marches, protest sit-ins (including one by 2,000 fans on the pitch during a game), protest petitions, protest letter campaigns. You get the picture. There was protest. Feisty, remember.

Maxwell dug his heels in too. 'If they want to support another team, they are entirely welcome. If the deal does not go through, Reading and Oxford will be dead by the end of the season.' Two weeks later the *Reading Evening Post* carried the jubilant headline: 'We've won! Merger off.' Maxwell and his supporters on the board had been taken aback by the fan reaction and were beginning to realise that Ron Atkinson was right, they didn't have a captive audience of 12,000, they had potentially no audience at all. In the end, the businessman was undone by a lack of business.

'In the end, the businessman was undone by a lack of business.'

Millionaire builder Roger Smee, Reading born and bred and former player, had smelled a rat about the Reading directors who had sold Maxwell that controlling interest. He did some investigating and it turned out they may not have been theirs to sell in the first place. The High Court agreed and the Thames Valley Royals were gone before a ball was kicked.

Even better, it turned out well for all concerned.* Maxwell stayed as owner and presided over successive promotions that took Oxford into the very top league, and they were taken to Wembley in 1986 where they won the League Cup and Jim Rosenthal lost his hat.

---

* Although considering what eventually happened to Robert Maxwell, let's make that for 'most' concerned.

Then Maxwell left, bought Derby County and tried to buy Watford at the same time, leading to new rules being introduced to prevent that actually happening.

Oxford United have had ups and downs since then. Very down, actually: they briefly returned to the modern-day equivalent of the Southern League (the only major trophy winners ever to do so). But they are back now, and flourishing in a new stadium just a Harry Potter broomstick-ride away from the centre of that beautiful city.

Why You Shouldn't Support Them

- The Manor Ground was a genuine dump with proper wannabe hooligans. That's fine in London or Manchester but not on the edge of the Cotswolds.
- The new ground has a car park at one end. Not a stand and a car park, just a car park.
- I'm from London and even I think beer is expensive in Oxford pubs.

PETERBOROUGH
UNITED

'I told Posh fans I would get them out of Division Two when I arrived as manager. I did, by taking them straight into Division Three.'

BARRY FRY legendary Peterborough manager

'It doesn't look posh.'

Every single away fan arriving in Peterborough

Can I just start by drawing the attention of the people of Middlesbrough to the spelling of Peterborough? Thank you. By missing out that 'o' you may have spent marginally less on printer's ink over the years, but they have retained their dignity by spelling the name of their town correctly.

It pains me that one of my heroes had to go through life with the shame of coming from a misspelt town, because as you know from my previous fanboy gushings,* there was only one Brian Clough. But there were plenty of pale imitations, and among the most interesting, and the most passionate, was Barry Fry, a man who was manager, chairman-manager, director and director of football in a 23-year tenure at Peterborough United.

Here, some Peterborough fans will be saying, 'Oh, not Barry Fry again. There must be loads more to say about us than Barry bloody Fry!' Calm down, mate. I've checked and there isn't. If it wasn't for Barry bloody Fry you'd be the shortest bloody chapter in the book. Fry is the widest of wide boys and the flashest of Harrys, but he has a charm and self-deprecating humour that always makes him entertaining, especially for people who don't support Peterborough.

---

* I believe Fanboy Gushings is also a village in Dorset.

'Yes, yes,' I hear you cry. 'That's all very interesting. We look forward to hearing more about him, now tell us about the Posh thing. That sounds interesting.'

Well, this is not actually an interactive book, but as it's you …

… I'm going to disappoint you. Whatever you've told people in pubs, the word 'posh' does mean 'upper-class' or 'of high quality', but it is *not* an acronym for 'port out starboard home', which is supposedly where the best cabins on a steamship were located. There is absolutely no evidence for that at all.

It was probably Victorian slang for a coin and then for somebody who has lots of them, but no one really knows. And no one really knows why Peterborough are called 'the Posh' either, although as a previous incarnation of the club was 'the Brickies', it's possible that it may have been sarcastic.

And the club, at least, believes that may be true. A team called Peterborough and Fletton played at London Road (the current ground) until 1932 and a decade before that their manager had announced he was looking for 'posh players for a posh team', and fans being fans, that's what they've been called ever since, sometimes, the club says, in a 'derisory' manner.

In 1934, in the Angel Hotel, it was decided to set up a club to replace the now bankrupt Fletton version and a whip-round followed to raise the £20 deposit required for Peterborough United to join the Midland League. Rather sweetly, when they reached the Football League proper in 1960, they got their deposit back!

Now, I sort of lied when I said there wasn't that much interesting about Peterborough, because there is, but much of it is kit-related so it may not delight you as much as it does kit-boy here.

'Barry Fry is the widest of wide boys and the flashest of Harrys, but he has a charm and self-deprecating humour that always makes him entertaining.'

Their first kit was donated by a local tailor and was green with a natty white chevron. I like it. Peterborough fans didn't and after two years of terrible football they decided that green was unlucky and only blue could bring success. Sounds very olden-times superstitious, doesn't it? But even now there are fans who will blame a particular away kit for a bad season. Me, for example. The club chairman was fine with that and issued a very practical statement: 'Pay for blue shirts, and we will wear blue shirts.' Pay they did and blue they've been, ever since. Normally accompanied by a badge consisting of two winged lions carrying the town crest. They're meant to be fearsome but they look more like they are delivering a pane of glass in a Carry On film.

The first shirt sponsor they had was 'SodaStream' in 1981. SodaStream made a device that turned tap water sparkly, which was positively space age back then, but clearly it wasn't a happy relationship. It was very noticeable that the logo got smaller and smaller as each season went by until finally, in 1986, it was not only in tiny writing, it was actually vertical! They had a new sponsor the year after.

So let's fill in the rest of their history until we get to Barry Fry. They won the Fourth Division, twice. When they won it in 1961, they scored 134 goals. Palace scored 110 and finished two points behind them. Even when we scored our record ever number of goals, some bugger had to score more.

Right, it's Fry time! I remember him celebrating a goal at Selhurst by running half the length of the pitch to do a jig round the corner flag then running the full length of the pitch to do a little jig round the other one. For neutrals I imagine that was vaguely amusing, but for Palace fans it was really annoying, and a bit alarming. He was a chubby little feller and he was definitely struggling for the last 20 yards, to the extent that both medical teams started looking on with the air of helpful vultures.

It also sums up why he will always be just one of football's characters rather than one of its legends. Brian Clough would never have done something as unclassy as that. Fair enough, Barry Fry never actually punched a pitch-invader either, but that's another story.

I don't know what one down from journeyman footballer is, but that's what he was. He was also no more than a decent manager. His fame/reputation/notoriety mainly comes from his unorthodox methods, his love for attacking football and his occasional failure to engage brain before activating mouth.

'He has had two heart attacks, one when he was attempting to push the broken-down team bus at Barnet and one when he'd just taken over at Peterborough.'

And he stood up for himself. As manager of Barnet, he was sacked and reinstated eight times by the controversial chairman Stan Flashman, a name that was eminently more suited to the manager he kept sacking. He lives, breathes and eats football. And it's repaid him by nearly killing him. One of the reasons that corner-flag relay was genuinely worrying is that he has had two heart attacks, one when he was attempting to push the broken-down team bus at Barnet and one when he'd just taken over at Peterborough.

And he's given other people heart attacks too. To ease Peterborough's financial worries he remortgaged his own house without telling his wife, then remortgaged his mother-in-law's house, without telling her either!

At Birmingham he referred to owners David Sullivan and Karren Brady as 'the porn king and the bimbo' and once so incensed Brady that she stormed into the dressing room to vent her spleen, apparently not noticing that he was naked. As he said, 'she gave me a proper bollocking'.

But it is with Peterborough that he is most closely associated. In the past two decades and a bit he has been manager, director, chairman, director of football and owner, often at the same time. Although there was a short hiatus in 2019 when he was fined £35,000 and banned from football for four months after admitting he'd 'been a prat' to put £500 each way on one of his players to be top scorer in League One. Typically, he won the bet. Even more typically, he used the winnings to cover the player's bonus for being the club's top scorer!

In truth, his time at Peterborough has been more entertaining than successful, but some clubs would kill for two decades and a bit of entertainment like that.

Why You Shouldn't Support Them

- 1961.
- Barry Fry is a true old-school character, but sometimes true old-school characters are really, really irritating.
- Imagine the embarrassment of being sponsored by someone who made water fizzy.

PLYMOUTH ARGYLE

'It's official! Plymouth Argyle v Exeter City ranked English football's SECOND biggest rivalry!'

Devonlive.com

'The biggest sleeping giant in football.'

talkSPORT

Devonlive.com can add as many exclamation marks and capital letters as they want to that statement, but they still won't make it true, even if it is based on an actual survey. And even Inspector Clouseau would be suspicious of a survey that also claims only Portsmouth and Southampton fans hate each other more than these two vicious rivals from the hotbed of football that is, erm, Devon. But in an alternative universe it could be true, because talkSPORT have a point, and it's a point that will be raised in the early seconds of any conversation with any Argyle fan.

To the west, you have to go through Cornwall and off to America before you find another professional football team, which may be why the Pilgrim Fathers set off for there in 1620,* and in any other direction there isn't another League club for 45 miles. I know this because my mate Bristol Mark, who supports Plymouth,† reminds me every time he sees me. Every time. Still, I suppose in the absence of actual success, *potential* success is a great consolation.

And if Devonlive.com are right, imagine how much more Exeter fans would hate Argyle if they were huge. Although, as Bristol Mark will be reading this, I happily admit that they are huge – in Devon. They regularly get 12,000 at home in League One or Two where they live, and their away fans travel in incredible numbers considering how far away they are from everywhere. Or, how are far away we are from them.

Josh Widdicombe is a comedian and presenter of Channel 4's long-running *The Last Leg*. He is also from Devon and a proper Argyle fan.

---

* It's not the reason but it explains why Argyle's nickname is the Pilgrims.
† One of you will inevitably know someone called Plymouth Pete who supports Bristol City, don't worry about it.

He gets cross about a lot of things and geography is one of them:

> It kills every conversation. If I mention who I support, no one has anything to say apart from to tell me it's a long way away. Not if you're there, it's not! It's the most southerly, the most westerly and the biggest city never to have a top-division team. Not things to be proud of, Kev, but at least we have a massive away support. Just don't mention it's because everyone moves away from the area.

Oh, bugger, he said *not* to mention it. Josh is also a classic example of how some people just don't get it:

> I took my daughter to kids' football recently, in her Argyle shirt, and one of the other mums asked if I supported them 'to be different'. Supporting Plymouth isn't a decision like being a fan of the Fall!

I have a soft spot for Josh and for the city of Plymouth. My first serious girlfriend spent four years at college there, and it's hard not to have fond memories of a city where you were getting regular sex for the first time. It also had Monroe's, a club where the DJ's idea of an uplifting dance number was anything by Joy Division; and the Minerva, a tiny pub in the old part of town that had a punk-only jukebox and cider in barrels, which, they claimed, was only ready when the dead rat inside it had dissolved.

Well, they claimed that to Londoners like me, but as I loved Joy Division, punk and regular sex, I was happy to put up with the odd bit of powdered rat in my cider. And, of course, Plymouth had Argyle. The only team in England to be named after an army regiment. Well, in England anyway. Although they were a Scottish regiment. The Argyle and Sutherland Highlanders were apparently posted in Devon at the time, despite the distance from Argyle, Sutherland and the Highlands.

And, whisper it softly, but there are some unromantic souls who point out that there was a pub in the middle of the city called the Argyle Arms, and it's quite possible that the two local lads who founded the club in 1886 may have looked no further than the beermats for inspiration. A-ha, say the romantics. How come Argyle wore green and black shirts, similar to the green and black of the Argyle tartan? Fair point, but green and black are also the colours of the Borough of Plymouth.

Does it matter? Yes, actually. Such seemingly pointless, and hopefully unresolvable, discussions are like golden grist to the mill for those of us obsessed with the history and culture of football.

And, as a kid, I was amazed that they were even allowed to wear green shirts, because that's what *goalies* wore! To a seven-year-old, that's a conundrum to keep you awake at night. And it wasn't just any old green, it was a sort of olivey, dark green, officially known as 'Argyle Green'. They had their own colour! Football is brilliant, ain't it, Dad?*

Sadly, for fans like Bristol Mark, whatever the origins of the name or the kit, Argyle, the sleeping giants, have spent a lot more of their history sleeping than gianting. True, they've won the Third Division a couple of times, and yes, they got to the FA Cup semi-final in 1984. And they hold the record for the fastest five goals ever scored in Football League history – 17 minutes on their way to beating Chesterfield 7-0 in 2004. But this is a team whose record attendance is 43,596. In 1973, they got nearly 38,000 for a flipping friendly, although Pelé was playing for the opposition. Yes, you did read that correctly. His team, Santos, toured Europe, playing hastily arranged games for cash.† Plymouth won 3-2. They beat Pelé! They should be massive; although God knows what Bristol Mark would talk about then.

> "'If I mention who I support, no one has anything to say apart from to tell me it's a long way away.'"
>
> JOSH WIDDICOMBE

And my memories of watching Plymouth? Ah. There you have me. I've never been there, even though you could see the floodlights from my girlfriend's flat. I've seen them and their massive away following many times at Selhurst, but, let's face it, if you're a 21-year-old given the choice between an afternoon of passion with your partner or an afternoon watching a team you don't actually support …

Why You Shouldn't Support Them

- It's your own fault you're not a huge club. Get on with it.
- I was actually sick for a week after one night in the Minerva. Could have been the 13 pints of cider, could have been the dead rat.
- Turns out that drunken sailors and 21-year-old men with eyeliner don't always mix. Yet another reason I stayed in a lot.

---

* Currently the club colour is registered as 'Pine Needle Green'. The game's gone.
† Plymouth paid them £2,500, in £50 notes, after the game.

PORT VALE

'Tall chimneys and rounded ovens, schools, the new scarlet market, the grey tower of the old church, the high spire of the evangelical church.'

ARNOLD BENNETT literary giant of the Potteries, describing the fictional (but not at all disguised) town of Bursley

'The papers can talk about my personal life as much as they like, or whatever, but don't mess with me and the Vale.'

ROBBIE WILLIAMS

Here's your Port Vale question, no conferring, I will take your first answer. What is unique about Port Vale? And no, the answer is not Robbie Williams. Although, I will accept that because I don't believe he supports any other football team.

As most football fans will have lurking somewhere in their mind, the answer is that they are the only club in England not named after an actual geographical location. There is no town, village or city named Port Vale. Which makes them unique, and makes things bloody difficult for away fans. A lot of teams don't play in their original location (Palace and Millwall, for a start) but no one else plays somewhere that doesn't technically exist.

Yes, I do know there was no such place as Arsenal, but Herbert Chapman was not only a genius manager, he was very good at branding and, as we know, he had Gillespie Road Tube station change its name to Arsenal, so there is such a place now – hurrah, I win!

Interestingly, as we have seen, a lot of our more exotic team names have been left in the past, almost as though Ironopolis,‡ Harriers and Swifts lost a Darwinian struggle for existence to Uniteds, Cities and Towns. Or maybe it's just that most of our place names are more prosaic.

There are lots of teams in Scotland with names that give no clue to their actual location – St Mirren, Queen of the South, East Fife are in Paisley,

---

‡ I have no idea what the plural of Ironopolis is. Ironopoli? Ironopolises?

Dumfries and Methil – and their real town names sound nicer than a lot of ours too. Cowdenbeath, for example, sounds positively glamorous. So much so that one Saturday afternoon during the Edinburgh Festival, me and a group of other comedians thought we'd go to a game there.

It's not glamorous. But we had one of the most gloriously different football experiences ever, culminating in asking the lads behind us why one of their own players kept getting booed by a small section of the crowd: 'Ah,' he said, 'his dad owns the chip shop at one end of the street, and they own the chip shop at the other. He's as shite as his dad's chips.' It was a race to see which of us could get back to Edinburgh first to tell that story on stage.

But Cowdenbeath is a long way from Port Vale and we don't even know where Port Vale is yet. It's in Burslem. One of the six towns that make up the city of Stoke-on-Trent. One of the towns is *also* Stoke-on-Trent. I know, but it doesn't seem to bother them.

Actor and presenter Nick Hancock, a Stoke fan, is a delightful, calm, funny and patient man. But he is infuriated by three things and they are all related. First, the fact that no one outside the six towns seems to have a clue about their geography and history. Second, Port Vale. Third, the Stoke/Port Vale rivalry never gets mentioned in football writing or Danny Dyer hooligan documentaries.

He's definitely right about the first. Stephen Fry and Sandi Toksvig will converse happily on just about any subject, but ask them to name the six towns and they will pretend their taxi has just arrived.

He is absolutely right about the second as well. When Port Vale fan Phil 'The Power' Taylor was a guest on *They Think It's All Over*, which I wrote on and Nick presented, Nick kicked up a massive fuss even though Phil was the world champion of darts and pretty much a household name. 'I just won't talk to him then.' And he didn't. For the whole show.

As to the third, well, three out of three. I think it's absolutely right and honourable that Palace hate Brighton, but hating Port Vale? Get out of here. Sorry Nick. Pint?

So why aren't they called Burslem then? They were for a while, but possibly not at the start. Historian Jeff Kent, who seems to have spent his whole life researching nothing but Port Vale FC, writes, convincingly, that the club were formed in 1876 in Burslem and were named after a canal wharf called Port Vale. But he also reports another theory: there was a team called Porthill Victoria whose ground was perched on a hill. Some of the players, presumably fed up with the vertical trudge, formed a new team and ironically named it the Port Vale. Hmm, as Chris Kamara would say: 'Unbelievable, Jeff!' And using an ex-Stoke player in this chapter will really annoy Nick. Sorry, mate, two pints?

The club's official account is more convincing: they say that they were formed in 1876 following a meeting in Port Vale House in a suburb of Stoke-on-Trent* then became Burslem Port Vale when they moved there in 1884. Then they moved away, dropped the Burslem, and didn't bother to reinstate it when they moved back to Burslem in 1950. We can agree on 1876 then?

They are still in that ground, Vale Park, and nice and compact it is too. In stark contrast to 1950, when they planned to make it the 'Wembley of the North'. Good job they didn't. It's hard enough for most of us to work out where it is in the first place, without throwing a London borough into the mix.

One of the reasons I can't really understand the Stoke/Port Vale thing is that they get so few opportunities to play each other. In their entire history, Port Vale have never, ever been in the top division, and rarely ever in the one beneath it.

So, for a team the size of Stoke to find themselves in the same division as a team the size of Port Vale is a rare thing and, if anything, I would have thought that Stoke fans would patronise them the way Liverpudlians do Tranmere and Londoners do Leyton Orient.

Apparently I'm wrong, because Nick Hancock told me there's always trouble between them when they do play, with both sets of fans making a habit of smashing each other's toilets. Mind you, as Nick says, 'that may be because it also provides work for the local porcelain factories'.

So, there's not much else I can tell you. But if you can, read Arnold Bennett's description of the Bursley football team in his 1911 novel *The Card*, which has a wonderful passage about the mentality of fans: 'but when they happened to lose, the great football public merely sulked … it would not pay sixpence to assist at defeats.'

Why You Shouldn't Support Them

▪ You should support your local team and it's hard to be local to somewhere that doesn't exist.
▪ I really like Nick Hancock and he really hates them.
▪ Robbie Williams once drank my bottle of beer in the green room after a TV show. To be fair, Nick used to do it all the time, but not deliberately.

---

* Town or city?

PORTSMOUTH

'Play up Pompey, Pompey play up.'

The famous Pompey chimes

'The biggest betrayal possible.'

TERRY BRADY Portsmouth director, talking about a manager leaving Portsmouth for Southampton

Fratton Park is a much more pleasant place to visit with a camera crew than it is for an away game. As an away fan it has a frankly intimidating, hostile atmosphere created by fans who have never let a little thing like a lack of success stop them from filling the place and making a tremendous racket before attempting to make your journey off the 'island'* as difficult as possible.

There has been some redevelopment, but it's such a throwback that if I close my eyes, I can only see it in black and white. Even when you're there, it is so redolent of the past that you wouldn't be surprised to hear the tannoy announce an imminent air raid.† It really is one of those places where, as an away fan, you just get in and get out as quickly as possible, even if that means drinking enough on the train to not worry about finding an even remotely friendly pub.

On the other hand, I couldn't wait to go there when I was doing *Match of the Day 2*. They were the friendliest of clubs and I would visit a succession of welcoming pubs to meet fans who greeted me with open arms even as they reassured me it *would* be a different story if I tried going in there before a Palace game as well.

And their fans were always funny. I filmed there shortly after Harry Redknapp, their recently departed, much loved ex-manager, had taken over at bitter rivals Southampton, just two weeks after leaving Portsmouth because he 'needed a break' from football. I wanted to talk about this and one pub full of locals happily obliged, except they wouldn't say his name.

---

* Portsmouth sits on a peninsula surrounded by so much water it's almost separated from the mainland.

† All of which, it may not surprise you to know, I think is a good thing.

They referred to him as 'the ex-manager ... the baggy-faced fella ... that bloke ... Jamie's dad ... Sandra's husband' all the way through. It made me laugh a lot. Which, of course, upset the soundman. It seems they can deal with any sound except laughter (see chapter on Blackpool).

I'm not sure if 'rivals' is actually the right word when it comes to Southampton. It often slips under the radar in discussions on local derbies, but theirs is *fierce*. They properly hate Southampton with an intensity that I haven't seen at many other clubs.

Local legend has it that it stems not just from proximity but from the relative fortunes of the two dockyards. Southampton built passenger liners and were therefore considered more affluent than Portsmouth, where they built Royal Navy ships. There have been dark mutterings that after the *Titanic* sank, Southampton sailors refused to crew its sister ship because of a lack of lifeboats and Portsmouth crews were recruited instead. Similarly, Pompey fans claim that Southampton sailors helped break a Portsmouth dock strike in the 1950s. Who knows, it could also be that, as in the north-east, there was beef going back to the Civil War. Oddly, they seemed to get on alright in 1939 because when Portsmouth won the FA Cup in that year, the trophy was paraded around Southampton as well.

'A bit of mystery never did any harm. The important thing is that in 2020, fans of a team with a mysterious nickname are still singing a song from 1890.'

It's impossible to pin down just one reason, so let's just let them get on with enjoying the enmity, shall we?

Portsmouth have always been a very well supported club, intimately connected to their island fans in a way that reminds me of the way Millwall are rooted in *their* community – only Portsmouth fans have had a lot more to shout about over the years, having won the title in all four leagues and winning the FA Cup three times.

Their recent history has been more volatile: successive relegations, financial meltdown and a real danger of extinction. Happily, thanks initially to fan ownership and then the shrewd investment of Michael Eisner, ex-CEO of Disney, they seem to be beginning the long fairy-tale climb back to a happy ending.

But what about the beginning? There had been a very successful army team, Royal Artillery, in the town but they had been banned by the FA for the heinous crime of training, which violated the amateur code. In 1898 the gap was filled by the creation of Portsmouth FC, who initially played in a 'salmon pink' kit (possibly because they were founded by a Mr Pink!) before changing to their now famous patriotic blue, white and red combination.

And if the kit was famous, their nickname was even more so. I always knew as a kid that they were Pompey, and they had to 'play up', but I never knew why. I probably assumed it just sounded a bit like Portsmouth for lazy people (I might have been a precocious reader at the age of seven but the word 'onomatopoeia' was beyond even me. Spelt it right first time here though*).

As with many of these things, the most simple of all the explanations seems to be the most likely. Naval ships docking in the harbour would record the code 'Po'mP' in their logbook. And, er, that's it. Sorted.

The chimes, however, are a different matter. It *may* be true that referees in the Royal Artillery games used the bells of a local tower to tell them the game was due to finish and the fans joined in, but it probably isn't. It doesn't matter. A bit of mystery never did any harm. The important thing is that in 2020, fans of a team with a mysterious nickname are still singing a song from 1890. And what a noise they make doing it.

There, I got all the way through the chapter on Portsmouth without once mentioning 'Pompey John', their most visible supporter. Or, as the rest of us call him: that twat with the bell.

Why You Shouldn't Support Them

- It is a seriously intimidating ground. They seem to hate London clubs more than northerners do, which is odd, because to them, we *are* northerners.
- It's not an island. And even if it was, that's nothing to be proud of.
- They need to take that bell off him. It's like having tinnitus for 90 minutes.

* I did, honestly.

PRESTON
NORTH END

'If there's a goal scored now, I'll eat my hat.'

THOMAS WOODROFFE BBC radio commentator, in the last minute of the 1938 Cup final – there was, and he did!

'Tom Finney was the greatest player ever to play the game.'

BILL SHANKLY

Imagine that: a time when Preston North End won the Cup and a man upheld the honour of his profession by making good on his public promise. I checked a lot of sources in the hope of finding footage of the hat dinner, because I really liked the idea of starting this chapter with a quote along the lines of 'Mmmm, this bowler is delicious', but, sadly, no luck.

Of course, there is always the possibility that he was made to eat the hat by an early version of BBC compliance: 'I'm afraid you must eat the hat *and* unless you can show proof that your granny would have scored that, then you'll have to stop saying it.' Compliance are the bane of the life of any TV writer/performer but that's a story for another book (eh, Bloomsbury?).

In the early days of football broadcasting, and I promise this is true, the commentator would have a blind man in the booth with him to let him know if he was describing the game vividly enough. And the *Radio Times* would publish a grid with eight squares representing the pitch so the listening audience would have a clue where the ball was. It's probably the origin of the phrase 'back to square one', but there's no actual proof of that. I'm beginning to realise there's no actual proof of much of football's history, which is making life difficult. My next book will definitely be about something that is full of actual facts (seriously, Bloomsbury, I literally have nothing to do when I finish this).

As a kid, the name Preston North End was still one that resonated with football fans. I was always fascinated by any team name that wasn't a United or City or Town, and they had a really intriguing badge – a sort of lamb and flag affair that wouldn't look out of place on the walls of the many Catholic churches we were taken to on school trips (the headmaster's theory seeming to be that we would visit a museum *after* we'd seen every crucifix in London).

'I do like the fact that a no-nonsense northern town like Preston has a patron saint called Wilf.'

Also, they had the only player whose name was mentioned by grown-ups in the sort of hushed voice reserved only for Stanley Matthews, and later George Best. Tom Finney was a winger, like the other two,* and arguments will still rage about who was best until the generations that actually saw them play are gone forever.

Turns out they were called 'North End' for a very simple reason. They started life as a cricket club in the west of town and in 1863 someone suggested a move to new playing fields in the north end of town. Someone else disagreed so a breakaway club was formed and off they went. The rest, as they say, is history. Or as *they* would have said, the future.

In 1875 they rented some land on Deepdale Farm and not long after, looking to keep fit during the winter, they started a football team, which played its first game on the farm on 1878, thus making Deepdale the oldest stadium in the world still in continual use by a professional club. How good is that? Yes, I do remember that Mansfield's ground is older and still in use, but other clubs played there before them.

The lamb on the badge is not just any old lamb from Deepdale Farm. Oh no, it's the lamb of St Wilfrid, the patron saint of Preston. I have no idea what makes his lamb different to any other, but I do like the fact that a no-nonsense northern town like Preston has a patron saint called Wilf.

The badge also carries the letters PP, which stands for Princeps Pacis, the Prince of Peace, but most fans prefer their version: Proud Preston. And they have much to be proud about. They were founder members of the Football League in 1888, which they won and became the first team to win the double in the process; they were one of the northern rebel teams who defied the FA and turned professional; and they have twice won the FA Cup, although sadly the last time was when George Mutch's last-minute penalty led to that lunch of hat and chips in 1938. And, as

---

* Full-backs' names are rarely mentioned in hushed tones – unless you don't want Gary Neville to hear what you're calling him.

any football fan will tell you (or, more likely, Google), in 1887 they beat Hyde United 26-0 to register the highest ever victory in English football.

But it is one man who stands out in the history of Preston North End: Sir Thomas Finney CBE, a left-winger who is arguably the best player this country ever produced (although see the chapter on Blackpool for some fans who may disagree). Tom was born in 1922, about three hundred yards from Deepdale (which by now was very much *not* a farm any more). He was so good that after one single trial he was offered a professional contract at the age of 15 (£2.10 shillings a week, since you ask), but his father refused, insisting he finish his apprenticeship first. So Tom played reserve games as an amateur before joining PNE full-time and becoming the most famous plumber in the country. And, like so many of his generation, he saw action as a tank-driver with Montgomery in the desert; although, again, like so many of his generation, he was far more likely to tell you about football matches than battles.

When the war ended, there was plenty of work for plumbers, courtesy of the Luftwaffe, so Tom simply carried on playing *and* plumbing, standing out on the pitch so much that the *Daily Express* referred to the team as 'the Preston plumber and his ten drips'.

If you want to know what he looks like then I suggest a trip to Deepdale. The seats of the Sir Tom Finney Stand make up a giant picture of his face, and outside is the best football statue in the country. It's called 'The Splash' and recreates a remarkable photo of Tom taking on two Chelsea defenders on a water-logged Stamford Bridge pitch.

Despite offers from clubs here and abroad, Tom remained a one-club wonder and retired in 1960 after 433 games and 187 goals. I never saw him play but I was lucky enough to meet him towards the end of his life, and he was as graceful and charming as everyone said he was. And it was humbling to be in the presence of football history, a living reminder of a time when a plumber played football and the North End of Preston produced a genius.

'Freddie Flintoff is never a details person, mainly because so much has happened to him it would take far too long to tell every story in full.'

Tom Finney is not the only famous sportsperson from Preston. One of my favourite jobs is baby-sitting England cricket legend Freddie Flintoff on a TV show called *A League of Their Own*. I asked him recently whether he had any interesting memories of going to Deepdale as a kid. 'Not really Kev ... Oh, I did once accidentally start a pitch invasion.'

There is quite often a brief pause in conversations with Fred as the information sinks in. 'Fred,' I said, 'how do you "accidentally" start a pitch invasion?'

'It were last day of the season and I wanted a goal-net for the garden. I thought the game had finished. Everyone just sort of followed me on.'

I did press him for more on the story but Fred is never a details person, mainly because so much has happened to him it would take far too long to tell every story in full! Preston has a footballer and a cricketer we could all be proud of.

Actually, it also has another *team* we could all be proud of. Clare Balding spent many of our hours together telling me about the 'Dick, Kerr Ladies', and many minutes telling me off for sniggering about the name.

During the First World War, a morale-raising football match was suggested between the men and women workers at the Dick, Kerr Munitions Factory in Preston. The women won (how's the morale now, lads?) and Albert Frankland, a factory administrator, suggested the women could play the odd charity match to raise funds for injured soldiers. 'These girls could fill Deepdale,' he is supposed to have said. If he did say it, he was right. They filled everywhere. Women's football was incredibly popular back then and over the next few years, the Dick, Kerr Ladies played a remarkable series of exhibition games, often in front of newsreel cameras and crowds of 50,000 people. The women became household names, and, every single penny raised went to the soldiers in need. Despite all that, the FA, shamefully, decided the game wasn't for the girls. Health reasons, they said, but more likely they disapproved of money not going into their pockets. 'The game of football is quite unsuitable for females and should not be encouraged.' And they banned it. For 50 years. It's a story that Clare thinks the world should know. And quite right too.

Why You Shouldn't Support Them

- Not mentioning any other player ever. Come on, some of the others must have been alright.
- Caused a man to eat his hat.
- The Preston Central Travelodge. I'm still not ready to talk about it.

QUEEN'S PARK RANGERS

'Q … P … R … Q … P … R … Q … P … ha ha ha ha ha ha ha.'

Away fans at Loftus Road – not big, not clever, makes me laugh every time

'Supporting QPR is a hereditary illness.'

SEANN WALSH QPR fan

Thinking about it, perhaps I need a CD* to go with this book, or at least some musical notation so you can get the full musical fun of that song. Or perhaps I should just trust that most of you will have sung it at some time, so you know how it goes.

QPR is one of the few away grounds where we felt completely safe. It's not a posh area like Fulham, where the most dangerous thing that could happen is a Volvo running over your foot on the way back from Waitrose, and it's not an out-of-town ground surrounded by lots of lovely open space with no potential ambush sites. It's actually in quite a deprived area and it's surrounded by bleak housing estates with plenty of rat-runs from which to leap out on unsuspecting away fans, but it never happens. I don't know if they are just nice people or don't care enough about QPR to have a row with anyone. I reckon you could walk into the Springbok next to the ground in full red and blue face paint, whistling 'Glad All Over', rubbing a picture of Rodney Marsh on your crotch, and the home fans who drink in there will buy you a drink and ask where you got the picture of Rodney.

True, some of the worst crowd scenes I have witnessed happened inside Loftus Road, but we caused them, or rather Clive Allen did. It was the quarter-final of the FA Cup. Allen had gone back to his old club after a season with us and scored the winning goal. He is a radio pundit now

---

* Or download. I know what's happening in the modern world, even if I don't know how to do it.

and I often think of phoning in to ask whether it was strictly necessary to run the full length of the pitch to celebrate, given that it took several hundred coppers and a line of police horses to stop us getting at him when the whistle blew.

It's not something I was proud of being part of, but it's still a mystery why he enjoyed beating us that much, although not as big a mystery as where a whole line of police horses suddenly appeared from. It is true that he was sent to Palace from Arsenal against his will as part of a swap deal, and it is true that we finished bottom of the league, but that was only technically our fault, so it's still a mystery. And where were the QPR fans while this was happening? Looking on bemused that someone could get that excited about a football match.

Seann Walsh is a very funny comedian and a QPR fan. He told me they only really get annoyed by Chelsea, although he has to work at it: 'I can't be arsed arguing with my own fans, so I just decided it was easier to hate Chelsea.' The club he really dislikes is Arsenal: 'Their fans are all called Hugo or Jack and look like they went to Hogwarts together and eat rice cakes and drink pints of Wizard's Beard after a hard day's yoga.' So, if they don't have a problem with us, it may be hard for me to have a problem with them. I'm willing to give it a go, obviously.

By now you know how much I love Brian Moore, the presenter and commentator for London Weekend Television's *The Big Match*.* If George Best was the face of my childhood, Brian Moore was the voice. But if Brian had one fault it was an over-fondness for QPR. Maybe it was my jealous imagination, but he always sounded a little more jaunty when he commentated on QPR games. It felt like his voice had a spring in its step … oh, let's be honest, 'aroused' is the word I'm looking for.

'I would never be unfaithful to claret and blue stripes, but if I was tempted, it would be by minx-like blue and white hoops.'

And while we're being honest, I would never be unfaithful to claret and blue stripes, but if I was tempted, it would be by minx-like blue and white hoops. That's a good kit, or it was when it was just blue and white hoops rather than many of the subsequent clever/ironic/playful versions. They're hoops, they should go all the way round the shirt, *and* be blue and white. End of.

If QPR serve one useful purpose, it's keeping football historians in work. It's not that the origins of the club are obscure. In 1882

---

* You'd be downloading the theme tune now. It still stops me in my tracks when I hear it.

two local youth clubs, St Jude's Institute and Christchurch Rangers, combined to become Queen's Park Rangers. It is to the credit of the club that their current mascot is a cat called Jude to honour that history, although presumably a church costume would be quite cumbersome for a mascot.

It's because, in the 138 years of their existence, they have changed their ground 17 different times, and to complicate things even more, they have only had 13 different grounds. No team has been anywhere near as flighty. God knows how they managed to rent anything without being able to show two years' worth of utility bills.

If I was to list their meanderings in full I'd have to ditch the next two chapters, but in 1933 they settled at Loftus Road (having tried it out once before and left), although in 1962 they got itchy feet again and tried a move down the road to the White City Stadium before going back again for good.

'That's a good kit, or it was when it was just blue and white hoops rather than many of the subsequent clever/ironic/playful versions.'

Ironically, at the time of writing they are looking for a site to build a brand-new stadium. Whether that's because they need a bigger ground or just because they're really scared of commitment, I don't know.

They initially wore dark blue and light blue quarters (ooh, somebody had been to Oxbridge) before changing to green and white hoops, but changed to blue and white hoops after a while because the green and white ones were considered 'unlucky' – Jesus, imagine how many times Celtic would have won the League if they had a luckier kit!

Of course, all that faffing about with moving around and finding a kit left them no time to think of a decent nickname. Officially they are the 'R's. Which is terrible but marginally better than the 'Q's or the 'P's, although none of them sound brilliant if you put the words 'up the' in front of them. Unofficially, they are the 'super hoops', unofficial because for most of their career they have been anything but super.

True, they were the first Third Division to win a major trophy when they won the League Cup in 1967, and true they have spent a few odd seasons in the Premier League, but for much of their career they have moved between various leagues as often as they have moved between grounds.

But there was one glorious exception. Brian Moore may have been a Gillingham fan, but when he commentated on the QPR team of 1975/76 he didn't so much speak as purr. 'Swashbuckling ... inspired ... unruly

… scruffy' were just a few of the words the press used to describe a team that improbably pushed Liverpool all the way to the First Division title.

They had grizzled veterans Frank McClintock and David Webb tackling anything that moved, Gerry Francis ran the midfield and Stan Bowles did things up front that even George Best may have approved of. And they had Dave Thomas, a wafer-thin winger who, despite the fact he had to walk around in the shower to get wet, was absolutely fearless, facing the roughest of treatment without wearing shin pads.

For one glorious season, QPR played the sort of football that belonged in a school at lunchtime. Fast, furious and a joy to watch. The nation fell in love with them as much as Brian Moore did, and a team that had appeared out of nowhere were willed on to beat the perennial title winners in red. On the first day of that season they took Liverpool apart, and on the last day they were a point ahead of them. Unfortunately, it wasn't the last day for Liverpool. Because of European commitments their last League game was 10 days later, away at Wolves, themselves desperate for a win to avoid relegation.

The BBC, literally a stone's throw from Loftus Road,* invited the QPR squad to watch it live in their studio and for 70 minutes all was well until an exhausted Liverpool roused themselves and they took the points necessary to win the title.

But for that one season, the hoops really were super. Never happened again, of course. That's the nature of romance, and football economics, I'm afraid.

Why You Shouldn't Support Them

▪ Clive Allen. He also had a goal disallowed at Coventry when the ball went in and bounced back out off the stanchion. I'm blaming him for that too.
▪ Several Palace managers scarpered there when things got tough at Palace.
▪ Brian Moore jealousy.

---

* I've seen someone do it.

READING

'Reading supporters were the first supporters to get the number 13 shirt – and officially be named the 13th man.'

NIGEL ADKINS Royals boss, in 2013. Really, why not walk under a ladder and break a mirror while you're about it?

'Hob Nob Anyone?'

Reading FC fansite (makes me laugh every time)

Did you read the biography of me on the cover? You did?! Thank you, long train journey was it?

Well, Reading was the university I was thrown out of. I went there to study archaeology but was 'asked' to leave for having the temerity to fall in love with a student of agriculture who was three years older than me and much wiser in the ways of the world (and agriculture). I won't embarrass her by telling you her name, but it was a relationship passionate enough to completely distract me from becoming Streatham's very own Indiana Jones; my tutor reckoned I had attended exactly one and a quarter lectures in three months when he announced he was sending me home.†

Now, the more astute among you, or those on a *really* long train journey, will be thinking, 'Hang on a minute, just a chapter or two ago, in Plymouth, he was in a passionate relationship with his first serious girlfriend who was at college there. Was this happening at the same time?' Sadly, it was.‡ I'm not proud. Although I was a little bit at the time. Come on, I was 19.

So that's my personal relationship with Reading – what about my football one? Well, I always liked visiting Elm Park (although, as you know, I missed us winning 6-1 there because Chirpy was a whole day late picking me up). It was a ramshackle, run-down old place that you

---

† As it happened, 'home' didn't want me. I was the first in my extended Irish family to go to university and Mum didn't take it well when I became the first to get kicked out.
‡ Which didn't help with the 'home' situation. Mum adored my first girlfriend. As it happened, the girlfriend was very philosophical about the whole thing and we were together for some years more. And it turns out she was seeing someone else too.

couldn't see coming until you were virtually in the turnstiles. Officially the capacity was 33,000, but unless it was an actual Tardis it looked like you would have to shift the floodlights to get more than 10,000 in there.

In other words, in my eyes it was a 'proper' ground. And my mate Bill, who supported them, agreed. He was also rather proud of the fact that the club had to move from their original ground in 1889 because the local squire objected to 'rowdyism among the rougher elements in the crowd'. And I think we have a clue as to what caused the rowdyism, when a donation towards finding a new ground was given only on the proviso that 'no liquors were to be sold'.

Turned out, however, that Bill was a traitor to his own class. Driven by the Taylor Report's demand for all-seater stadiums, Reading moved to the brand-new, purpose-built Madejski Stadium in 1998, funded by their new (and not very modest) owner, John Madejski. The first time I saw it, my heart sank. Actually, my heart sinks every time I get off the train in Reading, although whether that's because of nostalgia or the architecture I don't know.

'My heart sinks every time I get off the train in Reading, although whether that's because of nostalgia or the architecture I don't know.'

It's a classic example of an identikit new stadium that could be anywhere in Europe and reflects absolutely nothing of the club or the town. Even worse, walking to the away end we passed a pizza restaurant and a jazz cafe, not near the stadium, *in* the bloody stadium.

After the game (we lost), Bill had asked us for a drink in a hotel bar. The Madejski Stadium Hotel bar. It was as bad as we'd expected. There was a grand piano. With a pianist who got really arsey when I put my pint on it. I hated it, but Bill was actually proud that the local boozer was a four-star hotel and served its crisps in bowls, not packets. He actually accused us of reverse snobbery and nostalgia for the bad old days of football. He was right on both counts.

I definitely yearn for the days when Reading had the lowest-rent nickname in football. As you know, I am a big fan of the clues left by nicknames to the occupations of the proud working folk that first followed them. Sheffield United, steelworkers: the Blades. Walsall, leather-makers: the Saddlers. Crystal Palace, builders in glass: the Glaziers. Proud, strong occupations giving proud, strong nicknames.

Reading had a Huntley & Palmers factory, so they were: the Biscuitmen. Come on, chaps, you can't look a saddler, a glazier or a steelworker in the eye and say 'move over, lightweights, I make custard creams'. Unless I'm much mistaken about the biscuit-making industry and there is the real danger of a crumb in the eye or butter-rash, in which case I apologise. The factory closed in the 1970s and, being in

'Come on, chaps, you can't look a saddler, a glazier or a steelworker in the eye and say "move over, lightweights, I make custard creams".'

Royal Berkshire, the club changed their nickname to the Royals, which is arguably worse but does sit better for fans drinking in a hotel.

They were the Biscuitmen for a long time because they are an old club, formed on Christmas Day 1871 – presumably by blokes who were desperate to go to a game on Boxing Day. So old, in fact, that for a long time they had no league to play in and got by against random teams who fancied a kick-about. Indeed, their first game at Elm Park (in 1896, a year after they turned professional) was against A. R. Bourke's XI, a scratch team not registered with the FA. So, naturally, the FA fined them £5. And the game was called off because of a thunderstorm when Reading were winning 7-1. It was an inauspicious start to life in their proper old ground. You may not have been able to get a pizza there or crisps in a bowl, but I know where I'd rather watch *my* football.

I can hear Bill saying 'I told you so' from here.

Why You Shouldn't Support Them

- A jazz cafe *in* the ground? That is all sorts of wrong.
- Their record victory was 10-2 against Crystal Palace.
- Biscuits. They weren't even specific about which type. I'd have more respect if they'd been called the Jammy Dodgers or the Pink Icing Ones That No One Likes Best.

ROCHDALE

'At a meeting convened by Mr Harvey Rigg in Fleece Street, Rochdale, last evening, with Mr H. Hopkinson in the chair, it was decided to form a club to be called the Rochdale Association Football Club.'

The Rochdale Observer, 15 May 1907

'Her story is the Cinderella story of all time. She went from a fish and chip shop in Molesworth Street, Rochdale, to a world-famous superstar in Capri.'

ROY HUDD comedian, unveiling a statue of Gracie Fields (the *Guardian*, 19 September 2016) – it was the first statue of a woman erected in Greater Manchester for over a hundred years

I liked Roy Hudd. He was from Croydon, he was a Palace fan and he was a walking encyclopaedia of the history of comedy. And I like the sound of Harvey Rigg. I assume he wore a bowler hat and had the flourishing moustache and slightly superior look that all middle-class men displayed in Edwardian photographs. A generalisation of course, but not the only one, because there's no getting away from the fact that if you ask anyone in the south to imagine anywhere in the north, it would probably look like Rochdale.

The great artist of industrial landscapes, L. S. Lowry, never painted Rochdale, but in my mind's eye Rochdale looks like every painting he did, which is odd, because I've been there so I know what it actually looks like. It has a magnificent Victorian Town Hall, a legacy of the wealth brought by industrialisation and cotton mills. Well, brought to the lucky few. The rest were pretty much stuffed.

Rochdale is the birthplace of Gracie 'Our Gracie' Fields, Mark 'Chappers' Chapman and Lisa 'Lisa' Stansfield, but I'm sure they would forgive me for saying it is also the birthplace of the Co-operative Movement, because all that cotton money that went to the few inspired some of the many to become fervent trade unionists.

Mark Chapman, as I'm sure you will know, is the voice of sport on

BBC Radio 5 Live and has now presented *Match of the Day 2* for many seasons. Because he's a mate, I asked him about Rochdale, specifically so I could out him for being a glory-hunting Man U fan and not supporting his local team. He reminded me that I'd already accused him of that 'many times' and he'd always told me the reason: he moved to Sale when he was a baby, so Man U *was* his local team. I still think that when you're old enough to pick a team you should be asking where you were born first, but I'm obviously more rigorous about these things than other football fans. Nonetheless, Mark is still very proud of being born in Rochdale, and it turns out that he has good reason.

Once firmly in Lancashire, it is now part of the Greater Manchester conurbation and Rochdale AFC are one of those clubs, like Oldham and Stockport, who miraculously survive in the shadow of United and City (Bury, of course, were not so lucky). They played their first ever league game in the Manchester League in September 1907 against a team with the splendid name of Tongue. The game was played at St Clement's Playing Fields, where they played until moving to their current home, Spotland, in 1920.

> 'I still think that when you're old enough to pick a team you should be asking where you were born first, but I'm obviously more rigorous about these things than other football fans.'

I have no idea where Tongue played. Or where it is. Or if it exists. There is a place called Tonge, so either they played an early misprint, or everyone realised that having a football team called Tongue was a recipe for too much double-entendre for a sexually repressed era.

Rochdale, I'm afraid, are remarkable only for how unremarkable their history has been. No club has been promoted or relegated fewer times than they have. In 1921, the Football League was expanded, and Rochdale were invited to step up from local football to join the brand-new Third Division North. Since that time they have only ever been in the bottom two divisions. The longest run of 'failure' of any club.

They were in the Fourth Division for 36 seasons between 1974 and 2010. That's a record. At the time of writing they have been promoted and relegated three times – basically, they get promoted every 33 years. Then relegated again.

It's actually quite fascinating to learn of a club where nothing fascinating has ever happened, yet 3,000 people happily turn up to watch it not happening. Except, no club can last that long without something happening, and it was something I didn't know about. This came as something of a shock to me because I thought I knew a little bit about most important things that had happened in the game. And it turns out that Gracie Fields is not the only trailblazer for the town to be proud of.

In 1961, the Football League decided they wanted their own cup competition and launched the League Cup. The FA were miffed and refused to allow the final to be at Wembley. A lot of top-flight clubs simply couldn't be bothered to enter so it became a chance for lower-league clubs to get a rare crack at glory. So, in 1962, the League Cup final was played over two legs between Norwich and … da-da-da-da-da … Rochdale.

That much I knew. Well, I knew Rochdale had been in the League Cup final, but what I didn't know until I did the research* for this book was that the man who had taken them to that final was English football's first black manager. I mean, you can still count the entire number of black managers on the fingers of not many hands, so how the bloody hell have I never heard of one in 1962? It's almost like no one wanted to give him any praise for his achievement.

Tony Collins was born in Notting Hill, played briefly for Palace,† then moved to Rochdale, where he was made player-manager in 1960. The chairman said: 'We are aware that some eyebrows will be raised because of his colour, but that made no difference and we hope it will make no difference in his managerial career.' That may sound patronising to the modern ear, but back then it was quite a ballsy statement and the club deserve enormous credit for giving Tony a chance, especially as Notting Hill was still smoking from recent race riots.

Collins was known by the local press as 'the professor of soccer know-how' and remains the only black manager to have led his team out in a cup final. Although surely that will change soon, won't it? Don't hold your breath.

'I mean, you can still count the entire number of black managers on the fingers of not many hands, so how the bloody hell have I never heard of one in 1962?'

Rochdale lost 4-0 over the two legs (11,000 cramming into Spotland), but there were no TV cameras so no record of Tony's proud moment. Perhaps if the final had been at Wembley, the sight of him striding on to the hallowed turf may have become an image so iconic and so inspirational that the sight of a black manager now wouldn't still be so rare.

---

* I use the word loosely.

† He was our first ever black player. I did not know that either.

He left Rochdale in 1967, fully expecting to get another manager's job soon. It didn't happen. I think we all know why, but he never accepted it was because of the colour of his skin. He went on to become one of the chief scouts at Leeds, providing those famous dossiers for Don Revie, and did the same thing for Ron Atkinson at Man United. But again, I didn't know that.

He was obviously a much admired man of football. No disrespect to Rochdale, who deserve a lot of credit for giving him a chance, but surely a pioneer like that should be more famous than the club he managed?

And no disrespect to Gracie Fields, but if anyone deserves a statue, it's Tony Collins.

Why You Shouldn't Support Them

- I spent hours looking for a Lowry painting of Rochdale.
- There really should be a statue of Tony Collins.
- Service in my local Co-Op leaves a lot to be desired.

ROTHERHAM UNITED

'To me, to you, to me, to you.'

Rotherham and Ipswich fans' tribute to Barry Chuckle at the first match after his death,
11 August 2018

'Rotherham could dedicate square to Barry Chuckle.'

bbc.co.uk/south-yorkshire

Not every team can boast a Prince William or an Elton John or an Oprah Winfrey as a celebrity fan. Some have to settle for lesser mortals, but the Chuckle Brothers made children laugh for nigh on three decades and they were as proud of Rotherham United as Rotherham United were of them.

Any foreign guests at the game against Ipswich, or people who don't have a TV, would have had no idea what was going on as both sets of fans took turns to chant the Chuckle Brothers' catchphrase for a whole minute rather than stand in silence, but it was genuinely moving, all the more so for apparently being spontaneous. There may have been a few 'let's do this' tweets going around but 73 minutes into the game, thousands of people stood to mark the passing of a clown. Further proof too, that football fans may bicker, bitch and battle but when real life intervenes they will rise above the game and unite in grief or injustice. Is there a more moving sound than the silence of 40,000 people?

The Rotherham United Barry Chuckle left behind are a well-run, financially stable football club, who refuse to gamble their future on a reckless spending spree to try and force their way into the Premier League.* How dull is that?

It's very dull. If only there were more clubs like them. They fight

---

* Well, they were at the time of writing. The way football is going, they could well have been taken over by a Chinese betting company and bought Lionel Messi.

their way into the Championship, compete with a wage bill so low it's almost laughable – one of their players was paid £3,000 a week last season. A *week*! David Beckham could get through that on pants alone, I reckon.† Then they accept relegation, knowing they have secured their financial future for another few years, and go on being the focal point of a community that has a far less secure financial future. My point being that £3,000 a week is a hefty chunk to most of us, but in modern football it is, I'm afraid, back-of-the-sofa change for some players.

At the risk of sounding patronising, clubs like Rotherham (and Palace, for that matter) are the backbone of English football. They will have years, maybe even a decade or so, in the sun, but then they will go back to being just another club, mostly unnoticed by the rest of us but doing their best to get by so that local people will still have somewhere to go on a Saturday afternoon in a hundred years' time.

'Football fans may bicker, bitch and battle but when real life intervenes they will rise above the game and unite in grief or injustice.'

One of my earliest memories at Selhurst involves seeing a group of elderly Rotherham fans in the away enclosure, all wearing rosettes and all having two programmes, one to keep fresh and one to write team changes. It's a memory so rosy I'm surprised my subconscious hasn't also provided them with rattles and flat caps. Who knows, maybe two of them were Mr and Mrs Chuckle having a romantic weekend away from the kids in Croydon?

For quite a small town there have been a lot of teams who have been called Rotherham something, although disappointingly not one actually called Rotherham Something. There have been Rotherham Wanderers, Swifts, Amateurs, Casuals, Grammar and Town. There was also a team called Thornhill, who became Rotherham County, and a team way back in late-Victorian times called Lunar Rovers because they played games by moonlight (was there really, bloke in a pub, was there really?).‡

It's really hard to say how all these teams were related – although anyone who has ever played Sunday league football will be able to relate to the Machiavellian politics that sees clubs emerge, fold, re-emerge, fold

---

† I decided not to name a current player as an example in case they do actually spend that on pants, or, even worse, don't and get annoyed with me. Plus David is a genuinely nice chap, apparently, and wears lovely pants.

‡ Yes, there was. And they did only play by moonlight. If they also avoided garlic I think we may be on to a horror franchise here.

again, then re-re-emerge until suddenly you've got a pub team called Manchester United.

As I don't support them, I won't try to explain, especially as it is really difficult to follow. There were only about 200,000 people living there, how many teams did they need? Suffice to say that in 1925, Rotherham County and Rotherham Town joined together to become Rotherham United, just about the only name they hadn't tried yet.

It is a town with a proud industrial and coal-mining heritage, although, sadly, the only word that is still relevant is 'heritage'. The mines, and the foundries that made cannons, ploughs and baths, are long gone, and so are most of the flour mills that give Rotherham their nickname. They are the Millers, and their badge commemorates that with a neat little windmill, although I suspect that would have been a more relaxing place to work than the actual giant factories of companies like Hovis.

They have a natty new ground called the New York Stadium (because it's in a part of Rotherham called New York). They won Division Three twice, had a couple of decent cup runs in the sixties, and they should have stuck with Rotherham Town's original brown and blue halved kit. Apart from that, there is not a lot to tell you. Except that, like many of the clubs in this book, they will only ever be really special to people like my rosette-wearing friends of 1975 – but, you know what, that's special enough.

Why You Shouldn't Support Them

- I needed a spreadsheet to keep track of all those names.
- New York? In Rotherham. Without irony. Really?
- People who bought two programmes really annoy me. All the team changes will be on your phone.

SALFORD CITY

'This club isn't a TV show, it's a serious football club.'
GRAHAM ALEXANDER manager

'Salford City is the 82nd most famous football club in England. Described by fans as fit, interesting, up and coming and powerful.'

YouGov.co.uk

The 82nd most famous, already? They've only been in the League two minutes!

This is Salford City's first season in the Football League, so this should be the quickest and easiest chapter to write; but of course, their late arrival to the party doesn't mean they haven't got a long and illustrious history. It just means it took place off the radar of many of us.

It's actually slightly disconcerting having them in the League in the first place. It's like a Sunday team is suddenly all over the telly because they are owned by some of the most famous footballers in English history.

Not as disconcerting as their crest, though. I think it's meant to be a menacing lion emerging from a shield or something, but it just looks a bit like Aslan has got his head stuck in a tea-towel holder. But before the history, we need to discuss the geography. Back in the day, the stage manager at the Comedy Store was called Salford Stan, because he was from Salford and his name was Stan. Stan was a Man U fan who constantly told me that they were actually a Salford club, not a Manchester one. And he constantly kept saying that to me because I constantly kept saying to him, 'How the fuck can you tell? And why is it called "*Manchester* United" then?' Honestly, sometimes the repartee just flew.

It turns out Salford is part of the City of Salford, which is part of Greater Manchester, and Manchester is also part of Greater Manchester, but Manchester is not part of Salford or the City of Salford. Now we've sorted that out, what about the football club? Well, not only are they new to the League, they are relatively new full stop. They were founded as Salford Central in 1940. That seems a really strange year to start a football club. Maybe it was a gesture of defiance, or a sign of optimism that there would be enough young men around to play for them despite the war and the Blitz. Whatever the reason, it paid off and they were a success in local football and in 1963 stepped up to the Manchester Amateur League, changing their name to Salford Amateurs in the process. Changing your name to Amateurs strikes me as slightly less optimistic than starting a football team during the war, but it paid off because amazing success followed.

In 1982, the Sunday league team were good enough to be invited to join the newly formed North-West Counties League at the very bottom of the pyramid. In 1989 they were too good to be amateur, so step forward Salford City.

And, 24 years later, step forward Nicky Butt, Ryan Giggs, Gary Neville, Phil Neville, Paul Scholes and David Beckham: the Class of '92, Fergie's fledglings, an extraordinary group of home-grown players who emerged together into the Man United team and took the decade by storm, despite Alan Hansen's famous *Match of the Day* declaration: 'You can't win anything with kids.' In 2013, in what appears to be a proper altruistic gesture, they approached the club with an offer to take it over and invest in the team, to 'put something back' into an area that reflected their own development and their passion for Manchester United, even though apparently Salford is a separate bastard city.

The ownership has not been without controversy. There was an unsavoury spat between Gary Neville and Andy Holt, the owner of Accrington Stanley,who accused them of trying to buy their place in the EFL by offering players wages of up to £4,000 a week. But if they were lucky enough to find people willing to finance their ambition, then good luck to them.

So, here they are, in the English Football League. Whether it's the start of a journey or the end of one remains to be seen.

Why You Shouldn't Support Them

- It's really hard to spend many, many seasons booing Gary Neville and Paul Scholes and then suddenly be expected to like them as benefactors.
- I mean, come on, it's Gary Neville.
- Seriously, Stan, if you can show me where Manchester stops and Salford starts, I'll believe you.

SCUNTHORPE
UNITED

'I'm getting first team football here. Should think if I went First Division, I'd struggle a bit.'

KEVIN KEEGAN 1970

'Ian Botham, the cricket superstar who is now a Scunthorpe footballer, is unlikely to forget his first taste of action in the Football League.'

Saturday Sports Telegraph match report, 1980

There is no doubt that I support the team with the most gorgeous name in English football. Only Aston Villa comes close (although I think their website may need to ponder that, when celebrity fan Tom Hanks said the name made him imagine it was on the Amalfi Coast, he may have been taking the piss). As we've seen, Scotland has some beauties, like Queen of the South and Heart of Midlothian; and the wider world has a few crackers as well, my favourites being O'Higgins FC in Chile and Swaziland's Eleven Men in Flight.

Unfortunately, and I think you know where this is going, Scunthorpe is definitely the worst name for a football club. Once you see the four letters hiding between the 'S' and the 'h', it is impossible not to see them every time you see the word. And the abbreviation – Scunny – only adds insult to injury. I very much doubt that their fans mind, though. It's a tough town built on a tough industry; having a poetic-sounding name for their football team has probably never been high on their list of priorities. And the team is one of those rare ones that isn't much older than the town itself.

A village called 'Escumesthorpe' (meaning 'Skuma's homestead') is listed in the Domesday Book in 1086, but it grew into a big town in just a few years in the 1850s and '60s following the discovery of ironstone in the local hills. Iron has sustained the town and employed its people ever since, meaning there could only be one nickname for the football team: the Iron. Their current badge is a hand holding a girder. Unfortunately, and I know I sound like a stuck record here, that industry is in serious decline and it probably won't be long before the football Iron is the last reminder of local prosperity.

Scunthorpe United were formed in 1899 and in 1910

> 'What? WHY? Why not drop the "Scunthorpe" bit? Lindsey United is a great name.'

amalgamated with another local club to become Scunthorpe and Lindsey United, which they stayed until the mid-50s when they dropped the 'and Lindsey' bit.

What? WHY? Why not drop the 'Scunthorpe' bit? Lindsey United is a great name. It wouldn't quite be up there with Palace and Villa, and Lindsey United does sound a bit like an insurance company in the Hebrides, but it's way cooler than Scunthorpe. What were they thinking of?

They wore claret and blue from the start (well, that's some consolation for the name) but flirted with white for a while because it would look good under floodlights, then tried red because it worked for Liverpool. Obviously it didn't take them long to work out that it was more the squad of world-class players than the kit that had worked for Liverpool, so thankfully they are now back on the good old claret and blue.

And mention of Liverpool will have Scunthorpe fans going 'I bloody knew it', because they are probably more famous for producing Kevin Keegan than anything they have actually won. If George Best was the face of football in the sixties, Keegan took his place in the seventies, forming a stunning strike partnership with John Toshack at Liverpool, before moving to Hamburg then returning to England to galvanise Southampton and, more famously, Newcastle.

For a decade he was probably the most recognisable footballer in the world. He must have a massive mantelpiece because he has won everything there is to win as a player, and he is also one of the nicest, most enthusiastic people you could ever meet. The first time I met him was on a TV show called *A League of Their Own*. As we were chatting, a producer tripped over a waste-paper bin and Keegan leapt to his feet shouting 'penalty, ref' before telling the producer off for diving. For someone my age, it was a moment of magic.

And he started his career as a teenager at Scunthorpe in 1968. He scored 22 goals in three seasons (as a midfielder) and played his last game for them against Workington in front of fewer than 3,000 people on 1 May 1971 before joining Liverpool for £35,000 (yes, young people, £35,000).

He has often talked (he did to me and the producer) about the values he learnt at his first club, values that the fans demanded: hard work, discipline, loyalty, togetherness, respect – so, I could carry on and tell you about Scunthorpe coming fourth in the Second Division in 1962, or winning League One in 2007, or the 20 times they have won the Lincolnshire Senior Cup. But I think it's enough that a team with an unlovely name produced one of the most famous names in football.

It's not enough, you say? Okay, how about it's enough that they briefly gave a home to one of the most famous names in cricket? Between 1979 and 1984, Ian Botham made 11 appearances in the first team of Fourth Division Scunthorpe as a non-contract player, and nobody seems to know why.

> 'As we were chatting, a producer tripped over a waste-paper bin and Keegan leapt to his feet shouting "penalty, ref" before telling the producer off for diving.'

Well, the non-contract bit is easy. He had a day job being the best all-rounder cricket has ever seen, single-handedly winning the Ashes for England. It's the 'why' he played for Scunthorpe that's the mystery. He lived nearby, which helps, but despite being one of our most talked-about and written-about sporting stars, there is barely a mention of his football career anywhere, even though he is now president of the club.

It's like turning up late for a game at Port Vale and seeing Freddie Flintoff up front. Although he could, of course, be invading the pitch.

Why You Shouldn't Support Them

- How on earth was copying Liverpool's kit going to make you successful? Even if you were putting Ian Botham in it.
- And much as I love Kevin Keegan, it's still hard to forgive him for the hair and the singing.
- 'Scunthorpe' or 'Lindsey'? As the ancient knight at the end of *Indiana Jones and the Last Crusade* said, 'he chose poorly'.

SHEFFIELD UNITED

'In a city with a burning passion for football, Sheffield United and Sheffield Wednesday can hold their heads high in having one of English football's oldest and fiercest derbies.'

Footballfanzine.co.uk

'You fill up my senses like a gallon of Magnet, like a packet of Woodbines, like a good pinch of snuff, like a night out in Sheffield, like a greasy chip butty, like Sheffield United, come fill me again.'

United anthem sung to the tune of 'Annie's Song' by John Denver – proof that football is still essentially a working-class sport

Sheffield is the oldest football town in the world. But, and here's the tricky bit, do I mention that in the United chapter or the Wednesday one?

Hang on. Heads, United. Tails, Wednesday. Heads.

Sheffield is the oldest football town in the world. Even if it turns out that Crystal Palace are acknowledged as the oldest football club in the *League*, there is no doubt that football was being played in the Steel City long before the League even existed.

Sheffield FC, known as the 'Sheffield Club',* were founded in 1857 and initially played games only among themselves, until Hallam FC took pity on them and formed the city's second club in 1860. If it *was* formed in 1860 they took a long time to arrange that first match because it didn't take place until 1862, so there are some who assume that was the year of Hallam's foundation.

It may be that they were arguing about which rules to use. At the time, different areas, different clubs, even different schools played their own version of the game, and often the only thing they had in common was that they were played with some sort of ball which had to go in the

---

* Sheffield FC are still going. They play in the Northern Premier League and their badge carries these proud words: 'The World's First Football Club'.

general direction of some sort of line or between some sort of stick.†

I think it's fair to assume that this game was played by 'Sheffield rules', which allowed barging in mid-air and catching the ball, but didn't allow shin-kicking or headed goals. The goalposts were 12 feet apart with a crossbar nine feet from the ground. There was no offside and no specified number of players. Although I do like to think there was a cartoonist who acted as an early version of VAR.

That first game was played at the home of Sheffield United Cricket Club, Bramall Lane, and legend has it that it lasted three hours and ended 0-0, probably because the goals were so tiny. In 1889 an FA Cup semi-final game between Preston and West Brom was played at the Lane, and caused such interest in the town that the cricket club decided they needed a football club as well, to rival a cricket club called Wednesday that had also started a football team.

Please don't quote me on any of that. More than any other two clubs, the rivalry between them is such that they reach back in history for anything that gives them a moral edge and it is quite difficult to find any two sources that agree on any of the details. Although it is 100% definite that they were nicknamed the Cutlers until Sheffield Wednesday changed their nickname from the Blades to the Owls in 1903. Or 1907. Or 1912. Make that 98% definite.

Whenever it was, United obviously saw an opportunity. I have no idea whether they asked politely before appropriating the Blades as a nickname, but that's what they've been ever since. And let's face it, Sean Bean wouldn't look half as tough if he had a knife, fork and spoon tattooed on his arm over the words '100% Cutlery'.

An exciting and energetic Sheffield United team are currently sitting fourth in the Premier League, but that may not last because they have an alarming habit of being relegated in successive years, then promoted back again in a similarly short space of time, although they seem reassuringly stable at the moment.

Bramall Lane is a great away ground. Sheffield is easy to get to, it has an array of ways to pass the time, normally involving eye-wateringly cheap beer, and United fans have all the passion and grit of other teams in the region, but seemingly far less of a desire to physically hurt soft southern bastards.

Mind you, the average South Yorkshire policeman, I have to say, was never that friendly. I remember them being furious with Palace fans

---

† As far as I'm concerned, it's only a 'ball' if it's round. Whatever that thing they chuck about in rugby is, it's not a ball.

because one game at Bramall Lane was so foggy it would have been called off if 600 of us hadn't had the temerity to travel there to (not) watch it, and the referee thought that we would kick off if he didn't. One copper in particular seemed intent on blaming me for the fact that he was at a freezing cold football match rather than toasting his toes back at the station. Having said that, I could be a mouthy little sod, so it is possible I had been reminding him of the toe-toasting potential he was missing.

He was right, though. It should have been called off. The second half was so foggy that some of us spent most of it chatting to the United goalkeeper, disturbed only once by a half-hearted Palace attack looming out of the gloom. Although, thinking about it, maybe it was Woodbine smoke, not fog.

'The second half was so foggy that some of us spent most of it chatting to the United goalkeeper.'

Whatever it was, we could only try to interpret what was happening at the other end by the sound of their fans, and as there wasn't any, we came to the correct conclusion that the game ended nil-nil. Why the referee thought there would be trouble from us if the game was called off is beyond me. We shared the toe-toasting dreams of the grumpy policeman and would happily have gone home early.

Still, when we did eventually get back to lovely London, we went straight to a party, where Roy met the girl he is still married to. Roy, as you know, was the smooth good-looking one with all the charm.

Well, some of the charm. She still doesn't know that three of us drew lots to decide who got the chance to chat her up and Roy won. I'm trusting that most of you are gallant enough not to tell her.

Why You Shouldn't Support Them

- Yes, Sean Bean, we know you have Sheffield United tattoos. Put them away, love.
- They made me pay money to watch fog for 90 minutes.
- A gallon of Magnet and a greasy chip butty. How is that a good night out?

SHEFFIELD
WEDNESDAY

'You don't choose Wednesday, Wednesday chooses you.'

GARY MEGSON Sheffield Wednesday player and manager

'We are historically the bigger club. Little brother always wants to be big brother and we had to put them in their place.'

TERRY CURRAN Sheffield Wednesday player and fan

It is a well-known fact (honest) that Sheffield is the only city that never produced a punk band. It produced a lot of steel but absolutely no punk bands. There is a theory that the industrial hammering that pervaded the city inspired a number of electronic drumbeat bands like Clock DVA, Cabaret Voltaire, Human League and Heaven 17, whose lead singer I failed to recognise at a party recently even as I was telling him how much I loved Heaven 17. Then we had a massive row about Jeremy Corbyn before hugging out over a lethal rum punch. Yes, showbiz is as glamorous as you thought.

Of course, the one place where industrial hammering is guaranteed is a Sheffield derby (you see, there *was* a reason for the musical interlude). In all the talk of Merseyside, Manchester and Glasgow, the Steel City derby often gets overlooked, possibly because it doesn't get played as often, as the shifting fortunes of each side have often seen them 3.5 miles in distance but divisions away in class.

The Blades versus the Owls. United's badge and nickname reflecting the city's heritage as the home of the British steel and cutlery industry,* and Wednesday's badge and nickname reflecting a load of trees near their first ground.

Eh?! Trees in which owls lived? Nope. Trees. The Wednesday

---

* Although surely you'd be more proud to be from the home of British steel than the home of British forks.

Football Club (they weren't 'Sheffield Wednesday' until 1929) moved to the suburb of Owlerton in 1898, but the 'owl' in question was actually a Yorkshire dialect word for alder tree. The Wednesday fans in their wisdom (owl/wisdom, get it?) obviously decided that the Trees wasn't a brilliant nickname and adopted the Owls instead. So their badge depicts an owl. Although, confusingly, it is sitting on the branch of a tree.

Just to cement matters, in 1912, one of their players, George Robertson, presented the club with a stuffed owl to replace the original mascot of a stuffed monkey, which hadn't brought the team, or the monkey, much luck, and they have been the Owls ever since.*

Okay, what about the Wednesday bit? Simple. As with many football teams, they began life as a cricket team looking to keep fit over the winter before realising that football was an infinitely better game. The Wednesday Cricket Club were so called because they were made up of shopkeepers and small merchants who had Wednesday afternoon off and passed the time playing cricket until football came along in 1867. The decision to form a football club was taken at the Adelphi Hotel, on a Wednesday of course.

There is a theory that the animosity between the two has its roots in Wednesday being the club of shopkeepers and merchants while United was the club of industrial workers. But there is also a much more sensible theory that the animosity stems from being the two biggest clubs in quite a small city. Particularly because United also started life as a cricket team.

Now pay attention, for fans of the Sheffield clubs this information will be imbibed through mother's milk, but for the rest of us it's a tad complicated. Initially, Wednesday also played at Bramall Lane and they were the team nicknamed the Blades before United appropriated it after Wednesday got all owled up. Yes, I did mention that in the last chapter, but it's *really* important that I treat both Sheffield teams as though I had no idea the other existed, because they have been going at each other hammer and tongs for a long time. Hammer and tongs presumably made in Sheffield.

And as this is Wednesday's chapter, let's ignore the other lot's best derby result† and explore a day of legend for the Owls: a 4-0 win on 26 December 1979 in front of a record Third Division crowd of 49,309 people, a game they still refer to as the Boxing Day Massacre.

---

* What is it with football clubs and stuffed animals? And where did a bloody stuffed monkey appear from?

† A 7-3 win in 1951.

And Wednesday have a bonus: in 1993 the two teams met in a pulsating FA Cup semi-final at Wembley. Mark Bright was part of the legendary Wright and Bright goalscoring partnership at Crystal Palace, but played for Wednesday in that semi-final. He told me: 'It's a two-team city, you are either red or blue. Everywhere I went, shops, petrol stations, restaurants, I would be told "don't you dare lose" or "you know we're going to beat you".' Then, echoing Terry Curran, he said, 'We had to win, we were the older, bigger, better club'.

Mark scored the winner in a 2-1 victory. How did that feel? 'Relief. Just overwhelming relief.'

But it's Boxing Day the fans still sing about. The game kicked off at 11 a.m. on the orders of the police and it was still dark when fans started queuing to get in. Apparently, it was Sheffield Wednesday manager Jack Charlton's idea that both teams walked on to the pitch together to ease the tension, but as Terry Curran explained that just gave the teams more opportunity for 'banter' in the tunnel. 'Banter' like 'you'll be carried off after 10 minutes', that sort of hilarity. United fans were just as funny: 'If I'd picked up all the coins that were thrown at me, it would have been more than my wages,' said Curran afterwards.

Curran scored twice to ensure that Christmas was ruined for one half of the city and I love the fact that for most of the country, Boxing Day is a time for recovery and relaxation, but for football fans it's a day that legends are made.

I don't know why but a derby win on Boxing Day is somehow twice as sweet. And while United are currently the City's top dogs, Wednesday will always have that to sustain them.

Why You Shouldn't Support Them

▪ For most of the first two decades of my life you couldn't buy anything on a Wednesday afternoon because shops shut early. If there was a team called Sunday I'd dislike them even more.
▪ Not happy that Mark Bright seems to have enjoyed his time there.
▪ I'm told that there is 'beef' between them and Brighton after a play-off game. How dare they? They're ours!

SHREWSBURY TOWN

'Is it "shrew" or "shrow"?'

Everyone who is not from Shrewsbury (or Shrowsbury)

'Salop, Salop.'

Shrewsbury fans' chant (the only Latin chant in English football)

I've always had the hump slightly with Shrewsbury. Well, since I was six and my friend Nicholas was cruelly uprooted from the loving embrace of south London and dragged away* to live in a tiny town none of us had heard of.

I have no idea what became of him, because in those days six-year-olds weren't entrusted with important information like phone numbers, so getting in touch would have meant writing an actual letter, saving up for a stamp and attempting to launch it into the slot of a letter box that was three feet taller than you. Besides, what news is a six-year-old sharing? 'Dear Nicholas, the conkers are here.'

But it meant that Shrewsbury were one of the first teams on my now 91-club-long list of football teams I dislike for no logical reason other than they are not Crystal Palace. Which is a shame, really, because they always seem to me like the bumblebee of the football world. Just sort of harmlessly bimbling around the bottom of your league, minding its own business, you leave him alone, he'll leave you alone, that sort of club. With quite a nice kit. Well, sometimes. They started with various plain blue numbers but then settled for variations of dark-yellow and blue stripes. Very fetching. Although occasionally someone at the club will decide it's too fetching and introduce a boring plain variation until fans get the hump. Luckily, Shrewsbury fans get the hump quite well, as you will discover.

It was a bugger to get to, and it was disturbingly close to the countryside for my liking, but it was always a nice day out even if their ground did have all the atmosphere of a large allotment. It had its

---

* By his parents, not kidnappers.

advantages, though. For the average Palace fan, the first visit there led to many other new experiences, like fresh air and a cow that wasn't between two halves of a burger bun.

The ground had two distinguishing features. One, it was called Gay Meadow. Beautiful that, isn't it? Possibly the nicest, quaintest name of any football ground ever. And it was called that because there used to be a fairground there, which I can only imagine was exactly like the one in *Mary Poppins*.

Two, it had a river running behind it, into which the occasional ball would be lofted by the errant boot of a lower-league centre-back. When that happened, the emergency services kicked into action and a bloke in a coracle would paddle his way out to retrieve it. My theory was that teams playing there for the first time would deliberately kick the ball out just to see if that really would happen. It was a quaint and charming sight and an endless source of amusement to Brian Moore, my beloved presenter of *The Big Match*, London's TV football show.

About once a season we would see two minutes of highlights of a Shrewsbury game and about once a season he would chuckle his way through the latest footage from the faraway river and explain to us yet again what a coracle was.† They really were kinder, gentler times. These days the coracle would be sponsored, and coracle-cam would bring us really close to the watery action.

I say 'kinder' and 'gentler'. You can also add to that list 'duller'. The annual Christmas treat on *The Big Match* was a Palace player called Peter Taylor doing his Norman Wisdom impression. As I was a Palace fan, I dutifully found it hilarious, but it also explains why grainy images of a bloke trying to reach a ball with an oar was such a refreshing annual occasion.

Shrewsbury Town's official website admits it has no insight into the whole 'Shrew/Shrow' thing, presumably working on the basis that if you live there, you know the answer. But it does rather sheepishly admit that their history has been 'one of mixed fortunes'. Frankly, that's an over-optimistic summing-up, because it implies there have been ups to go

---

† It's a tiny round boat. It was actually quite a small river so I reckon a net on a pole could have retrieved the balls just as easily, but we townies assumed it was another harmless and unnecessary countryside tradition, like morris dancing and staring at strangers.

with the downs. True, they did win the Welsh Cup in 1891, and they did once spend several seasons in a row in the old Second Division, and yes, they did win the Midland League at their first attempt in 1938 – but otherwise, erm, well that's about it really.

Oh hang on, there was one more thing. The club website also contains one of my most favourite sentences ever: 'In the 1880s Shrewsbury became a hotbed for football.' Obviously that's hilarious to a hard-nosed city dweller like me, but it's true. At that time there were over 40 clubs in the town and surrounding area, so how they got any apples picked or fields ploughed is beyond me. But even now, with only one team left, it's still a mini-hotbed; and a brilliant illustration that football fans who support a small club are just as passionate and angry about things as the rest of us.

The badge of the football club, like the coat of arms of the town, had on it three medieval leopard-ish animals, which were known as 'loggerheads' – possibly because they look like the sort of thing that may have been carved on a battering ram made of logs. Although I'm sure if you ask a bloke in a different pub you'll get another equally dubious theory.

'These days the coracle would be sponsored, and coracle-cam would bring us closer to the watery action.'

In 2007, in an unnecessary attempt to jazz things up a bit, the club decided to replace the three sort-of-leopards with a sort-of-lion, which was probably meant to look fierce but looked instead like it was wondering where it had left its keys. The fans were furious and remained furious until 2015 when, after an eight-year campaign of petitions, boycotts and angry letters, the club agreed to a vote. Of the 1,170 votes cast, 90% wanted the old badge back. And they got it. Now, 1,053 angry fans may not seem a lot to you, but to me it proves it doesn't matter how big your club is, what matters is that it's yours, and you don't mess with it.

Why You Shouldn't Support Them

- Friend stealers.
- The air is way too fresh. Away fans want to be singing, not gasping for breath. I nearly had to suck an exhaust pipe.
- Latin chants, medieval leopards. I'm surprised their kit hasn't got a ruff on it.

SOUTHAMPTON

'A prince? Pah! You had the Queen.'

The Southern Daily Echo's '10 Things Only a Southampton Fan Would Understand' (the last time the Queen gave the cup away, it was to the Saints)

'The 32,000 people who came on Tuesday won't forget him. How much of a failure is that?'

MICK CHANNON (great Southampton striker) on Matt Le Tissier (genius Southampton midfielder)

It's very easy to write about the club you love. It's quite easy, and very good fun, to write about the clubs you hate. It gets a bit harder when you are writing about those few teams you have no real animosity towards, so I imagine it's going to be really difficult to write about the one side for which you feel total indifference. And so we come to Southampton FC, a club for which the word 'meh' was surely invented.

We'd all get along alright without Southampton, wouldn't we?* The world would still keep turning. Yes, they once had a quaint old ground; yes, they once had some right old characters in their team; and, yes, they did cause one of the biggest FA Cup final upsets of all time, but still, you know, meh. And that takes some doing, considering they actually knocked Palace out in the semi-final on their way to Wembley. I cried for two days after that, so I should hate them with a passion, but I simply can't be arsed.

Not even the single most unpleasant club official I ever met filming *Match of the Day 2* can nudge me out of my indifference. He repeated the phrase 'you are only allowed to film inside the ground and nowhere else on the St Mary's footprint' so often that I began to suspect he was a robot who had lost the ability to use any of the expressions he'd been programmed with. I'm not a violent person but he came very close to getting *my* footprint up his arse.

But I am nothing if not professional, so let's do this. The St Mary's footprint is very close to where they were originally formed in 1885

---

* Well, Liverpool wouldn't. Where would they get half their players?

as the St Mary's Church Young Man's Association Football Club. In around 1887 one of the young men in question distributed hundreds of little shields bearing the words 'Play Up Saints', and the Saints have been playing up ever since. I like to think that, inspired by his success, the young man moved on to selling badges and half-and-half scarves outside the ground.

In 1894, growing ever more popular, and now all grown-up in the Southern League, they changed their name to Southampton St Mary's FC, and two years later they dropped the 'St Mary's', retaining their holy links only in the nickname. I wish they'd kept the St Mary's and dropped the nickname, because, sweet Jesus, 'When the Saints Go Marching In' is one of the dreariest songs in football, especially in the dirge-like monotone style in which they sing it. And I wish they'd never moved to the new St Mary's with its bloody-impossible-to-film-on flipping footprint.

It's none of my business because I'm sure there were commercial imperatives/growing the brand/attracting overseas investors reasons, but the Dell was a proper old ground and a half. And those of you who are paying attention will have realised by now that when I say 'proper' old ground, I normally mean likeable mixture of ramshackle with a dash of 'unfit for purpose' thrown in.

I am aware of the irony that I complain how football fans were treated in past decades while simultaneously moaning about modern attempts to treat us properly.

It's not new stadiums as such I don't like. It's identical new stadiums designed by people with no notion of how a football ground should look, feel and sound. They should be rectangular, for a start, and all four sides should join up. It's not rocket science.

'It wasn't hostile or intimidating but there was at least, mild taunting ...'

The Dell was sort of rectangular. It also had the feel of Escher's stairs, because you couldn't really tell if the stands were going down or up, and it had a sort of two-tier triangular wedge at one end. But it had an atmosphere that the new stadium simply can't recreate. It wasn't hostile or intimidating but there was at least occasional mild taunting.

Although the one time we went there expecting it, even that didn't materialise. In 1989, on the Saturday after losing 9-0 to Liverpool in midweek, we were away to Southampton. The away end was packed and defiantly noisy but the expected onslaught of abuse we were expecting simply didn't happen. I don't know if they couldn't be bothered or genuinely thought we had suffered enough. Even after they had beaten us in the FA Cup semi-final in 1976, a family of Southampton fans genuinely tried to console me afterwards and I was genuinely fucking furious. Maybe there's a psychologist reading this who can tell me the expression for subliminal anger being expressed as indifference.

As I said, Second Division Southampton beat Man United 1-0 in the final that followed, a result that went beyond shock into sensation. Saint's striker Mick Channon said himself they 'didn't have a cat in hell's chance', but manager Lawrie McMenemy saw good omens. They lost the toss and had to wear their away kit of yellow and blue, exactly the same colour combination the Queen was wearing. Although she wasn't wearing shorts, obviously. And for quiz lovers, that was the last FA Cup final the Queen ever attended. To be fair, it is difficult to get tickets.

'For quiz lovers, 1976 was the last FA Cup final the Queen ever attended. To be fair, it is difficult to get tickets.'

Most of their career before that cup win was spent outside the top flight, but much of their career since has been in it, including one glorious spell that started by signing the actual Kevin Keegan in 1980 and finishing second in the League in 1984. In Keegan's two seasons, Southampton scored 148 League goals but sadly conceded nearly as many. It was a problem that dogged the career of arguably their greatest player, which – considering he is in competition with Kevin Keegan – is a pretty mighty claim.

I've seen them both play, though, and if I had the choice of only seeing one again, it would be Matt Le Tissier. And let's face it, if your nickname is Le God, chances are you are good. He's from Guernsey (really? he rarely mentions it) and joined the Saints as a teenager in 1985. In the next 17 years he played 443 games and scored 161 goals, mostly, I reckon, against Palace.

But that doesn't tell the whole story. He was a scruffy-looking sod but he didn't believe in scruffy-looking goals. Forty-seven of those goals were penalties (he missed one) and that was probably the closest to the net he ever scored from because he was a one-man goal of the month machine. And wasn't even a striker! He was a creative, audacious, breathtakingly skilful midfield player and, even when he was scoring against you, you couldn't help but produce a noise somewhere between a groan and a purr, like a cat discovering there's a second bowl of food.

He was a magical footballer, genuinely up there with George Best, I reckon. The fact that he only got eight caps for England at the same time as the lumbering Carlton Palmer, football's equivalent of an Ent,* was getting 18 is shameful. Le Tissier stayed with Southampton for his whole career, turning down many opportunities to go to 'bigger' clubs. That was taken by some idiots as a lack of ambition, as failure, but it wasn't. It was loyalty.

And it's a mark of how loyal he was to a team nowhere near as good as he was that Southampton are the only team to have lost two Premier League games when a player scored a hat-trick. Both, of course, scored by Le Tissier.

Le God has morphed now into Sky Sports pundit Le Tiss and, to his enormous credit, his one-eyed reporting on Southampton games is a sign that not everyone is as indifferent to them as I am.

Why You Shouldn't Support Them

- Made me cry for two days after that semi-final.
- Tried to console me after that semi-final, leaving me feeling vaguely guilty for calling them bland now.
- That bloke at St Mary's was an absolute bell-end.

---

* The trees that can talk in *Lord of the Rings*.

SOUTHEND UNITED

'Couple of pints by the sea, hopefully three points, and fish and chips on the way home. Lovely.'

MARTIN TRENAMAN actor and Southend fan

'It must have been very stressful for Bobby, working there.'

STEPHANIE MOORE wife of England legend Bobby (and not a Southend fan)

Football humour rarely translates well. It tends to be very specific and is usually very much of the moment. So when a Southend fan said to us: 'Our ground is called Roots Hall, but we've won nothing so it should be called Fuck 'all', it got a big laugh round the pub table, mainly because we had been sitting round that pub table for some hours drinking lager in the Essex sun, waiting for an evening kick-off. But by the time I'd got home and woken Ali up, explained the history of Southend United for some context, given her a brief update on Gaz's marriage then told her the joke, it didn't seem quite so funny.

As you know from previous chapters, I adore my wife, but I have met no other woman capable of expressing such displeasure with her eyebrows, and that night they reached an angle Pythagoras would have been proud of.

Similarly, when I was working with Martin Trenaman on a TV show recently, he told me about being in the away end at Selhurst Park on the night we beat them 8-0 in the League Cup:

> As we were walking towards the station, a battered old car covered in Southend stickers screeched to a halt by some Palace fans. We thought there was going to be trouble, but instead a heavily tattooed geezer stuck his head out of the window and shouted 'that fifth goal was definitely offside' then drove off again.

I laughed and obviously tried to convince him I was one of the Palace fans that bloke in the car had shouted at. But the two producers in the studio with us just looked baffled because they weren't football fans. Intelligent and creative they may be, but what joy those producers miss out on because they find football 'all a bit rowdy'.

But would you believe it? At the Roots Hall/Fuck 'all game, something even more hilarious had actually happened (this is the first time Ali knows though, I didn't risk telling her anything 'not remotely funny' for a while afterwards). Halfway through the second half, an announcement was made over the tannoy that the wife of Terry Fletcher,* a Palace fan, had gone into labour and could he please go back to Croydon immediately.

There was a spontaneous round of applause from the entire ground at this lovely news. Then Terry stood up, waved sheepishly at the Palace fans and made his way out of the ground, whereupon every single person in there began to sing 'part-time supporter' at him. What instinct kicks in to make about 5,000 people spontaneously chant something clever *and* witty I don't know, but I felt like writing to *Private Eye* to tell them not to bother any more.

My dad gets all misty-eyed at the mere mention of Southend. In the 1950s they used to run paddle-steamers down the Thames to Southend Pier. God knows what he got up to down there, but it seems to have involved the fairground and a girl called Elsie, or, occasionally, Pauline – like me, he tells a good story, but he's not big on detail. What I do know is the merest whiff of a cockle takes him to a happy place.

Sadly for Southend fans, there isn't much for them to get misty-eyed about. There was a team called Southend Athletic in the 1890s, but they played at a ground that had no actual room for supporters so presumably they went skint because the club shop did a terrible business; but Southend United filled the void in 1906. Since then, sadly, pretty much 'Fuck 'all'. They did win the Essex Professional Cup a fair few times, but to be fair there are only two professional clubs in Essex.

According to the official club history, the trophy was 'shared' in 1955. I still can't find out whether that was because the final was a draw, or because they simply couldn't be arsed to play it that year. As we know, they also have shrimp on their badge, which is way cooler than Morecambe's, and they once had a player called Prince Blott.†

Their mascot is a shrimp as well. Sammy the Shrimp, who, according to the club's marketing manager, has 'taken shrimping to a new level'. Which can't be easy, given that other mascots at least have the advantage of legs to play with. He's quite an articulate shrimp as well, he actually gave an interview in which he admitted being nervous about the players'

---

* Not his real name. Apologies if there is a Terry Fletcher out there. If there is, I imagine he's a boxer.

† Definitely his real name.

reaction: 'Did they want a big pink shrimp mucking about with them?' Does anyone, Sammy, does anyone?

Bobby Moore never shared a pitch with a big pink shrimp. 1966 is the most famous year in English football (yes, Scottish readers, I know it was a long time ago and we are still banging on about it – the Battle of Bannockburn happened in 1314, and that's in your national anthem so we're not the only ones). And arguably the most famous image in that most famous year was Bobby Moore wiping his hands before lifting the trophy. For most people, that summed him up. As neat and tidy and respectful to a Queen as he was to a football. The epitome of the cultured defender, who rarely had to get his shorts dirty by doing something distasteful like tackling someone. He was all about positioning and anticipation and passing. It was his long ball that found Geoff Hurst for England's fourth goal of the World Cup Final. He played for England 108 times. He was awarded the OBE. He won BBC Sports Personality of the Year Award. He was selected by FIFA for the World Team of the Twentieth Century. And he finished his football career as manager of Southend United.

He had managed in Hong Kong and with non-league Oxford City before taking over at Roots Hall in February 1984 with not enough time to save them from relegation to the Fourth Division. And even with enough time the following season, he only just kept them off the bottom. While all that was going on, the club's owner, Anton Johnson, was being investigated by the Serious Fraud Squad – I'm not entirely sure why, but my guess is that it was serious. And fraud.

He was banned from football and in April 1986 the club's new owner, Vic Jobson, argued with Bobby about team selection and got rid of him.

From Wembley Way to Fuck Hall in just two decades. Heartbreaking.

Why You Shouldn't Support Them

- They've got a shrimp on their badge. And Sammy needs to wind his neck in. If he has a neck.
- No one treats Bobby Moore like that.
- That fifth goal was definitely not offside.

STEVENAGE

'When you're Hertfordshire's other team you know you're in trouble. I can't find a quote anywhere.'

ME to Ali when she asked why I'd been staring at the laptop for two hours

'Stevenage FC fans lobbing bottles at your head because your football team had the nerve to defeat them.'

Hertfordshire Mercury, October 2019, reason number 10 in an article asking why the town of Stevenage gets a bad name

Well, I finally found a quote but I'm not sure that Stevenage fans will like it. If your own local newspaper decides to fill some column inches by refuting the 12 reasons people hate your town, then you definitely *are* in trouble. Fair play, though, the *Mercury* sticks up for the town. Reason number four is 'It's full of the overspill from London', to which the response is: 'People who work in London are paid more and they spend that money in Stevenage.' And reason number five is: 'There is nothing for young teenagers to do.' There is, says the *Mercury*: 'There's a trampoline park, mini-golf and a bowling alley.' Yeah, teenagers, stop moaning.

And the answer to the bottle-lobbing complaint? 'Anyone would naturally be upset if their team was beaten at home, but most of us wouldn't lower ourselves to those standards.' Most of us?!

Stevenage fans, you may have already surreptitiously glanced at the bottom of this chapter and noticed that it's quite short. Your fault, I'm afraid. You're just too new. As a town and a club. There has been a Stevenage for a very long time, it's in the Domesday Book and the name means 'stiff oak', presumably to distinguish it from all those limp oaks you see all over the place. But you've only been a town since 1946* and you've only been a football club since 1976.

Seriously, 1976?! There will still be people now, walking their dogs in the King George V playing fields, wondering what happened to that

---

* It was the first designated 'new town'.

nice group of lads playing in the Chiltern Youth League. As we're being honest with each other here, I have to admit that I originally started this chapter by writing Stevenage Borough at the top. I genuinely thought they were still called that, because they were when we sort of began to half notice them worming their way up through non-league football. Actually, they were doing it quite quickly, but my search engine failed to provide me with an example of a fast worm.

I assumed that lazy reporters were simply dropping the Borough bit, but no, they dropped it themselves when they arrived in the Football League in 2010. Although the club nickname is still 'Boro' so the memory lingers.

So that worm I was googling (sorry, search-engining) would have to have been meteoric to reflect the speed with which they went from playing in front of a couple of Labradors and a spaniel in that park to playing in front of 5,000 actual people in Broadhall. OK, 5,000 is a bit of an exaggeration, but I need to get back in their good books before they start reaching for the bottles.

They were formed to replace the bankrupt Stevenage Athletic, and where a lot of clubs grow up and eventually start a youth team, they started as a youth team and went on to become a grown-up team in 1979,† competing in the gloriously named Wallspan Southern Combination. Then Stevenage Borough Council, no doubt flattered by the bold request of this cheeky new club to become Stevenage Borough FC, rented them Broadhall Stadium‡ and on 16 August 1980 they played their first ever game in senior football, in the United Counties Football League in front of 421 people and no dogs.

'Stevenage fans deserve more than that. They're good people. With weapons.'

I could tell you which counties had united to form that league but it would take too long and Stevenage fans deserve more than that. They're good people. With weapons. And they witnessed an almost blemish-free progression through the ranks.

That meteoric rise of theirs could have been even more spectacular. They won the Conference in 1997 but were denied their place in the Football League because their facilities weren't good enough.

To have gone from park football to the Football League in just 21 years would have been extraordinary. Instead their achievement is only amazing.

---

† That's a roundabout way of saying they grew up, ain't it?
‡ 'Stadium' is pushing it a bit as well, but I'm still trying to keep them happy.

Their progress has stalled a bit now, obviously, and here's a bold prediction: they will never, ever, win the Champions League, but they are still a good story.

So the next time you're walking your dog down the local common on a Sunday, take a good look at those lads playing football on the roped-off pitch. You never know where they may end up. And watch out for bottles.

Why You Shouldn't Support Them

- When you're writing a history book, it's really helpful if your club has an actual history.
- I'm still owed money for the last gig I did there.
- Stop throwing bottles, it's dangerous.

STOKE CITY

'Could Lionel Messi do it on a cold rainy night in Stoke?'

The *Daily Mirror* (yes, he could)

'You could do with losing a bit of weight, Kev.'

TONY PULIS (yes, I could)

Unless Steve Parish is right about the age of Crystal Palace, Stoke City are the second oldest professional football club in the world. As you'll know if you've ever sat next to one of their fans at a wedding.

I always ask if, back in 1863, they started their first game by lumping the ball aimlessly towards the mixer,* thus starting a proud tradition they have pretty much kept up ever since. Come to think of it, I've not been invited to many weddings in Stoke recently.

Stoke fans will never answer my innocent question. Instead, they will almost certainly move on to telling you that Stanley Matthews was still playing for them at the age of 50. He was also the only player to be knighted while still playing football. Did you know that? You will have done if you've ever been to a wedding in Stoke.

I've never been quite sure why I'm meant to be impressed that he was still playing at the age of 50. When I was playing Sunday football for Venn Street we played against a team who had a 50-year-old, and he was shit. We kept hearing about this bloke who used to play for Brentford and who couldn't run but still strolled around the midfield like a colossus. What we actually saw was a bandy-legged Norman Wisdom lookalike who reeked of White Horse and went off after 10 minutes for a roll-up. Even I was faster than him and I was once beaten in a race by two blokes carrying a crossbar. By the way, White Horse is liniment, for those who thought this book was taking a turn for the kinky. And if you don't know what liniment is, look it up. We'll be here all day otherwise.

The other thing Stoke fans will inevitably tell you, or rather, shout at you, is that they are the loudest fans in the country. For some reason the

---

* For some reason, advocates of long-ball football prefer 'mixer' to '18-yard box'.

Premier League decided to measure the decibel level at each club and Stoke fans were officially the loudest. Unofficially, as a Palace fan, I say that's bollocks, but who am I to gainsay the notoriously accurate sound-scientists of the Premier League.

And most of that noise is made singing 'Delilah'. Just how Stoke fans adopted Tom Jones's 1968 chart hit as their club song is a mystery, but legend has it they were singing rude songs in a pub before an away game and the landlady asked them to sing something nice instead. The next song on the jukebox* was 'Delilah', and history began. Ironically, it's not a 'nice' song, it's about a murder, but I have to say it does sound impressive when it's sung by thousands of Stoke fans.

Anyway, they may like to think of themselves as the second-oldest club with the loudest fans, but the sad fact is that in recent years Stoke City have become the byword for an 'up and at 'em give them the cold steel put it in the area, test the goalkeeper LUMP IT' style of play. Or as they would call it, 'good old-fashioned English football', roared on by the loudest fans in football as officially measured by the FA.

The good old-fashioned English football reputation was cemented under the stewardship† of manager Tony Pulis, who revelled in the role of pantomime villain as his pesky team of hard men and hoofers continued to beat Fancy Dan teams like Arsenal on those cold, rainy nights in Stoke, and, indeed, on sunny Saturday afternoons in north London.

It wasn't only Pulis who relished the reputation: 6'7" striker Peter Crouch could have been designed for a Pulis team as the ideal recipient for all those long balls. He told me one of the reasons he loved playing for Stoke was *because* of that fearsome reputation: 'The away team would walk on the pitch and you could see the blood drain from their faces.' And Crouchy was not surprised when I told him what Tony Pulis had said to me about my weight. 'You got off lightly, he could be brutal unless he liked you.'

'Are you saying he didn't like me, Peter?'

'No, I'm saying that wasn't brutal. In fact, that sounds positively affectionate for him.'

I was at Stoke to report on the fascinating news that Stoke fans could be noisy and I was interviewing Tony Pulis on the pitch minutes after the end of a game – because, hey, nothing says noisy fans more than an empty stadium! Luckily, Stoke had won because, according to Crouch,

---

* A jukebox was like an iPad that hung on the wall of a pub.
† The word 'stewardship' is only ever used in two contexts: football management and *Game of Thrones*.

if they had lost, Pulis would not only have called me fat, he would have made me get down and do 20 press-ups followed by three laps of the pitch.

To be fair to Tony Pulis, there is more to him than the dour throwback football he is famed for (he actually saved Palace from relegation a couple of seasons later). Actor, presenter and uber-Stoke fan Nick Hancock told me that, 'yes, he did once hide a player's phone and lock him in a hotel room so his agent couldn't contact him on transfer deadline day; but he also walked from Land's End to John O'Groats and cycled from London to Paris to raise money for a local hospice'.

Damn. You'd think that level of commitment to charity work would outweigh one humorous remark about my weight, wouldn't you? You'd be wrong.

My favourite Stoke manager was Tony Waddington. Partly because he looked more like a 1970s' manager than any other, partly because he guided Stoke to their only ever trophy, the League Cup in 1972, but mainly because he had the same name as the Waddington's board games I loved to play with my family. That's true, I'm afraid, and weird because I'm an only child, remember.

Tony Waddington was also very unlucky. He was genuinely building Stoke into a decent side when the roof blew off one of the stands in a storm and they had to sell their best players to buy a new one. I love telling that story. Mind you, it's probably another reason I'm not getting asked to those weddings any more.

Why You Shouldn't Support Them

- I don't care how effective it was, that style of football was bloody painful to watch. Although recently Stoke have tried to play a more passing game, a transition that's even more bloody painful to watch. It's like seeing a werewolf get stuck halfway.
- Stoke fans are nowhere near as loud as Palace fans. Fact.
- I am *not* overweight. I'm underheight, if anything.

SUNDERLAND

'The most surprising result that Wembley has seen in its 50 years of FA Cup finals.'

BRIAN MOORE commentator, addressing his TV audience in 1973

'People from the north-east don't understand business … you have less entrepreneurs up here.'

CHARLIE METHVEN club director in 2019, addressing a meeting of Sunderland fans (he subsequently resigned … another surprising result)

The Black Cats have been anything but lucky lately. As I write this, they languish in the bottom half of the third tier of English football. A succession of owners have treated the fans with indifference at best and contempt at worst.

The Stadium of Light increasingly sounds like it has been named ironically and while the fans still turn out in force, their numbers are dwindling; one of the saddest sights in football is seeing the stadium nearly empty in the closing minutes of yet another defeat. Indeed, Sunderland fans, ever funny in adversity, got in first with the joke: 'Shall we stay to the end to beat the rush?'

Some commentators* may tut at leaving early, but who can blame Sunderland fans for being dispirited? And who among those fans is old enough to remember when they were the 'Team of All Talents', the biggest in the country? Although many will be old enough to remember them taking part in what I consider the greatest Cup final that ever took place. It certainly produced the greatest save ever, not just in a Cup final, *ever*, and one of the greatest managerial responses to the final whistle the game has ever seen.

On 5 May 1973, a Saturday, the glory days were already a fair way behind Sunderland. They were about to finish a distant sixth in the old

---

* BBC Radio 5 Live's Alan Green is the worst culprit. He moans when fans leave early at half-time to join the queue for a pie and a pint and he moans when fans don't stay to the end even if they are 5-0 down. He doesn't moan when his pie is brought to him or when he strolls out of the stadium long after the traffic has departed.

Second Division, but an arduous cup run (three of their games went to a replay) saw their coach dawdling up Wembley Way to face dirty Leeds in the final. Leeds were the holders and were third in the old First Division. Sunderland had beaten Arsenal and Man City in that cup run so they weren't exactly no-hopers, but the most you could say was they were glimmer-of-hopers.

By the way, I say 'dawdling' because it seemed like half of Sunderland were surrounding it. Indeed, there was a remarkable report on local TV showing the streets deserted like a cowboy town waiting for a baddie to get off the train. And every shop is festooned with red and white, and 'closed' signs, obviously.

As we have already discussed, dirty Leeds were hated by most football fans in those days, and by most players; one local paper even suggested that the Sunderland team may have sharpened their studs before the game! And there was particularly bad blood between them because a few years before, their captain Bobby Kerr had his leg broken in an 'accidental' challenge by Norman Hunter.

I can watch highlights of this game over and over again. I'm not nostalgic about the past in general, but all bets are off when it comes to football, and somehow this game seems to represent the high-water mark of my childhood love of football. Dirty Leeds in their ironic snow-white kit, gallant Sunderland in their bold red and white stripes. Not a sponsor's name to be seen, referee in black, scruffy-looking goalkeepers in gardening gloves, crowds surging around like water on a windy pond, all the pre-match build-up on telly and my beloved Brian Moore commentating.

On the Leeds bench, Don Revie (boo), and on Sunderland's Bob Stokoe. I haven't got time for his history, so all you need to know is that, as the game kicked off, he was sat there in red tracksuit bottoms, a beige raincoat and a trilby hat. It was cold and rainy so he also had a blanket over his lap. Even for the decade that fashion forgot, that wasn't a good look.

It was a physical, yet unremarkable game. Except for two things. First, that save: Ian Porterfield had given Sunderland the lead, but halfway through the second half, an equaliser seemed inevitable. Then a diving header from Trevor Cherry was somehow palmed away by Sunderland keeper Jim Montgomery, but it left him prostrate on the ground as the ball fell to Peter Lorimer. He smashed it towards the empty net, but even as Brian Moore shouted 'it's a goal', Montgomery somehow scrambled up and at full stretch tipped it on to the bar.

It is the greatest save ever. Gordon Banks fans may tell you otherwise, but I will accept no argument. And it is a tribute to the power of nostalgia that I seem to have described that save in the manner of a 1970s tabloid newspaper.

Then, second, that celebration. At the final whistle, Stokoe cast the blanket aside and ran in wild jubilation to hug Montgomery. His coat whipped behind him and he held his trilby on with one hand. It's a beautiful image and one you can see captured for posterity in a brilliant statue at the Stadium of Light.

'... legend has it that a German ship went to action-stations, alarmed by the noise of a goal being scored.'

Two bits of trivia for you. Sunderland had a League game against Cardiff on the Monday night so stayed on, so didn't bring the cup home till Tuesday. And, it was the only FA Cup final ever to be played with an orange ball.

So what of those glory days? Well, the Sunderland and District Teachers Association Football Club were founded in 1879 but either the teachers weren't very good or they needed to spend their Saturdays marking essays, because a year later they opened their doors to any player and became simply Sunderland Association Football Club.

They became a powerhouse of English football, mainly by recruiting a lot of Scottish players who played a passing game rather than the dribbling game more usually favoured south of the border.

Known as the 'Team of All Talents', they attracted massive support and moved to Roker Park, which was so raucous, legend has it that a German ship went to action stations, alarmed by the noise of a goal being scored.

They won everything there was to win, and then just sort of stopped winning anything, with the odd glorious exception. What must be really annoying for Sunderland fans is that even though Newcastle United have under-achieved in recent years, they have still stayed comfortably ahead of them on and off the pitch. Theirs is a fierce rivalry, although they seem to me like a married couple who argue all the time but would both turn on you for insulting either of them.

And it's a rivalry that has manifested itself in strange ways. In 1996, sales of Sugar Puffs plummeted on Wearside after Newcastle legend Kevin Keegan appeared in an advert for them. Seriously, sales only properly resumed after the Honey Monster appeared up there in a red and white striped shirt in 2009!

But whatever you do, don't ask either of them why they are called 'Mackems' and 'Geordies', you'll be there all bleedin' night. They are probably both derogatory: 'Mackem' from the claim that Sunderland shipbuilders would make stuff then take it home and 'Geordie' because the people of Newcastle supported King George in the 1715 uprising while the rest of the north-east supported the Jacobites.

So now you don't need to bother looking it up. Instead, use the time you saved to type 'Jim Montgomery save' into your search engine. You're welcome.

Why You Shouldn't Support Them

- An online poll in the *Mirror* in August 2016 revealed that 63 per cent of Sunderland fans hated Palace more than any other team in the Premier League. To be fair, Newcastle were in the Championship at the time.
- Dragging the Honey Monster into a small local dispute.
- My cousin's husband supports them and really rubbed it in the last time they beat us. And he's a magician. So that's two reasons.

SWANSEA CITY

'I think Cardiff has always been perceived to get whatever funding is going.'

ALAN CURTIS who played for both Cardiff and Swansea (brave man)

'So I now believe in the team too. I'll invest in it too!'

OPRAH WINFREY offering to make up the funding shortfall

Oprah was talking after finding out her friend, the actress Mindy Kaling, had shares in the club. The club have invited her to a game but she hasn't been yet, and I think I know why.

I know this sounds odd, considering Palace's most bitter rivals live 50 miles away, and I know it reflects poorly on the average Londoner's knowledge of anywhere that can't be reached with an Oyster card,* but I'm always surprised by how much further on from Cardiff Swansea is.

I mean, they properly hate each other, it is literally all police leave cancelled in South Wales when they play each other, so surely they should be closer to each other than they bloody are! Technically, it's only 42 and a bit miles. Well, not 'technically', actually, but it's a long 42 and a bit miles. Whether by road or rail, it seems to take forever as the scenery changes and everything seems to get a bit more Welsh, which of course it's entitled to. But then suddenly, all is forgiven, as the sea bursts into view and you arrive in Dylan Thomas's 'ugly lovely town'.

All of this is by way of saying that travelling to football in Wales does have an exotic feel to it, and prompts the question of why there are Welsh clubs in the English League in the first place. A question normally asked by Celtic and Rangers in one of their periodic attempts to join them here. I'm not opening that can of worms, but the simplest reason is that until 1992, there was no Welsh league for them to play in, and they declined to join the Cymru Premier when it was set up in that year. Other reasons are available if you fancy an argument.

Swansea has had a football team for a lot longer than Wales has had

---

* Seriously, don't ask me about anywhere that isn't between Borehamwood in the north and Gatwick in the south.

a league. There is some dispute as to how long, because it seems various attempts were made to start a football team in a hotbed of rugby, but the club celebrated their centenary in 2012, so unless their maths is as bad as mine is, let's go for 1912.

Swansea Town† faced Cardiff City in their first ever game. Their goal, in a 1-1 draw, was scored by Billy Ball, who went to become their first player to score a hat-trick and their first to be sent off. The club's official history refers to him as 'Swansea's first hero', but whether that was for the goal, the hat-trick or the sending off, they don't specify.

It says much for a largely success-free century that their club history also records the first season they were ever on *Match of the Day* (1979/80), but that was the Swansea team that my generation will remember. After growing up completely untroubled by footballing events in South Wales, on 29 August 1981 the rest of us suddenly realised that Swansea were somehow in the First Division. Managed by legendary Liverpool striker John Toshack, they were led on to the pitch by legendary Everton striker Bob Latchford, who scored a hat-trick as they slaughtered dirty Leeds 5-1. That season they were never out of the top six, an amazing achievement for a club of their size, whose far-flung location made it difficult to recruit players.

Buoyed by that success and backed by a financially responsible board, they consolidated their place in the top table and have been there ever since ... would be a lovely thing to write once in a while. Sadly, people who ran‡ football clubs in those days were often idiots and by 1985 the club were back in the Third Division and on the verge of receivership. They survived, just, and since then they have been even closer to liquidation; but, aided by the remarkable efforts of their Supporters' Trust, they are in sound financial shape now, even if the whole being a long way away thing can still make it harder to recruit top-class players.

Time was when that was an advantage. They kicked off the 1952 season with a team that included ten Welshmen, eight of whom were from Swansea and six of them were brothers! That's three sets of two, not a litter of six.

They certainly seem to think they are more Welsh than Cardiff, and I have to say that interviewing Max Boyce§ pitch-side before he led the whole ground into singing 'Men of Harlech' was the most Welsh thing I have ever done. It brought tears to my eyes.

† Not a misprint. They became City when the town became a city in 1970.
‡ I say 'ran' because I know the bloke who runs ours and he's very clever.
§ Look him up, kids.

As Cardiff fans may do after reading that last bit. Ah, Cardiff, 42 and a bit miles away but the focus of a bitter mutual hatred. The irony is that, for various reasons, the two sides rarely met in their early years and relations were considered cordial – when Cardiff won the FA Cup in 1927, many buses were laid on for Jacks to support their fellow Welshmen.

Jacks? Swansea City's nickname is the Swans, but unofficially they are the Jacks, a name given to all residents of Swansea (along with others given to them by Cardiff fans), Swansea Jack being a black Labrador who made himself useful by rescuing people who had fallen into the sea, which is a much better trick than fetching sticks.

But things changed somewhere after 1927, who knows when or why, because if the history of a football club is hard enough to piece together, then the history of a rivalry is much worse. The first report of real violence between the two wasn't until 1969. Certainly, Cardiff-born John Toshack having such success didn't help, but whatever the cause, after the infamous 'Battle of Ninian Park' in 1993, away fans were banned from subsequent fixtures for several seasons, the first time that had ever happened.

And there were political reasons too, with the perception that Cardiff received a bigger share of public money than Swansea. And in 1997, following the devolution vote, the new Welsh Assembly (Senedd) was built in Cardiff, despite way more people in Swansea voting for devolution. Still, Swansea got a new swimming pool so that was alright.

Whatever the reason, if you find yourself in Wales, trust me, don't mention it.

Why You Shouldn't Support Them

- Are we there yet? Are we there yet? Are we there yet?
- I have never seen my dad more angry at a football result than when they scored twice in added time to beat us 5-4 in 2016.
- I love club rivalries but even I think they hate Cardiff too much.

SWINDON TOWN

'If the Swindon team could only have more practice shooting at goal, any club in the South of England would have a difficult task to beat them.'

North Wilts Herald, 1887 (quoted at swindon-town-fc.co.uk)

'I saw a sign on a train that said "Do not flush this toilet at a station. Except Swindon."'

ARTHUR SMITH comedian, also around 1887

You have definitely seen Swindon. Even if you haven't actually been to Swindon, you've been *through* it, because just about every train heading westwards will hurtle past its rather impressive station. Legend has it that sometime in the late 1830s, Isambard Kingdom Brunel and his chief engineer Daniel Gooch were searching for somewhere halfway between London and Bristol to build a repair works for trains on their new railway line. Unable to agree as they trundled through Wiltshire on one of the soon to be defunct stagecoaches, Brunel is reputed to have said that he would throw his half-eaten ham sandwich out of the window and build wherever it landed. And it landed in the tiny village of Swindon.

Which proves that railway fans are just as happy to believe bollocks facts as football fans. How far do you reckon you could throw a half-eaten ham sandwich? Even if you stuck it on a javelin, you're chucking it 90 yards tops.

Whatever, trains turned Swindon from a farming hamlet into an industrial town, and men of a certain age will go misty-eyed at the mere mention of GWR, Great Western Railway; or, as Ali's grandad used to call it, 'God's Wonderful Railway', he being one of the misty-eyed men in question – although for a long time I just put that down to age and cataracts.

The last time I went to the County Ground was by car. We were very late for some reason (probably Chirpy) and we jumped out of Roy's car just before kick-off while he tried to find a parking space. Miraculously, he turned up in the ground about a minute later, muttering something about a stroke of luck. Whatever county the ground was named after, it didn't appear to be Wiltshire. It's a low-slung, nondescript affair, although it does have a giant Rolex watch, which is actually quite cool and is apparently the only one in the world.* And the County Ground is apparently the only club in England that was requisitioned to hold prisoners-of-war in 1940. Italian, I presume. It would have been very embarrassing for a German to be captured as he chased us to Dunkirk.

Anyhoo, the giant Rolex counted down the minutes to a Palace defeat and we headed home. Turns out that Roy's 'stroke of luck' was that he had just left the car across someone's drive – and when we bowled up two hours later, 'someone' wasn't very happy about it because he was supposed to have taken his wife shopping in his now trapped vehicle.

Mrs 'someone' wasn't very happy either, especially when we shared our opinion that we'd actually done her old man a favour by getting him out of an afternoon in Sainsbury's. And 'someone' didn't help his own cause when he said he was a Swindon fan and he was glad we'd lost. Even though he lived close to the ground, he wasn't prepared to go to the game even when the shopping option had been removed. This confirmed all my long-held prejudice. Long-held since the first time I got my scarf nicked as a kid by Swindon fans.

Scarf-nicking, by the way, was a strange phenomenon of the 1970s. Kids would wear a club scarf around their wrist and bigger kids who supported the opposition would nick it from you. There was no violence involved, normally the implied threat of it was enough. In the end you just sort of factored it in and wrote 'new scarf' on the end of every shopping list. But I won't hold that against Swindon because I'm a big man and I have many spare scarves.

Also, one of my favourite ever players, Don Rogers, came to us from Swindon. He was a dashing winger with shaggy black hair and a huge black moustache. I met him years later when he had shaggy white hair and a huge white moustache. He was delightful and offered me a discount in the unlikely event I ever visited his sports shop in Swindon (and I really hope we didn't lose him a customer when we parked across that driveway).

He also had a West Country accent, which was lovely but quite distracting when he was telling me about the old days. In the old days, Don scored two goals on one of Swindon's few days of triumph. In 1969, Third Division Swindon beat the mighty Arsenal in the League Cup final.

---

* At a football ground, that is.

It was a bizarre game. Arsenal assumed until around 11 a.m. that the match would be postponed because the pitch was a swamp and six of their players had flu. But the game went on, with both teams wearing their away kit because that was the League's bizarre way of resolving a colour clash. Arsenal fans are still moaning.

Swindon AFC were (probably) started in 1879 and merged with a team called St Marks Young Men's Friendly Society and a cricket club called the Spartans before deciding on Swindon Town in 1883. No one seems to know why. Possibly because they weren't very friendly and people pointed out that real Spartans probably didn't talk like Don Rogers.

Whatever they were called, they became very good very quickly, good enough to be invited to tour South America in 1912, and I would love to have seen the looks on the faces of the posh passengers when a bunch of railway-workers piled on to their ship, laid into the buffet and started trying to rake the moon out of the sea.

I get really irritated when clubs miss the opportunity to officially adopt an unusual nickname and opt instead for the Robins. 'Moonrakers' was their unofficial nickname for a long time, based on the impression that the locals were so dozy they thought the moon's reflection in a pond was actually a cheese. The local spin on it is that a couple of smugglers, surprised by excise men from London, dumped their barrel of brandy into the pond and fooled them by saying they were trying to rake the cheese out of a pond.

It is, however, quite possible that they were looking for a discarded ham sandwich.

Why You Shouldn't Support Them

- I'm still psychologically scarred by the scarf stealing. Not really, but I remember it vividly so I might be. It was outside Selhurst station in 1974.
- Yet another bloody Robins!
- Yeah, we parked across his drive. It was only for two hours. Not even that.

TOTTENHAM
HOTSPUR

'My son will be a Spurs fan whether he likes it or not.'

STEPHEN MANGAN award-winning actor, shortly after his son's birth

'It's been my life, Tottenham Hotspur, and I love the club.'

BILL NICHOLSON legendary double-winning Spurs manager, shortly before his death in 2004

I don't want to make Tottenham fans jealous here but I think I have probably met more Spurs legends than you have. I should probably say 'more jealous', because most Spurs fans live in a permanent and confused state that is part-jealousy at more successful London rivals and part perpetual sense of entitlement, even though they haven't won the League title since those great Bill Nicholson days of 1961.

Their state-of-the-art new stadium will only add to that emotional mindset. There's no point having the best ground in the country if your trophy cabinet is gathering dust in the corner. It is a magnificent stadium, though, apart from one major design fault: it's still in Tottenham. I mean, Arsenal are a north London team, but when you're there it's still recognisably London, albeit an inferior northern version, but Tottenham is so north London I'm amazed the buses are the same colour. You can tell the Palace fans visiting for the first time – they have the same look on their face as Dorothy has when she arrives in Oz. 'Toto, I've a feeling we're not in Kansas any more.'

And speaking of Arsenal: Paul Hawksbee is one half of Hawksbee and Jacobs, talkSport's equivalent of the ravens in the tower of London. He is a massive Spurs fan, and I asked him the same question I asked Alan Davies about Chelsea replacing Arsenal as the main rivals: 'Definitely not. Arsenal are 100% the ones I want to beat the most and dread losing to the most.' So Andy Jacobs being a Chelsea fan doesn't make things awkward? 'No, we just get excessively polite to each other as the game approaches. We are both big believers in karma. Sticking it to your mate in victory is almost certainly setting up crushing defeat.'

'And,' added Andy mischievously, 'he used to work for Chelsea as head of media.' Paul nodded 'I caught myself describing Chelsea as "we" one day. That was troubling.'

Palace were Spurs' first opponents at the new ground,* and only on the day did they seem to realise that an extra 30-odd thousand people trying to get there may have required a slight tinkering with the transport system, just a small adjustment, maybe doubling it in size, something like that. Still, it did mean that by the time we'd negotiated their ticket system, been sniffed by three types of dog – I'm guessing the first two were bombs and drugs, I think the third one may just have been out for the night – and queued for ages at their guaranteed-no-queue bar, we'd missed most of their interminable opening ceremony, which seemed to consist of 'Oh when the Spurs go marching in' sung in many different musical styles. Seriously, if you're going to nick a song, nick a better one than that bloody funeral march.

To their credit, though, even in a stadium of the future, they are a club who proudly display their history, rather than hide it to avoid embarrassing the current team, who are doing their best to add nothing to it.

And what a history it is, although oddly, like Arsenal, they do have a connection with south London, albeit a more tenuous one than actually starting as a south London club. They were formed as Hotspur FC in 1882 ('Hotspur' being the glamorous but feisty rival to Prince Hal in *Henry IV, Part 1*), but added the 'Tottenham' two years later to avoid confusion with another Hotspur FC, which had already been started in Wimbledon.†

They won their first FA Cup in 1901, becoming the first, and only, non-league club to do so. They were League Champions in 1951, playing an attacking brand of football known as push-and-run; and they won the double in 1961 (they have won trophies in years that don't end in a 1, but not many). They were the first team to win a European trophy when they won the Cup Winners' Cup in 1963, and way before that, about 40 years way before, they had become the first team in England to have an animal crest on their badge. It was a cockerel, based on the bronze one gifted to the club by an ex-player in 1909 to commemorate Harry Hotspur's apparent love of cock-fighting.

---

* We already have the proud distinction of being the only club to have lost there twice. You're welcome.

† Also by Shakespeare fans, presumably.

It's a spurious reason, I reckon, and it was an even more spurious cockerel. It would definitely not have passed Colonel Sanders' quality control. It had a tiny breast, huge wings and virtually no legs.

In the years following that double, despite a cup win, Spurs gained a reputation for playing attractive but ultimately fruitless football. It was that later history that gave me two very happy moments. And trust me, Spurs fans, as a passionate student of football history, I was almost as excited to meet these people as you were.

As I said, Spurs are not a team afraid of their history and they invited me and the *Match of the Day* cameras to basically spend a Saturday following 'some legends'. So, I found myself in a room with footballers that would have made the eight-year-old me explode with joy. These really were players stepping straight out of my telly. All it needed was Brian Moore, chuckling as he introduced them. Irish goalkeeper Pat Jennings was there, and he really did have big hands.* Tough-tackling ticking time bomb Steve Perryman was there, and Martin Chivers, the urbane and sophisticated centre-forward who looked more like a James Bond than a footballer. And then, oh bliss it was to be in that dawn alive,† here comes Ralph Coates. Ralph Coates was a flying winger who joined Spurs from Burnley and had a comb-over so sparse it made Bobby Charlton look like a Wookie. As he arrived, Chivers looked up and said, 'Hello Ralph. Don't be afraid, these are called electric lights.'

'Ardiles and Villa showed there were other ways of playing football than aiming the ball somewhere in the direction of a floodlight and hoping for the best.'

Ralph laughed, then looked at me and muttered in his Durham accent, 'He bloody said that first day I arrived in 1971 and he's been saying it ever since. And he still thinks I've never been on an escalator.' I was in Heaven.

In 1978, days after bouncing back from a very rare season in the Second Division, Keith Burkinshaw stunned the world of football by announcing the signing of Ossie Ardiles and Ricky Villa from Argentina, a country still throbbing from winning a pulsating World Cup. Legend has it that Burkinshaw had been there to scout Diego Maradona but couldn't afford him so went for the next best thing.

---

* Brian Moore was obsessed by the size of his hands and always made him pick up a whole football with just one of them to prove it.
† Wordsworth. You knew that.

The English game was very insular at the time, buoyed by the belief that the country who had won the World Cup in 1966 didn't need Johnny Foreigner to play his football for him, and if they did, they'd whistle towards the Scottish border and get one of them down. Ardiles and Villa, then, came as something of a glamorous culture shock, especially after adjusting to our game and showing there were other ways of playing football than aiming the ball somewhere in the direction of a floodlight and hoping for the best. Villa, of course, won Spurs the FA Cup final in 1981 with a dribbled goal straight out of *Roy of the Rovers*.

Imagine my excitement then when, on another visit to White Hart Lane, I found myself sitting in the directors' box with Ardiles and Villa. I happened to mention how impressive the executive facilities were, whereupon Ricky launched into an impassioned lament at how the working classes were being priced out of football while Ossie explained how the game was one of the very few ways out of poverty in Argentina. Half an hour later the three of us were still talking about the history of the game and the economics of working-class football, until Ossie was finally gracious enough to agree to my eager young producer's request to say 'Tottingham' in that funny way he had.

God knows what they would make of the new stadium, a space-age architectural marvel plonked slap bang in the middle of one of the most economically deprived areas in the capital. But their respect for the past hasn't diminished, which means part of me, very deep down, wouldn't begrudge them continuing to make history in a stadium of the future.

Why You Shouldn't Support Them

- Every second TV sports producer seems to be a Spurs fan. Their sense of entitlement is baffling, matched only by their amazement that they haven't signed Neymar, Ronaldo or Messi.
- The new stadium is trying a bit too hard to be liked, if you ask me.
- I genuinely hate that song.

TRANMERE ROVERS

'He belongs in the company of the supremely great like Beethoven, Shakespeare and Rembrandt.'

BILL SHANKLY on Dixie Dean, who started his legendary football career at his home-town club, Tranmere

'I'm quite proud of being the worst left-back in Tranmere's history.'

RAY STUBBS who started his brilliant broadcasting career after being released by his home-town club, Tranmere

It's hard enough being the so-called second club in a city, so being the third must be a nightmare. Especially when my mate Stu, who's from there, insists that Tranmere is a 'separate bloody place, it's not in Liverpool, you ignorant git'.

Seriously, Salford Stan has nothing on Stu. Stan will at least try to patiently explain things to me. Stu just goes straight to angry. Which is always fun. He gets even more annoyed when I say, 'Well, you sound like it's in Liverpool', but he loves me really and he loves Tranmere, although not enough to live there, obviously. And he supports Liverpool. No wonder I get confused.

Wherever it is, and whatever they sound like, they have always been considered Merseyside's third team, although, unfortunately, in terms of resources and success, it is a very distant third. I've not actually been to their ground, Prenton Park. Partly because we haven't often been in the same league (humble brag) but mainly because they used to play their home games on a Friday night to avoid clashing with Liverpool and Everton – you know, the two teams that they are definitely not in the same place as.

Between 1992 and 1997, Pat Nevin played 193 games for Tranmere and scored 30 goals during one of the most successful periods in their history, including three successive seasons when they reached the Division 1 play-offs. He was a proper old-fashioned winger – a joy to watch – and one of the few footballers unafraid to express left-wing views or play Joy Division and The Fall in a DJ set. He also played for Everton, so I asked him whether Tranmere felt like a different place. 'When I was there, no, but older fans certainly spoke as though it was. Liverpool and Everton fans considered them as belonging to them, but obviously not as rivals. They were seen as harmless.'

Uh-oh. I asked Pat if that annoyed Tranmere fans as much as it annoyed Orient fans in London. 'Seriously, Kevin, *nothing* annoyed Tranmere fans. They were the nicest club and the nicest fans you could meet. I was probably the most aggressive person there! They were almost fey.'

Tranmere fans being called 'fey' by Pat Nevin is what I call a compliment.

Prenton Park is in Birkenhead on the Wirral Peninsula, directly across the Mersey from Liverpool. So yes, geographically it's separate, but only in the same way Croydon is separate from London and Palace are very definitely a Croydon team and a London team. Oh, actually, I suppose that could be quite confusing too.

Until about 1750 Tranmere very definitely was separate, being a sort of rural retreat for the wealthy folk of Liverpool, but the Industrial Revolution turned wood into iron and it became famous for shipbuilding. In 1886, the Mersey Rail Tunnel (the first in the world to be built under a tidal estuary, you're welcome) linked the town to their new big brother, and Tranmere Rovers' journey to being the city's third team had begun.

Formed in 1884 as Belmont Football Club, they became Tranmere Rovers in 1885 and, ahem, roved about various grounds before settling at Prenton Park in 1912. They tried out a fair few kits as well, my favourite being a natty orange and maroon number, before settling on blue shirts and white shorts, which they wore until 1962 when a new manager changed it to all white because it was too much like Everton's (although why would that matter if they were from a completely different place?).

Tranmere Rovers have had a history mainly untroubled by trophies and a recent history mainly troubled by finances, but they have seen some famous names. Some, like Ian St John and John Aldridge, at the end of their career, and one at the very beginning. Dixie Dean scored 60 goals (*sixty*!) in one season for Everton, and 323 more in all his other seasons there. He scored 18 goals in 16 games for England. But before all that, he joined his home-town team, Tranmere, as a teenager, and scored 27 goals in 30 games for them. He would be worth a gazillion pounds now, but what amazes me is what he was wearing while he did it. He scored those 60 goals in the 1927/28 season. Google a photo of him at the time and marvel at the fact his football kit probably weighs about as much as Tranmere's back-four does now.

I love performing on stage, but I don't tend to make life more difficult by wearing a suit of armour and a parka, which is pretty much what old-time footballers did. Remember those nipple-scratchy nylon shirts you wore playing Sunday football? They were uncomfortable, but they were light. In Dixie's day, shirts and shorts were made of heavy cotton, or wool, both of which absorb water, perfect for an English winter. Those shorts came down to the knee, where they were met by socks made of wool so thick you could lag your boiler with them. Club badges added to the weight. Some of them were the size of corner flags and were sewn on by hand with stitches the size of wine gums.

And as for the boots! They look like their primary purpose was to hold deep-sea divers down, but players were expected to run, kick and score goals while wearing about three piglets worth of leather on each foot.

Any spare piglets went on the ball. I have held a genuine 1920s' fully inflated leather ball; it was like lifting a toddler, only toddlers don't have inch-thick laces to hold them together. It was often said that really good wingers could cross a ball with the laces on the side away from a centre-forward, but how anyone could do anything that accurate wearing boots that heavy is beyond me.

And the really amazing thing is that those players would have thought they were wearing the very latest cutting-edge sportswear, and probably spent half-time laughing at photos of Victorian players in their knickerbockers and peaked caps.

Tranmere's motto is 'Ubi fides ibi lux et robur': 'Where there is faith there is light and strength'. It takes faith and strength to support a team like Tranmere when virtually everyone you go to school or work with is wearing red and blue. Even I wouldn't begrudge a little light in their lives as well.

Why You Shouldn't Support Them

- Stu can be quite insulting.
- Friday night games are really hard for away fans.
- If they want to be different that much, they really need a different accent.

WALSALL

'Football is the working man's ballet.'

BILL SHANKLY

'They don't know what prawns are at Walsall.'

PETE WATERMAN music producer, giving one of his reasons for being a Walsall fan

Pete was of course referring to Roy Keane's famous outburst about the 'prawn sandwich brigade' of corporate football fans changing the atmosphere of football. I totally agree, but I've never understood why ballet can't also be the working man's ballet. I'm quite partial to it (*The Sleeping Beauty*, since you ask) and I've always been annoyed when people assume that a love of football must mean you have no love of culture, art and beauty. Similarly, I also hate football fans who resolutely believe that going to a theatre is a betrayal of your working-class roots. I'm working-class (I have a chip on both shoulders to prove it) but I'll talk *Cyrano de Bergerac* with you all night.

For all the razzmatazz, football is still a working-class game. A Premier League player may be getting £100,000 a week, but the simple fact that we talk about his *weekly* wage, and not his salary, is an indication of the roots of our game; and the nicknames of many clubs is another; and it's the reason why football fans have a bizarre sort of general knowledge unavailable to the unlucky millions who have no interest in the beautiful game.

I knew as a five-year-old that if I wanted a saddle, hat or biscuit, I would have to go to Walsall, Luton or Reading. True, I didn't know where those places were, but I knew because their football teams were the Saddlers, the Hatters and the Biscuitmen, even if I didn't realise quite how low-rent it was for Reading to have a nickname that dissolved in tea.

Walsall, like Tranmere and Leyton Orient, are another of those teams who are overshadowed by bigger clubs in their area. And, probably worse, patronised by their fans as well, constantly being told that a dad/ brother/cousin/cellmate used to go there as a kid and what a friendly little ground they have, good luck in the FA Cup, etc.

I've lost count of the number of times I've been told that Selhurst Park was the first ground they went to as a kid because it was 'safe', to which my response is always: 'Well, how come you support Man United then?' And if it annoys me that much, how much must it annoy fans of a club who aren't a Premier League behemoth like Palace?

So, the Saddlers. Walsall Town were formed in 1877 and Walsall Swifts were formed in 1879. It didn't take much research to discover why the first club were called 'Town' but no one seems remotely bothered why the second were called 'Swifts'. Obviously, one reason is that 'Town' was taken, and I'm guessing there must have been some sort of bird-related reason because there has nearly always been a swift on Walsall's badge.

'I've always been annoyed when people assume that a love of football must mean you have no love of culture, art and beauty.'

Sorry, I should have said, in 1888 the two clubs merged. Apparently they had been fierce rivals, which perhaps explains why the new club was called Walsall Town Swifts until 1896, when presumably they decided to resolve 12 years of Jets/Sharks-type bickering by changing their name to Walsall FC.

Ironically for my thesis on class, Walsall Town were originally a cricket team and played their first few games wearing their whites as a kit. Luckily, it seems they went downmarket quite quickly and used a dye freely available in the tanning industry to turn the white into maroon.

Most of that leather went on saddles. In 1851 there were 75 firms making saddles in the town. In 1889 the Sweated Trades Commission reported to Parliament that the average wage for a leather-worker was 28 shillings (about £1.40) for a 55-hour week, but that was before the factory owners deducted the cost of lighting and heating the factory.

'… football fans have a bizarre sort of general knowledge unavailable to the unlucky millions who have not interest in the beautiful game.'

My one Walsall football memory, though, doesn't involve Walsall FC. The night before the 1990 FA Cup semi-final at Villa Park, six of us stayed with a mate who lived in Walsall. After a night out we were walking down the main street when we spotted a couple of Palace fans we recognised. We said a wary hello. Wary because they were standing outside a kebab shop and were carrying a large wheelie bin. They said hello back, followed by 'I tell you what, they love a bit of banter up here', then threw the wheelie bin through the kebab shop window and legged it.

We apologised to the shop owners on behalf of all Palace fans, then bought some more lager and went to my mate's house to discuss symbolism in Shakespeare.

Why You Shouldn't Support Them

- Loads of teams have a bird on the badge. At least give the bird a saddle.
- All those Midlands clubs to choose from and their main rivals are Shrewsbury. Lacks ambition.
- Much as I agree with Pete Waterman's sentiments, he was responsible for *The Hitman and Her*, arguably the naffest late-night TV show ever. It ran between 1988 and 1992 and no matter how full of adrenalin I was after a gig, that show would cure it.

WATFORD

'I think Watford FC might have saved my life.'

SIR ELTON JOHN when he was owner of Watford

'I'd rather win 5-4 than 1-0.'

GRAHAM TAYLOR when he was manager of Watford

It's a new phenomenon, but Watford really don't like us. In the 2013 Championship play-offs final at Wembley, a tense game between us was settled by a very late penalty given for a tackle on Wilfried Zaha and scored for Palace by Kevin Phillips, an ex-Watford legend.

Watford's management and players took defeat on the chin and accepted it was a stonewall penalty. Their fans, however, despite the evidence of many slow-motion replays, still insist that Wilf dived, thus proving my point that fans of every other club except Palace are irrational idiots. Our games against them ever since have been played in a very hostile atmosphere. At first, this was quite amusing, and being a physically and morally bigger club than them, we shrugged it off. But just as, eventually, even the most amiable puppy will snap at a teasing toddler, we/I are beginning to dislike them just as much. And it doesn't help that their mascot, Harry the Hornet, is on a one-furry-man mission to annoy us by throwing himself to the ground when Wilf gets the ball and/or 'hilariously' pretending to dive in front of the away end.

Try as I might to suggest that despite petty rivalries, we are all united by football, I'm afraid I have to admit that I only hate some of the other 91 clubs for comedy purposes. One or two or 38 of them I genuinely do not like. And, for the moment, until their fans grow up, Watford is one of them.

It's a shame, really, because for a neutral there is much to admire even if you're not a fan of Elton John.* According to the club's official history, they were formed in 1881 when the Earl of Essex gave permission for

---

* He's not a fan of me either. During a big gala gig at the Old Vic I opened a swing door without looking and knocked him over. I tried to help him, but he was flailing around like an up-ended tortoise and called me something very unpleasant.

some local teenagers to 'kick a ball around in the park'. But, as local teenagers have been kicking something around somewhere local since the first mammoth coughed up a furball, I'm taking that with a pinch of salt, so let's start in 1898 when the West Herts Club absorbed Watford St Marys to become Watford FC.

I don't know where Watford St Mary's is. To be honest, like most football fans, I don't really know where Watford is, and I only got back from there an hour ago.† Actually, it may not be a good idea to write this 10 minutes after getting home from a bad-tempered away game against a team that really doesn't like you, but I've been sat on a train seething for an hour, and I want to channel the energy.‡

It used to infuriate my dad when Watford were included as a London team on *The Big Match*, but I don't think he knew where Watford is either. He just knew it wasn't in London. Yes, it's in Hertfordshire, so they're not local rivals, but you can use your Oyster card to get there, so maybe it is a derby after all. It's all very confusing – perhaps the whole Zaha thing is a blessing because it gives us a reason other than geography to not like them.

It's not the only mystery about them, either. Why have they got a moose on their badge, for a start? Well, actually, it's a hart, which is a reference to Hartfordshire, sorry, Hertfordshire. If it is a hart, it's drawn by someone who has seen a lot of mooses, or meece, or whatever the plural of moose is.

And why are they the Hornets? Well, that one's easier to answer. In 1959, they changed their kit to yellow and black. Before that they played in blue and their

'If it is a hart, it's drawn by someone who has seen a lot of mooses, or meece, or whatever the plural of moose is.'

nickname was … the Blues. Not very clever but that must have been the shortest club nickname decision meeting in history. Of course, if Elton John had a sense of humour,§ he could have sung 'I Guess That's Why They Call it the Hornets'.

And it was under the chairmanship of Elton John and the management of Graham Taylor (see the chapter on Lincoln City for more details) that Watford had the most fun. Between 1976 and 1982, the pair took Watford from the bottom of the Fourth Division to the top of the First. Two years later they reached their first ever FA Cup final, a game only

---

† Nil-nil. Horrible game.
‡ Strictly speaking I was sitting on Gaz's lap for an hour, so he's not happy either.
§ He may have a wonderful sense of humour, but he didn't when I accidentally floored him.

memorable for Elton John's tears. And despite not being a fan of his music, I still get very moved at the genuine emotion of a man watching his beloved football club walk out at Wembley.

They were the tears of a man who was not only supporting his local club but acknowledging that his involvement with them led him away from a potentially destructive lifestyle. It should be hard to dislike a club like that. But I'm giving it a go.

'... and if Watford fans think I'm being illogical and childish, then tough, you started it.'

Taylor left in 1987 and the club were relegated the year after, but in his climb up the table, Watford played a sort of sophisticated direct football that was lambasted by pundits, but which I found quite compelling to watch; and it was played by a team that, unusually for the time (except, I'm proud to say, for Palace), reflected a growing social diversity with black players like Luther Blissett and John Barnes lighting up the pitch, despite the despicable abuse from many Neanderthal fans at away games.

Sadly, the current team seem less concerned with lighting up the pitch than with kicking Wilf Zaha off it; and if Watford fans think I'm being illogical and childish, then tough, you started it.

Why You Shouldn't Support Them

- It couldn't have been more of a penalty if he'd brought Wilf down with a lasso.
- The bar in the away end doesn't open when we play there. Possibly wise, but in the context, childish.
- Most annoying mascot in football. I know he's a Hornet but he really gets into character.

WEST BROMWICH ALBION

'Boing, boing.'

WBA fans

'I love going to West Brom, it's a proper place.'

NEIL WARNOCK manager of many football teams

Yes, Neil, it *is* a proper place, but as a child I was genuinely intrigued by the name West Bromwich Albion because it didn't sound like one. I was a curious* little kid and loved history and mystery, so 'Albion' conjured up images of King Arthur and a land of mist and chivalry; and I was genuinely interested in what the rest of Bromwich must be like and why *they* didn't have a football team too.

Those of you who have been there will know that I was in for a disappointment when I grew up and actually went there. There is some mist, but there is a noticeable absence of chivalry. On the other hand, there is a pub that serves brilliant Indian food and at my age, that is way more important than history and mystery.

Not that West Bromwich Albion are short of either. As a child, I had no idea what a 'throstle' was, let alone a 'baggie', but West Brom seemed to be called both. Turns out that a 'throstle' is a thrush, which was an early reminder for a seven-year-old that not only are there places outside London, but they also have the temerity to make up their own words. Actually, I wasn't entirely sure what a thrush was either, although I later surmised it was a small bird that seemed to have given my cousin an embarrassing itch.

'Baggie', however, remained a mystery, and still does really. Because while everyone happily refers to them as the 'Baggies', no two West Brom

* As in, I was curious about things. Not as in I was strange. Although all kids are, so I probably was.

fans can agree what it means and why they are called it. There seems to be a lot of 'probably' about their early history, but most people agree that there was a team called 'West Bromwich Strollers' in 1879, who had no actual ground and used to carry goalposts around with them, looking for somewhere to play.

I'm not going to disagree with 'most people' but that sounds a bit unlikely, doesn't it? Carrying goalposts around on the off-chance. Still, if Rotherham had a team that played by moonlight, let's go with it.

Then, there was 'probably' an area full of steel foundries known as 'The Albion', which inspired their name change in 1880. And it's definitely 'probably', because the locals seemed to have been too busy carting goalposts around or making steel to write anything down for posterity.

What is definite is that, in 1900, after a few years of having to move to bigger and bigger grounds because of growing support, they finally moved to the Hawthorns, which may or may not have once formed part of the ancient Hawthorn Estate. And, as the hawthorn bush is the favourite nesting ground of the throstle, that became their nickname. I don't know why thrushes like nesting in prickly bushes – I wouldn't put it past somebody in 1900 making that up as well. Nevertheless, an actual thrush did live in a cage above the players' tunnel – and given previous chapters in this book, I'm amazed it didn't end up stuffed after it died.

So, that's 'cleared' that up. What about the 'Baggies'? Well, let's start by getting a cup of tea and a biscuit, because this could take some time. Make that two cups, because after that we still have the whole bleeding 'boing boing' thing to explain.

Right, I'm donning my deerstalker hat for the full Sherlock Holmes detective experience here, so let's examine the evidence.

It could be because in the early years at the Hawthorns there were only two entrances and the gatekeepers had large cloth bags to take the entrance money. At half-time, a policeman would escort the gatekeepers and their bulging bags of coins along the touchline and 'here come the bag-men' became 'here come the baggies'. Hmm. If the club had to move to a bigger ground because of the growing number of fans, why only two gates? Answer me that, Watson.

> 'Most people agree that there was a team called 'West Bromwich Strollers' in 1879, who had no actual ground and used to carry goalposts around with them, looking for somewhere to play. '

Or, in 1904, a match report described a burly defender, Amos Adams: 'His thickness of hips made his baggy pants look even more huge.' So he became known as 'baggy' and so did the rest of the team. Meh. By that logic, Watson, we'd have teams nicknamed the 'Lazies' or the 'Useless Wastes of Space'. What's next?

Well, the club was short of money in 1905 and fans went from pub to pub collecting money in bags. Any information on the type of bag, Watson? Uh-uh. Well, let's not speculate in the absence of facts. And I'm beginning to believe that the 'Absence of Facts' would be a more suitable bloody name. Send in the next candidate.

> 'What about the "Baggies"? Well, let's start by getting a cup of tea and a biscuit, because this could take some time.'

In 1918 they signed a player called 'Magee', only he pronounced it 'Maggie' and that somehow got turned into 'Baggie' and they became known as 'Baggie's team'. Sorry, Watson, I couldn't hear that last one over the sound of a barrel bottom being scraped.

Any other options? Perhaps because of financial reasons they had to replace big strapping professionals with skinny little amateurs and the kit didn't fit properly. That *is* one of the theories?! Watson, have you been drinking?

Any other serious options? Well, many of the fans worked in steel foundries, which were very hot, so they wore loose-fitting, baggy clothes when they turned up for a game after a Saturday morning shift. Well, that at least sounds plausible, although many other teams were built around steelworkers and none of them got called the Baggies.

But Sherlock Day here is going for something similar as the real option. (I'm sure West Brom fans will be delighted that a Palace fan will be deciding. On the other hand, it will also confirm their belief that London thinks it knows everything, so I'm doing them a favour.) In a 1963 newspaper interview, an elderly chap known as a fountain of local folklore explained that the foundry workers of West Bromwich wore thick moleskin trousers as protection, but wore them without belts as that would make them too hot. Sometime in the 1890s, after a morning shift, a group of them walked together to an away game at Aston Villa and because of the whole belt situation, they were taunted by Villa fans outside a pub with 'here come the Baggies of Bromwich', or words to that effect. That rings true, if only because football fans have often turned insults into a badge of pride (the 'Smoggies' of Middlesbrough, for example), so, for the moment, I declare it the winner.

Right, have we got time for 'boing boing'? Not really, but I did promise. Sometime in the eighties or nineties,* West Brom fans started jumping up and down on the terraces in unison, chanting 'boing boing'. There are as many explanations for why as there are for the whole Baggies thing, and West Brom fans are still arguing about it on message boards as we speak.

They are still doing it, although it's much harder in all-seater grounds, and whatever the origins, it is unique and funny. And not knowing why they do it in the first place makes it even better.

One more thing. Ali's parents live in Birmingham. My lovely father-in-law was delighted when he told me a football fact I genuinely didn't know. Apparently, if you travel across Europe, the next ground as high as the Hawthorns is in Siberia.†

Although if he was told that by a West Brom fan, I would take it with a pinch of salt.

Why You Shouldn't Support Them

▪ It's bad enough that West Brom fans believe some of the Baggies stories, but, seriously, 'Strollers'? When I played Sunday football you couldn't get anyone to carry the posts from the changing room, let alone wander round Clapham Common for hours looking for a spare pitch.

▪ 'Boing boing' is funny, but only for about 15 seconds.

▪ On Christmas Day 2004 they were bottom of the Premier League, but rallied to pull off 'the great escape' to avoid relegation on the final day of the season. Palace were relegated instead.

---

* Only 30 years ago, but they still can't agree. Seriously, these people need to start making notes.

† It's true in the way that all football facts are true.

WEST HAM UNITED

'I'm forever blowing bubbles, pretty bubbles in the air.'

West Ham fans' anthem – a surprisingly gentle choice, I've always thought

'The crowds at West Ham haven't been rewarded by results, but they keep turning up because of the good football they see.'

RON GREENWOOD manager, 1961–1974 (not any more they don't, Ron, not any more)

I want to reassure West Ham fans from the start that this chapter will contain no reference to the acquisition of the London Olympic Stadium by your club. Apart from that one, obviously. And I'm not saying that just so I can very cleverly lull you into a false sense of security before ambushing you with a lecture on taxpayers' money. Your club is owned by people whose reputation is based on a lifetime of making shrewd deals, so we can hardly be surprised if they took advantage of the situation to get you that massive stadium at a bargain price.‡

I'd have been delighted if Steve Parish had done the same thing. Well, not delighted, it's a bloody long way away from where I live, but you know what I mean. I do, however, have one complaint to make about your new stadium. It ain't Upton Park, is it? Now, that *was* a stadium. If I was there as an away fan or as a broadcaster, the hairs on the back of my neck would always tingle as you lot belted out 'Bubbles' at the top of your voice. Although it has to be said, there was less actual fear in the tingle when I was there as a broadcaster.

Yes, I know that technically it was the Boleyn Ground, but if Upton Park was good enough for Brian Moore it's good enough for me. Besides, it was called the Boleyn Ground after a grand house nearby that was known as Boleyn's Castle, because Anne Boleyn lived there. Only she didn't, and couldn't have because it didn't exist when that poor soul was Queen of England. As a history buff I insist on historical accuracy at all times, if not necessarily in all the chapters of this book.

---

‡ The cost of converting the Olympic Stadium to multi-use was £323 million. West Ham paid £15 million of it. You paid the rest. They also pay £2.5 million a year rent, which includes policing, pitch maintenance and, of course, corner flags.

Whatever it was called, it was the only ground I ever went to that I actually didn't dislike. In fact, if you took Selhurst Park out of the equation, it would be my favourite ground. Admittedly, the bits *outside* the ground could be a touch hazardous, but inside, it was grand. Intimidating, but grand.

Most West Ham fans still miss it, but there are contrary voices. My old chum, TV sports presenter and uber-cockney-even-though-he's-from Kent, Mark Webster, has been going dahn the 'ammers since he was knee-high to a jellied eel.* He reckons the nostalgia is 'sentimental bollocks' and as soon as West Ham start winning, the fans will stop moaning about the stadium.

His three boys, Jamie, Mark and Luke, are much more emotional/angry about it, though. I went to a cup game at West Ham with them a few days ago (purely for research, Palace weren't playing) and they told me they still yearn for Upton Park and the rituals that went with it. One of them (I can't remember which; we drank a lot of 'research') said: 'The worst thing is, it's like starting again. Grandad went with his dad, dad went with Grandad, we went with Dad. Our kids will never know that world, that legacy, they'll only know this posh bollocks.'

Some of you will be thinking 'they only know a warm, comfortable stadium with good views and decent catering, that's good'. And some of you will understand.

The club has never strayed far from its roots (well, until now; the new stadium is metaphorically so far from its roots it's in a different garden) and Upton Park was full of people I reckon probably hadn't strayed more than a couple of miles from home to get there.

Those roots were the Thames Ironworks, a shipbuilding yard on the Thames, run by Mr Arnold Hills. In 1895, Mr Hills encouraged, or allowed, his men to start a football team as a way of letting off steam, which hopefully amused those men whose job was actually letting off steam. Not long afterwards, Mr Hills paid £2,000 to move the club from the homely little cinder heap they had been playing on to a massive stadium called the Memorial Recreation Ground. It's a familiar story, isn't it? Except they paid for it, not the taxpayer.

Problem was that the new stadium helped get them elected into the Southern League and, to survive there, they needed their players to be professional. This Mr Hills did not like. No one seems to know whether it was because he was horrified by the very idea of professionalism or

---

* Or, as they now call it in Shoreditch, 'cockney sushi'.

whether it meant he would lose half of his best boilermakers and a welder or two if they became full-time footballers, but whatever the reason, he was angry enough to stop bankrolling the team.

They disbanded in June 1900 and reformed in July 1900 as West Ham United. There are those who insist that the club history should only start from that date, but there are also people who insist that Upton Park was the Boleyn Ground *and* that acquiring a new stadium cut-price was a fair deal for all. Last time I mention it, I promise.

Also, fans still call themselves 'Hammers' and 'Irons', so why would you want to deny the heritage that supplied those names? I accept that 'Hammers' may derive from West *Ham*, but the giant hammers on the badge look like working ones to me.

'Hammers' and 'bubbles' has always seemed an odd combination. Sadly, the former make a lot more sense than the latter. The song was first heard in a Broadway musical in 1918, but no one knows why West Ham fans sing it. They may have had a player nicknamed 'Bubbles' because he looked like the boy in an advert for soap. They may have copied it from Swansea fans. It may have been a morale-booster in East End Tube stations during the Blitz. The only truth is: it really works. God knows why, the lyrics are terrible.

Of course, the really big year for West Ham was 1966. That was the year they won the World Cup. Not that they go on about it or anything. In fact, I'd say there was at least one square metre of wall in the Press Room at Upton Park that didn't have a photo of a West Ham player holding the trophy aloft.

Not to mention the giant statue down the road.

Yes, all England's goals were scored by West Ham players, and yes, the captain was a West Ham player, but that coincidence is no reason why, even now, if Mark Webster, his sons or his three-year-old granddaughter are losing an argument, out it comes: 'We won the World Cup for ya.'

Could be a while yet before we see another statue of West Ham players holding a trophy, which is a shame because they have a lot of concrete to fill around that new ground of theirs.

Why You Shouldn't Support Them

- Branding themselves as the London club.
- The new ground. Nothing to do with the finances, I just prefer to be able to see a game without the aid of binoculars.
- Did not win the World Cup in 1966.

WIGAN ATHLETIC

'Wigan to unveil statue of Dave Whelan in honour of his 80th birthday.'

BBC Sport, 2016

'Will it have a plaster-cast on its leg?'

Everyone on Twitter

It almost beggars belief that in the early years of the second decade of the 21st century, Wigan Athletic were an established Premier League team *and* won the FA Cup. Basically, it's the football equivalent of me winning the Nobel Prize for Literature and the heavyweight boxing championship of the world, one of which, let's face it, would be highly unlikely, what with me having no sort of jab whatever. Sadly, football is sometimes no lover of romance. Days after lifting the trophy, Wigan Athletic became the first club ever to win the FA Cup and be relegated in the same year.

In truth, the romance lies in the fact that the place has a flourishing football team at all, because Wigan is not only a rugby town, it's a rugby league town, and that's different. With the possible exception of Gloucester, no rugby union team can match a football team as the focus of local pride. But in places like Hull and Leeds, the rugby league team does exactly that; and in Wigan, it was the sporting success of the Warriors that sustained a town through years of economic decline. In terms of history, support and economics, Wigan Athletic lagged a long way behind, but for a brief spell they were the team that made the headlines that made the town proud. Each season of survival in the top flight was a triumph of bloody-mindedness and half-decent football. It truly deserved celebrating.

'So, why are we talking about bloody pies then?'

'Because their pies are famous all over the world,' said the eager producer.

'Exactly. They're already famous.* We should be telling the world about their triumph of bloody-mindedness and half-decent football.'

'We are. Via pies.'

'And do we have to start on Wigan Pier? It's such a cliché. It had better not be because "pier" has got "pie" in it.'

'Ooh thanks, I hadn't thought of that.'

'Well, can I at least say that there were a number of attempts to start a football team in the town but they were all rebuffed by the lure of rugby league until Athletic finally managed a foothold in 1932. That they only reached the Football League in 1978 and with the help of genial millionaire owner Dave Whelan they went from the bottom of the Fourth Division in 1995 to the middle of the Premier League just a few years later?' I said, after taking a deep breath.

'You can, but we've stopped filming. Why not save it for that book you're always threatening to write?'

I didn't know there was such a thing as a 'genial' millionaire, but Dave Whelan was certainly genial and he was definitely a millionaire.

His playing career had ended when he broke his leg playing for Blackburn in the 1960 Cup final and he'd used the compensation to grow a retail business that became the hugely successful JJB Sports. There was a certain irony to this because after the Second World War, when Wigan were looking for a new kit, the local sports shop, suffering from the same shortages as everyone else, could only offer them a choice of blue, or blue. They went for the blue.

I'd been looking forward to meeting Dave that day because he had a reputation as a man of enormous energy and enthusiasm, a man with a sense of humour as well as huge pride in the football club he had nurtured and which had flourished in the new stadium he'd built, called, natch, the JJB Stadium. He was also immensely proud of the whole pie thing, his club having won various fan-based awards for them. And by now he was also apparently very proud of that broken leg: 'He may mention it once or twice,' said the press officer, wearily.

Before meeting Dave, in a restaurant in the ground called 'Puccino's', the press officer tipped me the wink: 'Dave's dad was a local singer, he was very good and Dave's very proud of him. He sang a bit of opera. That's why it's called Puccino's.'

'But ...'

'Yeah, we know it's spelt wrong but it's his club. Just mention his dad and you'll be fine.'

I did, and I was. Dave Whelan was utterly charming and talked with great passion about many things. He also talked me through that leg break in wince-making detail and, of course, he asked if I had tasted the pies.

By this time I was thoroughly pissed off with the mere mention of the word 'pie', as I said to the producer in the car on the road from Wigan Pier. I explained that pies were freely available in London, the greatest city in the world, and that I knew my way around a pie. Not steak and kidney, of course. Steak's great but kidneys are the work of the devil. As long as a pie was hot, in a shiny metal case and free from kidney, how different could these northern pies be? Stop going on about pies. Let's celebrate the achievements of this football club with the man whose money made that achievement possible, shall we?

Go on, then, let's taste one.

Oh my God, the pies! Those pies were a-ma-zing, darling, it's a 10! I mean, I'd tried balti pie (see chapter on Man United) but these were different gravy, literally. For a start, the filling actually filled it. I was used to pies that had so many gaps in you could use them as a flute. And what fillings! I think they were *actual* meat, with not a kidney in sight. And which evil genius would put cheese and onion in a pie? It was like eating hot melted crisps in puff pastry, and it turns out I'd always wanted to eat hot melted crisps in puff pastry.

Thankfully, you can now get them in London – well, pale imitations of them anyway, but they taste just enough right to remind me of a great day in Wigan.

I know that, even now, I still haven't celebrated their achievements enough. At the time of writing they are in the Championship, which is remarkable enough for a club the size of theirs. But there are many success stories in football, and sometimes a pie is as good as an FA Cup. Wigan have got both. Now, that *is* an achievement.

Why You Shouldn't Support Them

- The minced beef pie was arguably a little too peppery.
- Spelling mistakes really bother me.
- Not long after I met him, Dave Whelan made some unpleasant comments about Chinese and Jewish people. I doubt they were meant to be malicious and, yes, he is a man of his generation, but he was quite rightly given a six-week ban from football and fined heavily. Although they concluded that 'he is not a racist'.

WOLVERHAMPTON WANDERERS

'Oh, Stevie Bull's a tatter, he wears the England cap, he plays for Wolverhampton and he is a lovely chap.'

Fans' song, to the tune of 'My Old Man's a Dustman'

'Out of darkness, cometh light.'

Motto of the City of Wolverhampton

I don't want to alarm my younger readers, but imagine a world without apps. Imagine sitting on a train with your mates going to an away game trying to decide which pub you'll be welcome in when you get there, *without* flicking through a multitude of apps giving you a multitude of options, from the best curry in Burnley to the cheapest cabs in Newcastle and the friendliest football pubs in Watford. (If you're interested: Burnley fansites tend to go for Usha or Aroma; every cab in Newcastle is cheap – most of my journeys there have ended with one of us saying 'two quid, are you sure?'; and Oddfellows, Fearnley St, near the ground – very friendly, for Watford.)

But in the old days (I wonder when the old days stopped?) on the way to Molineux, we'd be sitting on a train trying to remember directions that someone had given you in a pub in Croydon the night before to a pub in Wolverhampton that definitely used to allow away fans but now he comes to think of it, may actually have been in Leicester.

Then imagine getting off the train at Wolverhampton, after four cans each and needing to find a pub. With a toilet. Because *not* finding a pub isn't an option. Then, wonder of wonders, it turns out that copper you asked at the train station wasn't lying, because lo and behold, there it is, the pub he told you about, and, yes, there is a sign saying 'away fans welcome'.

So, in you go. Then out again as the bouncers tell you to hide your scarves and cover up your shirts.

'It says "away fans welcome".'

'Not that welcome, mate.'

And then, of course, the traditional dance of the away fan trying to get served in a pub full of locals. There is an unwritten law, that any Londoner having waited more than half a minute at a bar without being asked what he wants will inevitably begin waving a £10 note in the belief that this will so impress the natives that a magical gap will open up, and we will not only be asked what we want, we'll be asked to stay and be kings. As it happens, it did work in Wolverhampton, the sight of a £10 note weaving a sort of magic on the bedazzled bar staff.

It *was* quite friendly in that pub, actually. Unfortunately, between the pub and the ground was an underpass flanked by locals of a less friendly type, but this is not a Danny Dyer book so let's not dwell on it.

Incidentally, away fans are quite welcome in my local pub, if only because none of them will ever be able to find it. But if you do manage to get there, I will be served before you are, partly because I've been drinking in there for decades, partly because I mention it at every opportunity I get. That's the Pawsons Arms, Pawsons Road, Thornton Heath. Hi Bev, hi Graham.

The next time I went to the famous old ground of Molineux was to film for *Match of the Day 2* and be given a tour of the place by Wolves legend Steve Bull. Every club has legendary players (Wolves have many), but I don't think I've witnessed anything quite like the reaction Steve Bull gets at Wolves, and I've walked into Newcastle following Alan Shearer.

They love 'Bully' with a passion. He played for them across 13 years in every division of the Football League, scoring 306 goals, including 18 hat-tricks. He is one of the few players to win an England cap from outside the top division. And he is from just down the road in Tipton.

Only one problem: I had trouble with his strong Black Country accent and he had trouble with my perfectly normal south London one, so we spent a lot of the afternoon nodding and smiling at each other, hoping that was the right reaction.

Nice bloke though. And for any football fan with a love of history, Molineux is a wonderful place to be. They once had a reputation that resonated round the world and in the 1950s were arguably as big a club as Man United and Liverpool are now; and that was way before apps, remember?

I really hope this is true, because if it is, it's probably my favourite origin story of all clubs (apart from the one about the glaziers, obviously). Apparently, the club first started in 1877 when the headmaster of

St Luke's school gave a football as a prize to a group of pupils for having a very good term. Two years later, the boys merged their team with a local sports club called Blakenheath Wanderers and the Wolves were born. If the boys had been *that* clever I reckon they should have nicknamed the club Romulus and Remus, but I suppose there was only ever going to be one nickname for a team called Wolverhampton.

They played in their school colours of red and white for a while, but adopted the unique old gold kit in 1891 and have played in variations on a theme ever since. And if you're wondering why they adopted it, check out the quote at the start of this chapter. The black represents the darkness and the gold is the light, according to the official club website.

Founder members of the Football League, they have won 11 League titles, four FA Cups and two League Cups. But in the 1950s they became 'Champions of the World'. In the early years of that decade, with Europe still struggling to return to some sense of normality, there was a series of high-profile friendlies between top clubs across the continent. Borussia Dortmund came to Molineux and lost. Real Madrid came to Molineux and lost. Then, most famously of all, just before Christmas in 1954, Honved came to Molineux from Hungary, went two-nil up at half-time … and lost. 'Most famously' because that Honved team contained many of the Hungarian national side that had just beaten England over two games, home and away, by an aggregate of 13 goals to 4. A result that almost shook the FA out of its arrogant and insular belief that we still led the world in football.

Gabriel Hanot, editor of *L'Equipe*, the French football journal, was delighted. He had long advocated a Europe-wide, floodlit tournament to help heal the scars of war: 'Before we declare that Wolverhampton Wanderers are invincible, let them go to Moscow and Budapest.' The European Cup was born. Wolves were never to win it, and began to suffer near-terminal decline shortly after, but they are back in the big time now, and – who knows? – they may yet win the Champions League. Steve Bull and Gabriel Hanot would be very proud men.

Why You Shouldn't Support Them

- They took full tactical advantage in that bloody underpass.
- I really, really want to be in Europe. Not fair.
- How did Steve Bull get in the England team?

WYCOMBE WANDERERS

'If you live in Wycombe, support fucking Wycombe, not Liverpool. It does my nut in, Kev.'

DANNY DYER English actor, during impromptu interview

'Kev, Wycombe are the best and I'm happy to tell the world.'

HENNING WEHN German comedian, during impromptu interview

I hate being called Kev. Kevin, I like as a name. It comes from the Irish for 'handsome from birth' and St Kevin seemed like a decent lad. Kev, eeurgh. It just sounds harsh, but as most people apparently can't be arsed to add the last syllable, I grin and bear it. Didn't help that one* of my nicknames at school was 'Middle Kev' because there was a short Kev and a tall Kev. And me.

For years I was convinced Wycombe's nickname was the Choirboys – an easy mistake to make when it's the Chairboys, and you'd only occasionally seen the name written down in small newsprint. I just assumed there was some kind of famous church there or their fans were famous for singing. And it made as much sense as Chairboys did when I eventually realised my mistake – chairs are not the first thing you think of when Wycombe is mentioned, are they? The first thing I think of is what a weird town it is. It feels like an even more sinister version of Milton Keynes.

Palace have never played them, but I've done a few gigs there and it always seemed to be the same 50 people who turned up for all of them. Trust me, that's rather an unsettling feeling.

And why Chair*boys*, not Chair*men*? Or just the Chairs? Or if you're going full furniture, the Chippendales. Might help get more fans if they call themselves that.

---

* The other was Doris, obviously.

Actually, they don't need more fans. As a non-league club they had a *huge* away following, nearly always outnumbering the home fans at every game they played. And they still get healthy support now, considering where they are in the table, and considering the amount of glory-hunters there are who get right up Danny Dyer's hooter by choosing a team based purely on success.

I imagine some people would pick Wycombe just because of their shirts, which, knowing my kit fetish, you'd think I would love. I don't. I love Bristol Rovers' blue and white quarters kit but for some reason Wycombe's dark blue/light blue quarters really annoy me. Don't know why. Trying too hard maybe. Or it's a subliminal reminder to the chip on my shoulder that the country is still run by two universities.

Henning Wehn is a very funny and occasionally jaw-droppingly inappropriate comedian. He is also obsessed with football. Conversations with him can be tricky because (a) he was a football journalist back home, and (b) he's German so he wins every football argument every time, except in the Fulham chapter, of course.† When he first came to this country he worked for Wycombe Wanderers in their commercial department and became a proper fan:

> I vividly remember getting on one of the official supporters' coaches at Adam's Park for my first away game. I was carrying my lunchbox, which consisted of four pints of Stella, only to be told that alcohol was not allowed on board. No one had told me that. Getting hammered is the whole point of football. How can you watch football stone-cold sober?!

I asked Henning a complicated question about club ownership and fan-involvement models in Germany compared to here:

> Kev, the only difference between our football and yours is that in Germany we are allowed to watch it hammered, because we're grown-ups.

He'll be pleased to know, then, that Wycombe Wanderers were founded in a pub called the Steam Engine in High Wycombe (Buckinghamshire) in 1887. Any team founded in a pub is fine by me, and I suspect by most people reading this as well, because let's face it, the only football most of us will have ever played will be for a team founded in a pub.

They are also one of those rare teams who resisted the temptation to turn professional for a long time. A very long time. Indeed, they didn't

---

† If you do ever talk to him about football, don't mention the Dutch. You'll be there all night, and not in a good way.

even have a proper manager until 1968, with the team being picked by committee. Again, something we have in common. All the Sunday league teams I played for picked the team by committee, because there was no manager, or, in one case, because there *was*. Sorry, Roy, but it's time you knew. We let you be manager because you had the biggest washing machine.

Of course, professionalism had to come eventually and a club that was probably always too big for the amateur leagues they played in eventually made it to the Football League in 1994. They have had some very successful managers (and Tony Adams, who was successful, but not as a manager). Martin O'Neill took them into the League, Lawrie Sanchez took them on a brilliant Cup run all the way to the semi-final in 2001, and Gareth Ainsworth is Buckinghamshire's leading Liam Neeson lookalike.

So, Chairboys? Well, the town is very proud of their furniture-making reputation, and they did specialise in chairs. In the 17th century Wycombe was surrounded by forest and what do you do with all that spare wood you're not chucking on the fire? Build ships obviously, or chairs.

And, it turns out, the subliminal instinct of the chip on my shoulder may have been right all along. Apprentices and beer-drinkers they may have been, but those lads in the Steam Engine were clearly aspirational because the kit was, indeed, chosen to represent the universities of Oxford and Cambridge.

The nuances of English elitism may have baffled Henning when he first arrived (he's caught up now, obviously) but I'm glad that a German football fan likes Wycombe so much; and, who knows, maybe that surprisingly large fan base will have a European trip of their own one day, and attract glory-hunting fans of their own. That really would annoy Danny Dyer.

Why You Shouldn't Support Them

■ The whole town genuinely unsettles me. Even when you pass it on a train, it just sits there looking like it knows something you don't.
■ It annoys me that a Wycombe fan is right when he says a lot of English fans can't hold their drink. Or words to that effect.
■ Lawrie Sanchez recently took exception to me calling him 'taciturn'. He emailed my podcast to tell me.

ABSENT FRIENDS

'Doesn't matter what league they are in. What you're shouting at is your youth, your family, your soul.'

CHARLIE BAKER comedian, talkSPORT presenter and Torquay United fan

'The action of a sociopathic asset stripper.'

KIERAN MAGUIRE lecturer on football finance at Liverpool University, on Steve Dale, owner of Bury FC

When I was a kid, if a team fell out of the 92 it was a major event. The two clubs who finished bottom of the Fourth Division had to apply to be re-elected for the start of the following season, and the top clubs in the regional leagues below stood for election against them.

Football being an industry that is conservative by nature, the other 90 clubs invariably voted for the status quo, so when Workington and then Southport were replaced in 1977 and 1978 by Wimbledon and Wigan Athletic respectively, it was a huge shock. I couldn't imagine what that must have felt like for the Workington and Southport fans, but mentally braced myself for when it happened to Palace, convinced even at a young age that if a bad thing could happen to anyone, it was going to happen to us eventually.*

Nowadays, of course, there is automatic promotion and relegation between League Two and the National League, so clubs are up and down all the time, although bouncing straight back is becoming increasingly difficult. To fill the 92nd chapter of this book I want to tell you about a few clubs who were always in the League when I was growing up.

Torquay United

Torquay had palm trees and Agatha Christie. It was known as the English Riviera, which didn't mean much to me, because even as a five-year-old I

---

* It already had. In 1949 and 1956 we successfully applied for re-election to the Third Division South. Being young, that news had been kept from me, but I would probably have been delighted that we'd won something.

had a vague grasp of what a 'palm tree' and an 'Agatha Christie' was, but no idea of where the other Riviera might be.

It just seemed to be an unlikely place to have a football team, especially one called United, which I associated with big teams like Manchester and dirty Leeds.

Torquay Town and Babbacombe United merged in 1921 to become Torquay United, and almost immediately applied to join the Football League. It was a bold move, which failed initially, but in 1927 they tried again and successfully took the place of Aberdare Athletic. However, Torquay either felt guilty about taking another's place or were scared by their own audacity, because everything else since could only be described as modest, properly modest, covering-the-piano-legs-and-sleeping-in-separate-beds modest.

They also had two weird chevrons on their chest, which I later discovered were meant to represent seagulls. I thought that was fair enough because seagulls are hard to draw, but with hindsight it may be that, being modest, they just didn't want to draw attention to the fact that they had a raucous toddler-terrifying bastard of a bird on their shirt.

Notts County

To be honest, I hadn't even registered that Notts County had dropped out of the League. They were the oldest Football League club* in the world, so it just didn't occur to me that they couldn't still be there. Plus, to my shame, seven consecutive seasons in the Premier League has clearly turned me into one of those Fancy Dan, big-time Charlies who can't be arsed to look down at what's happening elsewhere.

They are a club with such history and tradition: the club that gave Juventus their kit, and inspired many others to adopt the famous black and white stripes, but, oddly, not much in the way of actual success has come their way. Being the oldest club in the League was their success and hopefully they will reclaim their title shortly.

And, unlike just about every other club in this book, much of their history and tradition was not working-class. Indeed, Nottingham legend has it that after a few games against Forest, the County committee refused to play them again because of their 'humble and artisan' origins.

---

* There are older clubs, as discussed in the Sheffield United chapter for example, but they have never been in the Football League.

Chesterfield

Chesterfield were once the victims of a shamefully poor refereeing decision, one that robbed them of a place at Wembley. David Elleray was Head of Geography at the very exclusive public school, Harrow. Except on the days when he was a referee. In the FA Cup semi-final of 1997, Third Division Chesterfield scored a goal that should have given them a 3-1 lead against First Division Middlesbrough with just minutes to go. Even though everyone watching in the stadium and on TV saw the ball cross the line and roll towards the net, Elleray decided it had not gone in. Boro equalised, and the Crooked Spireites lost the replay.

Elleray has since apologised, but Burnley manager Sean Dyche, who was Chesterfield captain that day, has never forgiven the ref and I don't blame him. I interviewed Elleray for a TV show I hosted and he was a pompous arse who had the temerity to suggest that his experience of public school football gave him more insight into the game than my actual attendance at hundreds of matches.

I would love to see Chesterfield back in the League because of that injustice. And also because it will give me a chance to properly have a go at them for being so proud of a wonky church.

Wrexham

There is currently no team from North Wales in the English Football League. For years, Wrexham clung on valiantly while most of the local football fans crossed the border to support Liverpool and Everton instead (passing Chester City on the way, another club lost to the League).

Ali was brought up in Llandudno, and the first time she took me there I was amazed by the number of red and blue shirts I saw, and even that wonderful North Wales accent seems to have acquired a slight Scouse note to it, which, if anything, renders it even more poetic.

On 10 October 1981, Palace had gone from the top of the First Division to near the bottom of the Second Division, in just two years. We were on our fourth manager in 11 months. And we were 1-0 down at home to Rotherham in front of a meagre crowd of pissed-off fans, including, of course, me and the boys. One of us jokingly said that if we turned this game around we would all go to Wrexham next week. We won 3-1, and, boys being boys, we bloody well had to go to Wrexham next week. It took forever to get there on that clapped-out locked-up train I told you about, the ground was falling down, and it poured with rain. But we won 1-0, and Steve Lovell, the scorer, fell into our arms at the end, so it was worth it. And, the 4,000 or so Wrexham fans were very generous in defeat, even if most of them pointed out how long it would take us to get home. Given the size of the crowd that day, and the state of the stadium, it came as no surprise when, after one financial crisis too many, Wrexham fell out of the League.

They were formed in 1864, which means there was football in North Wales long before they kicked off in the south, and they have won the Welsh Cup more times than any other team. If Welsh teams are allowed to compete in the English League, it would be nice to see the most Welsh of them all back there someday.

Dagenham and Redbridge

The Big Match had disappeared from our screens long before Dagenham and Redbridge took their unlikely place in the League in 2007, which is a shame because Brian Moore* would have been delighted to welcome another London club to the fold. Leyton Orient fans were even more pleased than Brian would have been – finally they had someone to patronise as well.

Around the outer rim of London there are a huge number of non-league clubs and most of us keep an eye out for our local ones: many Palace fans will have been to Tooting and Mitcham or Carshalton Athletic or Sutton United at some stage, normally around about the fourth round of the FA Cup when we've already been knocked out.

But sometimes, once illustrious amateur teams simply can't carry on in the face of professional neighbours. Thus, in north-east London in 1979, Leytonstone, Ilford and Walthamstow Avenue merged to become Redbridge Forest, who in turn merged with Dagenham FC in 1992 to become, as they call themselves, Dag and Red. And for a kit they chose stripes of blue and red, which immediately sent them up in my estimation.

Remarkably for a team whose record attendance is just short of 6,000, within two decades they had climbed out of the middle ranks of non-league football and reached the dizzy heights of League One, playing their first game away at Sheffield Wednesday and getting their first win of the season a fortnight later when they beat, oh yes, Leyton Orient.

---

* Has a man ever had such contrasting idols as Brian Moore and George Best?

They couldn't sustain League status but they are doing alright in the National League and sustaining 2,000 or so fans in the far north-east of London who refuse to have their heads turned by West Ham, Spurs or Orient.

York City

Mention the name of York and many people will say 'ah yes, the Minster'. Some people will say 'ah yes, the Vikings'. And a few people, like me, will say 'ah yes, the kit'.

I love the magnificent Rose Window in the Minster and I'm fascinated by the Viking history, but the first thing I think of when I hear York mentioned is a maroon shirt with a large white Y on the front. Those without poetry in their soul called it the Y-front,† but for me it was a thing of beauty – a combination of a lovely, different colour with the first letter of their name proudly emblazoned across the whole thing. It was worn for four years in the seventies and coincided with one of their very few spells of success. There is, of course, no scientific link between the success of a football club and the shirt they are wearing, but I think there is, so take that, science.

And York had history when it came to kits. In the mid-30s, as a tribute to the tradition of confectionery-making in the city, they wore chocolate and cream stripes. That could only be more cool if it had buttons made of Smarties and a Curly-Wurly collar.

Sadly, not everyone is so mindful of heritage. In 2002, the club was saved from bankruptcy by John Batchelor, the owner of a motor-racing team. He changed the club crest to a shield, which was half chequered flag and half maroon, superimposed with the letters SC. The flag bit was bad enough, but the SC stood for Soccer Club. York City Football Club, who are nicknamed the Minster Men after one of the oldest churches in England, was now York City Soccer Club in a vain attempt to attract US investment. After a year of unfulfilled promises, Batchelor left the club and it was taken over by a Supporters Trust, who, being actual supporters, immediately dropped the name and the crest.

They are now a couple of levels below League Two, but are still part-owned by supporters and looking forward to a move to a brand-new community stadium. All they need now to bring back the glory days is a maroon shirt with a great big Y on it.

---

† Young people will probably need telling that 'Y-fronts' were the ubiquitous white underpants worn by most men for decades. Although they were never white for more than a day, obviously.

Yeovil Town

Professional football has very strict rules about how long and wide a pitch should be, but no one ever thought to mention how flat it should be. That was handy for Yeovil Town, because for many years their USP was a slope. Despite being arguably the most famous giant-killers in FA Cup history, Yeovil Town's pitch was probably more famous than their team. Everyone goes on about the slope at Lord's, but you can barely notice it even when you're there. In yet another example of football being way better than cricket, the slope at Yeovil's ground, The Huish, was so pronounced that you went to adjust your TV set before realising it was meant to be there. It looked like you needed crampons just to walk up it, so God knows what it was like to play on.

Basically, one touchline was eight feet lower than the other. That's Peter Crouch with a baby on his head. It's possible that the pitch gave them an advantage when it came to all those giant-killings as a non-league team. One source reckons they beat 20 League teams before they became one themselves in 2003.

The first was against, of course, Crystal Palace in 1934, but the biggest came in 1949 when they beat First Division giants Sunderland, Len Shackleton and all, in what the FA's own website reckons is still the greatest FA Cup shock of all time. It was a game played in freezing fog and it went into extra time because post-war fuel and travel restrictions meant replays were banned. Yeovil won 2-1 and were rewarded with a trip to Maine Road to play Man United in the next round. Yes, Maine Road: Old Trafford was still too badly bomb-damaged. Yeovil's goalkeeper was badly hurt in the opening minutes, but there were no substitutes in those days and he was more or less a spectator as United scored 8 without reply.

Yeovil's nickname is the Glovers (after the town's main industry) but it could have been much worse. In the early years of the 20th century there were two teams in the town: Yeovil and Petters United. They amalgamated in 1914 to become Yeovil and Petters United, which sounds like a trade union from a 'Carry On' film, before finally dropping the Petters in 1923. Probably for the best, I reckon.

They have a new ground now, with a nice, flat, boring pitch; and I suppose if there is any consolation to no longer being in the League, it does give them a lot more giants to kill.

Stockport County

At least two or three times while writing this book I wondered why I hadn't got on to the Stockport chapter yet. Of all the clubs that are not currently in the 92, they seem to be the most surprising, for some reason. I don't know why, but it may be because two of Palace's best results were against them.

In 1979 we beat them 7-0 in the League Cup. I walked away from Selhurst Park that night secure in the knowledge that at the age of 18 I had a whole lifetime of 7-0 wins ahead of me. Hah!

Then on 6 May 2001, just about recovering from a financial crisis that nearly saw us go out of business, Palace travelled to Stockport on the last day of the season needing a win to avoid relegation from the Championship following a disastrous run of results that had seen us plummet from mid-table security to the edge of disaster. Going down would undoubtedly have us flirting with bankruptcy yet again. Three minutes from time, unseen by the referee, Dougie Freedman controlled the ball with his hand before swerving his way past two defenders and scoring the winner. It was seen by at least 8,000 travelling Palace fans. I wasn't one of them.

Just before that disastrous run of results began, Ali announced that to help me recover from the stress of working seven days a week for three months as script editor on a struggling topical TV show, she had booked a trip to Naples so I could finally fulfil my ambition to visit Pompeii. 'Sweetheart,' I said, 'that's brilliant, but it's the last weekend of the season.'

After a hard stare that Paddington Bear would have been proud of, she said she was aware of that, but we were in mid-table with 10 games to go; would I rather be in Stockport or Naples? So it was that my one and only trip to Pompeii passed in a blur as I spent the entire afternoon desperately shinning up ancient Roman columns trying to get a signal on my phone while Ali pretended to be married to somebody else.

It was two hours after the final whistle when (and this is true) a bloke in a Palace shirt came tearing down the train corridor towards me yelling and laughing, then ran straight past me. I went after him, hoping that he'd heard some really good news, and hadn't just had a baby or something. He had. I will go back to Pompeii one day, but not during the football season.

Stockport were formed as Heaton Norris Rovers in 1893, changing their name when the town became an independent county borough in

1890. They lost their League position in 2011 after 107 years. I don't know why their particular absence saddens me so much, maybe it's just because they were always there – they certainly did nothing much to distinguish themselves, which was always going to be difficult anyway as the influence of United and City grew stronger and stronger in the area.

Like Luton, they were also the Hatters; but unlike Stockport County, Luton never had to ask permission from the Football League to change their kit three-quarters of the way through a season.

In 1979, inspired by the dashing football of the Argentina national team, Stockport County changed their kit to light blue and white stripes with black shorts, and very nice it was too. Unfortunately, it was still their kit when the Falklands War broke out in April 1982 and they hurriedly asked for permission to change it. Amazingly, the League said no, but the club quite wisely ignored the decision and turned out for the last few games of the season in plain white shirts.

Aldershot FC

On 25 March 1992, Aldershot FC became the first Football League team to fold during a season since Accrington Stanley way back in 1962 and the beginning of this book. Sadly, they weren't the last, as we shall see in a moment.

Football has been played in Aldershot since the 1850s but mainly by soldiers, as a tiny Hampshire village became home to the biggest British Army camp in the world.

It wasn't until late in 1926 when the Town Clerk decided that the civilians should muscle in on the action and formed Aldershot FC, who did indeed muscle in on the action because the first thing they did was recruit a few local Army physical training instructors as players. And the military connection continued with the kit. The Royal Engineers, who played in the very first FA Cup final, had been based in the town and they played in red and blue, as copied by the new club.

In truth, not much happened between then and 1992 when the fightback from the fans began with phoenix club Aldershot Town. They began life in Isthmian League Division Three, which, trust me, is properly three-men-and-a-dog territory. For a glorious few years they enjoyed the unusual feeling of being Big Time Charlies, regularly taking 1,000 away fans to roped-off village pitch 'stadiums' and getting home crowds of 3,000 plus. In truth, as many AFC Wimbledon fans will attest, they were probably the happiest days because the eventual return to League status brought with it many new financial problems, which brought them dangerously close to the phoenix needing to hatch again.

Currently they are in the fifth tier of English football, but to a couple of thousand people in north-east Hampshire, they are the centre of the universe.

Bury

If Chesterfield were the victims of a shameful refereeing decision, Bury were the victims of a shameless chancer and self-proclaimed asset stripper – Steve Dale – who bought the club for £1 and then proceeded to do exactly what asset strippers do: he began to strip the club of their assets into two holding companies he set up days after coughing up that quid in 2018.

Player and staff wages went unpaid, and he started a tedious game of cat and mouse with HMRC while introducing ludicrous schemes like mortgaging individual spaces in the club car park.

After it became clear that he wasn't going to stop and didn't care if the club folded, a number of potential buyers appeared, only to be deterred by his refusal to reveal the extent and nature of the club debts. With the EFL (to whom Dale was considered a 'fit and proper owner') shamefully standing by and refusing to intervene, and with fixtures going unfulfilled, the club were liquidated. Dale, I have to stress, did nothing illegal, but only because breaking the hearts of football fans is not a crime.

Being relegated from the League is one thing. Chances are you'll be back. Bury FC won't. But Bury Something will, because you can physically break a football club, but the fans will find a way to restore its soul.

Not goodbye, but *au revoir*

I could have included many, many more clubs in this chapter. Names that sounded exotic and remote when I was a football-obsessed child: Workington, Southport, Barrow, Chester City, Hereford, Darlington, Boston United and more. They may be out of sight, but they are not out of mind. They all still exist in one form or another, and all are still the most important football team in the world for those that stick with them through thick and thin.

POST-MATCH ANALYSIS

As I was writing this book, everything came to a shuddering halt, and suddenly, Bill Shankly's tongue-in-cheek comment about football being more important than life or death never felt more inappropriate. But another quote became even more pertinent. It was new to me, and there is some dispute over who said it originally (probably Arrigo Sacchi), but when I first heard it during a podcast in the first week of lockdown, it was as though a light bulb had pinged on the top of my head, and I was given a way to crystallise everything I think about our wonderful game into just a few words: 'football is the most important of the unimportant things'.

God, I missed it. Although not so much the game itself. In fact, I quite enjoyed the respite from result-based anxiety. What I really missed was what Ali describes as the 'peripheral bollocks'. The genuine joy of entering a pub you have been in a thousand times before and seeing people you saw just a week ago, even that bloke whose name you can't quite remember who just has to tell me that I'll never be as funny as real comedians like Jim Davidson.

So thank god it's back now, sort of. I missed the transfer rumours, conspiracy theories and alarming injury news brought to you by a bloke whose cousin sometimes takes Martin Kelly to training. At the moment *we* are not allowed back yet so I still miss the optimistic walk to the ground, turning left out of the rail tunnel because we'll lose otherwise. I missed cheering the team name announcements and belting out 'Glad All Over' at the top of my voice.

But that sense of loss was replaced by something else. Pride. Football clubs and football fans stepped up to the plate and became the focal point for so many official and unofficial support networks, helping the community that surrounds each club to get through those awful weeks and months.

It simply confirmed something I knew before I wrote this book; indeed, one of the reasons why I wrote this book. Despite our petty, childish, irrational, hilarious rivalries, much more unites us than divides us. Palace fans and Brighton fans play an annual charity match every year for a fund started in memory of a Brighton fan who died in the Twin Towers. When it looked like Palace were going bust in 2010, Brighton fans marched with us in protest.

Fans of every club will tell you a similar story. Football still has many problems, on and off the pitch, but I find a genuine magic in its capacity to bring people together.

I probably don't like your club very much, but if you like football, let's have a drink and talk nonsense about games gone by. Then we can talk about our families, about life, love and the universe. Then we'll be mates. That's how football works.

See you next season.

Acknowledgements

There are many people I want to thank for their help in writing this book and for being part of the story. The springboards for most of my research were thebeautifulhistory.wordpress.com and historicalkits.co.uk. I went into some dark and dusty corners but I always started with them. And I need to thank the authors of the histories on every single football club website, official and unofficial. Their knowledge and passion are an inspiration.

Every author thanks their publishing team and I always used to wonder how much bloody help an author actually needs. Well, now I know. Grateful thanks to Matt Lowing and all his team at Bloomsbury. It wouldn't have happened without you. Actually it probably would, but it might not have been as good.

I'd also like to thank David Hartrick for telling me this was *definitely* a book, and Richard Foster for agreeing!

And much love to Melanie, Dylan, Sophie, Rhonda and Jane at Troika, who did a marvellous job of agenting despite none of them knowing the first thing about football. Apart from Jane, who knows too much about it!

Now to the people who share my passion for Palace and a lot of my life: John and Ann Howes – founders of the dynasty. Steve, who is still tall; Gaz, who is still funny; Nick, who is still mysterious; Michael, who is still sensible; David, who tries to be; Dickie, with the twinkle in his eye; and Phil, the wide boy with the wide smile. Plus, of course, Roy, who is still handsome, and Chris 'Chirpy' Chapman, who is still always late. Then there's the offspring: Harry, Samuel, Mark, Charlie, Oli, George, Harvey, Eilish and Johnny, Daisy, Lily, Josh, Wilf, Matthew, Molly, Adam, my godson and Mark, his brother who will one day rule the world. Not forgetting (I wouldn't dare) Freya, Maddy, Adele, Sian, Tara and Meghan. Big love to them all, I cannot tell you how much joy their company has brought to me.

The FYP podcast boys, JD, Enders, Street, Sellsy, Rob, Dr John, Jesse and Travis.

All of the above can be found in the same pub pre-match, along with Neil the Fish, Barry, Griff, Sophie, Becs, Theatrical Julian, Andrew, other Rob, Jane, Martin, Akos from Hungary and Mikko from Finland.

Plus the special people who own and run the Pawsons Arms: Bev, Graham, Andy, Little John, Saffron and Jo.

Finally, of course, I would like to acknowledge the work of Palace For Life, the Foundation, of which I am very proud to be a trustee.

And everyone who has ever played for, managed, worked at, owned or supported Crystal Palace Football Club.

Permissions

The author would like to thank the following copyright holders and organisations for permission to reproduce copyright material in this book: p.11 Mark Lamarr; p.20 Andy Linden; p.24 Simon Inglis; p.27 EFL.com; p.33 Mark Fish; p.36 Historicalkits.co.uk; p.52 Millie Reeves/ Bristollive.com; p.58 *Lancashire Telegraph*; p.65 Max Rushden; p.86 Matt Barlow/The *Daily Mail;* p.105, p.202, p.287 *FourFourTwo*; p.110 *Liverpool Echo*; p.120 Forest Green Rovers; p.129 Martin Gritton; p.129 CodAlmighty.com; p.132 Tony Earnshaw/ReachPlc; p.148 Bob Mills; p.148 leytonorientblog.com; p.151 quotation from *A Town of Two Halves* (townsof2halves.co.uk) reproduced by permission of author David Guest; p.164 Simon Hattenstone/The *Guardian*; p.175 Teeside Live/The Gazette; p.178 quote from *No One Likes Us, We Don't Care* (John Blake, 2011) reproduced by permission of Bonnier Books; p.182 NorthStandChat.com; p.182 DreamTeamfc.com; p.192 Neal Heard; p.195 quotation from *Dixie: the Autobiography of Dixie McNeil* (Ylolfa Publishers, 2011) reproduced by permission of author Garmon Gruffud; p.219 StokeSentinel.co.uk; p.236 RochdaleOnline.co.uk; p.248 FootballFanzine.co.uk; p.251 *Yorkshire Post;* p.264 *Hertfordshire Mercury*; p.270 ChronicleLive; p.274 Stuart James/ The *Guardian*; p.277 Arthur Smith; p.290 quotation from *Me: Elton John* (Pan Macmillan 2019) reproduced by permission of the publisher.